OLD MEDIA AND THE MEDIEVAL CONCEPT

Media Before 1800

Under the co-direction of Daniel Kline (University of Alaska Anchorage), Fiona Somerset (University of Connecticut), and Stephen Yeager (Concordia University), Media Before 1800 brings cutting-edge discoveries from the disciplines of manuscript and early-print studies into conversation with the interrelated disciplines of media archaeology, infrastructure studies, and media ecology. The "1800" of this series title comes from Friedrich Kittler, whose description of the 1800 discourse network continues to influence the dominant periodizations of media history. Books in Media Before 1800 examine media from the medieval and early-modern periods to make challenging and politically efficacious claims that engage with the discourses of critical theory, cultural studies, media history, and media archaeology. In particular, they complicate the established narratives and counter-narratives of periodization, to look for alternative configurations of the relation between past and present.

Old Media and the Medieval Concept

MEDIA ECOLOGIES BEFORE EARLY MODERNITY

EDITED BY

Thora Brylowe and Stephen Yeager

Concordia University Press
Montreal

Cover: Sébastien Aubin
Design and typesetting: Garet Markvoort, zijn digital
Copy editing: Ian MacKenzie

Front cover image: Consanguinity diagram, France. © The British Library Board 15603, f.93

Printed and bound in Canada by Friesens, Altona, Manitoba

This book is printed on Forest Stewardship Council certified paper and meets the permanence of paper requirements of ANSI/ NISO Z39.48-1992.

Concordia University Press's books are available for free on several digital platforms. Visit www.concordia.ca/press

First English edition published in 2021
10 9 8 7 6 5 4 3 2 1

978-1-988111-28-5 | Paper
978-1-988111-29-2 | E-book

Library and Archives Canada Cataloguing in Publication

Title: Old media and the medieval concept : media ecologies before early modernity / edited by Thora Brylowe and Stephen Yeager.
Names: Brylowe, Thora, 1971– editor. | Yeager, Stephen M., 1979– editor.
Description: series statement: Media before 1800 | Includes bibliographical references and index.
Identifiers: Canadiana (print) 20210121300 | Canadiana (ebook) 20210121629 | ISBN 9781988111285 (softcover) | ISBN 9781988111292 (PDF)
Subjects: LCSH: Mass media—Europe— History—To 1500.
Classification: LCC P92.E85 O43 2021 | DDC 302.2309409/02—dc23

Concordia University Press
1455 de Maisonneuve Blvd. W.
Montreal, Quebec H3G 1M8
CANADA

Concordia University Press gratefully acknowledges the generous support of the Birks Family Foundation and Brian and Carolyn Neysmith.

ACKNOWLEDGEMENTS

The conversation between these essays crystallized around an event that took place at Concordia University in June 2017, and its contents have been shaped by the contributions of those who attended, sponsored, and/or facilitated that event. Special thanks is due in particular to Kat Morrissette and Katrina Tsimiklis, who contributed their organizational as well as intellectual labour, and also to event participants Patrick Outhwaite, Dan T. Kline, Elisabeth Buzay, Athena Pierquet, Damian Fleming, Arthur Bahr, Bill Buxton, Alex Custodio, and Michael Van Dussen. The event was made possible by the financial and in-kind contributions of the Interacting With Print project and Concordia University and on grants from the FRQSC and SSHRC, and we thank them for these. Thanks also to McGill University, McGill Medievalists, and the Osler library for their contributions, and to the many mentors and colleagues who may not even remember their own roles in shaping this project, but whose contributions are remembered by us, including Carolyn Jong, Lori Emerson, Amanda Phillips, Matthew X Vernon, Seeta Chiganti, Rob Gallagher, Breann Leake, Tiffany Beechy, Donna Beth Ellard, Mary Kate Hurley, Robin Norris, Jordan Zweck, Jill Hamilton Clements, Matthew Hussey, Will Robins, Suzanne Akbari, Holly Crocker, Alex Gillespie, Jessica Lockhart and participants, and Sarah Star. Thanks finally to Concordia University Press, and especially to Geoffrey Little, Meredith Carruthers, and Ian Mackenzie for their work bringing this volume to fruition, and also to the anonymous readers for their feedback.

THORA BRYLOWE is especially grateful to all members of the Mulitgraph Collective for helping to shape her thinking about print media—and to the contributors to this volume (and the conference that set us in motion) for helping her see ways to think about a world before print existed. She thanks Jonathan Sachs, for introducing her to Stephen Yeager, and her colleagues and family for listening to enthusiastic talk about all the new things she's learned.

STEPHEN YEAGER would like to thank those individuals from Concordia's English department who helped to shape this volume before, after, and during the event, in direct and indirect ways. These include especially Jason Camlot, Manish Sharma, Darren Wershler, Bart Simon, Nicola Nixon, Marcie Frank, Kevin Pask, Kate Sterns, Nathan Brown, Daniel O'Leary, Jonathan Sachs, Patrick Leroux, and Cynthia Quarrie. Thanks also to Liz Reich for her hugely important feedback on an early draft of his essay.

BRANDON HAWK is grateful to all of the participants of the Old Media and the Medieval Concept conference for their questions, comments, and discussion. I am especially thankful to Stephen Yeager, Thora Brylowe, and Kathleen Kennedy for reading and commenting on earlier drafts of this article.

FIONA SOMERSET would like to thank the organizers of the original conference and the British Library.

ALICE HUTTON SHARP would like to thank Stephen Yeager for his invitation to contribute, the reviewers and editors for their valuable suggestions, and her husband for listening to her endless conversation about manuscript formatting. She would also like to thank her children, Isaac and Hannah, for their daily lessons in how we learn—and for the animal facts.

CONTENTS

PREFACE: MEDIA BEFORE 1800

Stephen Yeager, Fiona Somerset,
and Daniel T. Kline

Description

The series that this volume inaugurates, Media before 1800, will present studies that span the disciplines of manuscript and early-print studies and the cognate disciplines of media archaeology, infrastructure studies, and media ecology. The "1800" of this series title frames its collective response to the work of Friedrich Kittler, whose description of the 1800 discourse network continues to influence the dominant periodizations of global media history.[1] Books in the Media before 1800 series will examine media from the periods preceding this starting point of Kittler's analysis, in globe-spanning investigations that will engage with critical theory, cultural studies, media history, and media archaeology. These studies will promote the new and overlooked voices that can complicate the established narratives and counter-narratives of periodization, and that can promote alternative configurations of the relation between past and present.

Media before 1800 assumes that the question of defining media in relation to specific historical periods is not a methodological question of establishing starting premises, but an epistemological question and an object of study in its own right. What is that distinction between material objects that bear human traces and those that do not, and hence between those that communicate facts about human subjects and cultures, and those that simply exist? Such investigations of "thingness" must consider the complex and embodied relations between subject-actors (whether human, post-human, animal; individual, collective; or otherwise) and material environments (whether political, historical, ecological, or otherwise). The definition of media is not a premise with which we ought to start, but a name for the goal where we ought to end.

The last ten years have seen the old antagonisms between methodological traditionalism and theoretically informed experimentation disappear from medieval studies scholarship. Meanwhile, practitioners of media archaeology like Sigfried Zielinski, Jussi Parikka, Lisa Gitelman, Lori Emerson, Darren Wershler, and David Edgerton have used their explorations of so-called historical media to push against the stream of progress narratives, so that they may—as Zielinski enjoined—"see the new in the old."[2] Books in the Media before 1800 series will bring these two developments into alignment, to find the "new" in the "old media" of not only European and settler cultures, but of the medieval and early-modern globe.

It is surely not a coincidence that these new scholarly interests have arisen during our transition into a media environment dominated by digital and telecommunications media. Not only is this development parallel to the transition from manuscript to print, but it has clearly been imagined and so designed through explicit reference to that parallel. The rise of digital technology is easily and quite closely tracked alongside both the scholarly ascendancy in medieval studies of "new philological" approaches to textual criticism, and also the broader growth in popularity of new- and multimedia medieval and neo-medieval fantasies like Tolkien's *Middle Earth*, *Dungeons and Dragons*, *Game of Thrones*, and even *Star Wars*, *Avatar: The Last Airbender*, and *Harry Potter*. There is a dense conceptual interrelationship between digital media design philosophies, scholarly trends in medieval and early-modern studies, and medievalism in pop culture that has been ill-served by our tendency to parcel out formal and technological analyses from historicist and cultural studies approaches. This inaugural volume of the series takes a first step in unpacking this interrelationship, but there is still a great deal of work to do.

Media before 1800 will provide a much-needed forum for the growing body of work that moves past traditional disciplinary boundaries of period and methodology, to engage with the understudied evidence of the past and the emergent concerns of the political present. Manuscript studies and early-modern book history have a somewhat deserved reputation for being fields that are focused primarily on the collection of data and the analysis of minutiae, so that they often miss opportunities to make synthetic claims that intervene in larger political and philosophical conversations beyond the discipline. Not unrelatedly, there is a tendency for the most adventurous and theoretically engaged research in early fields to focus on the representations that occur within literature, art, and historical records, more than the conditions of their production and circulation as manuscripts and books. Meanwhile, the studies of media history that apply theoretical breadth to materialist investigations are commonly so focused on the present that in its current usage, the term *old media* rarely looks back before print and sometimes even refers to technologies like film, tape recording, and 8-bit video game consoles. Media before 1800 aims to fill the urgent need for publication venues supporting the category of emerging scholarship rushing to fill the rather large gap that remains, and so push back against the structures of thought that created it in the first place.

The series' focus on the long period ca. 500–1800 C.E. will contribute substantially to our understanding of the history of media 1800–present and will enable us to remake the (historically and geographically bounded) theoretical paradigms that govern our engagement with that history. Studies in the series will ask, Why is the period that saw the foundation of the institutions that continue to govern the production and storage of media—not least of which is the university itself—nonetheless bracketed off as anterior to our own modernity? How determined are our conceptual categories by our history and circumstances, and what are the specific implications of historical determinations for our concepts of media? How much are our narratives of history shaped by our conceptual categories, and what are the specific implications of our concepts of media for our understanding of the place Europe played in global history, between the conquest of Rome by Alaric the Goth and the arrival of Columbus in Hispaniola? How did media history come to provide the central, authoritative evidence reinforcing the distinction between medieval and modern, in the face of a medieval studies that has spent decades exposing the implicit colonialism, racism, and sexism of that distinction, and a media studies that has spent decades self-consciously undermining such totalizing and deterministic narratives towards similar political ends? What other paradigms may we apply to think about developments like the popularization of print, that took place in media technology before they were transformed by industrialization? What hidden continuities exist between the present and the past, and which asserted continuities are in fact ideologically loaded myths of origin that distort the evidence of history in service of modern identities? In their approaches to questions like these, studies in the "Media before 1800" series will rethink late-medieval and early-modern developments like the rise of commercial book production, the popularization of paper over parchment, the development of the printing press, and the evolution of related media technologies like textiles, wood-carving, housewares, painting, and architecture. Their implications will resonate beyond the confines of manuscript studies, book history, and media studies, to reframe our approaches to humanistic inquiry itself.

OLD MEDIA AND THE MEDIEVAL CONCEPT

The Medieval/Media Concept

Thora Brylowe and Stephen M. Yeager

> The Second Age [of the videogame]: That was
> when the four central heroes made their first
> appearance: Brennan the warrior; Lorac the
> wizard; Prendar the thief, and Leira, the princess.
>
> —*Austin Grossman*

The early adoption of digital humanities (DH) technology in medieval studies is often cited only to acknowledge the counterintuitive fact of it, as raw data prove the continued relevance of the medieval period to the twenty-first century.[1] This volume presumes that the convergence of DH and medieval studies constitutes just one node in a far broader network of crosscurrents found between medieval and contemporary media, which demonstrate that memories of the medieval period have supplied much of the symbolic vocabulary we use to think about media technology. In the chapters collected here, we hope to contribute to efforts of medievalists and media studies scholars to traverse this network, through local analyses of texts and objects and through synthetic, diachronic studies. In this introduction we will briefly explain the starting formulation that informs our interventions. In brief, we suggest that a "medieval concept" has coincided with the emergence of what John Guillory calls a "media concept" in the "Western" intellectual tradition, and with the exclusion, definition, and limitation that have framed that tradition as "Western" in the first place.[2]

Since the Italian "humanists" first developed "Roman" scripts and typefaces in imitation of what are in fact early medieval, Carolingian letter forms, modernity has consistently refused to admit continuity with the medieval period, choosing to define the medieval as other and to root its own origins in classical antiquity instead.[3] The Latin period terms *modernus* and *antiquas* are contrasted as early as the fifth century,[4] but the logic of periodization that undergirds modernity follows the addition of a third, intervening, "middle" period of "dark ages," which is first referenced in the fifteenth century and explicitly designated for elision in the eighteenth.[5] The present volume, edited by a medievalist and an eighteenth-century specialist, acknowledges and pushes back against such master narratives, understanding (as, for example, Ted Underwood has shown) that periodization is a product solidified in the academy.[6] Our project began as a conference hosted by co-editor Stephen Yeager at Concordia University, also titled "Old Media and the Medieval Concept," which featured co-editor Thora Brylowe as a respondent, and early versions of many of the chapters you will read here. Following in the spirit of the event, we have planned this volume to start conversations that might extend well beyond the scholarly disciplines of the authors. In other words, you needn't be a DH scholar or a medievalist (Brylowe is neither) to recognize and appreciate our concerns, or to participate in the conversations we wish to begin.

In the remainder of this introduction, we will describe how the "middle" ages (*media æva*) are figured more precisely as "mediating ages" whose manuscripts both reveal and obscure the classical age that preceded them, before describing briefly how the period came to shape the ways in which mediation itself is imagined in the age of "new" digital media. As you will see, only some of the chapters here directly address DH and the forms of digital media. What binds them to the volume's themes nonetheless is their engagement with the discourses and methodologies of media studies, as investigations of traditional and non-traditional medieval corpora lend insight into the interfaces between the medieval and the digital, even—or perhaps especially—when they resist the obvious analogies to later phenomena between the different practices suggested by their juxtapositions. But before we describe these studies, we will briefly explain what we mean when we suggest that the medieval is itself a medium, and that the "medieval concept" of our title and the "media concept" of Guillory's are different faces of the same thought.

Old Media, Digital Media

This introduction began with an epigraph from Austin Grossman's 2013 novel *YOU*, in which the Hamlet-ish Russel, the English-degree-holding protagonist, joins his game-obsessed high school friends to work at their tech company.[7] The narrative toggles between the early days of gaming in the 1980s, when Russel and company were kids obsessed with series games like *Ultima* and *Zork*, and the world of 1997, where their company's signature game *Realms of Gold* competes with the *Warcraft* and *Final Fantasy* series.

Russel's "quest" to resolve a glitch in the code of the game becomes a heroic journey, in which the four heroes of *Realms of Gold* appear as life-size digital entities who assist him. In this narrative device, *YOU* draws on a long-standing practice of deploying the symbolic vocabulary of medieval romance to represent and comment upon video games and virtual realities, which is attested in games themselves from the self-referential jokes in Crowther and Woods's *Adventure* (1976) to the game-within-a-game framing device of the original *Assassin's Creed* (2007), and on into the formal experiments of influential independent games like *Braid* (2008), *The Magic Circle* (2015), and *Undertale* (2015).[8]

There is also substantial anecdotal evidence for such medievalism in programming communities throughout the history of computing, even beyond its well-known overlap with the history of gaming. In the Stanford Artificial Intelligence Lab in the 1970s, the technicians not only played *Adventure* but named the rooms in the facility after Middle Earth locations, posting signs on all the doors in both Latin and Elvish alphabets.[9] More recently, the AMC show about the early PC industry *Halt and Catch Fire* (2014–17) featured *Adventure* in the season 1 episode 5 titled after the game, and even ported it for the show's promotional website.[10] If medievalists have seen in digital hypertext a model that helps them better describe the medieval textual practices that Stephen Nichols influentially called "the manuscript matrix," programmers have also found models in medieval romance and its popular derivations for imagining what it is exactly that coders do. It is no wonder, then, that the "geek" cultures of fandom for Tolkien, Harry Potter, and other popular fantasies have long provided novice programmers with communities of practice that helped them to gain technical skills.[11]

As Andrew Taylor observes, Nichols's term "manuscript matrix" echoes the name of William Gibson's fictional VR network "the Matrix," most famously depicted in his novel *Neuromancer* (1984), which in turn popularized the genre known as "cyberpunk."[12] And as Wendy Hui Kyong Chun observes, the popularity of Gibson's "cyberspace" fantasy in public discourse about the digital appears related to a broader and ideology-driven tendency to imagine the internet as a spatial rather than a temporal, processual, iterative construct.[13] This framing figures the task of the programmer as analogous to that of the architect or worldbuilder. It is, then, pertinent to note that the play on "necromancy" in Gibson's title instantiates a broad-ranging analogy between hackers and wizards, programs and spells, virtual reality and Huizinga's "magic circle" manifest in a wide array of pop-culture tropes and programmer terminologies, dated both before and after Gibson's novel, which contribute to the construct of digital technology as a gateway to an imagined world.[14]

As even this brief summary should make clear, it seems that many people working in many sectors and fields have perceived an intuitive analogy between the tasks of designing games, writing code, and navigating user interfaces on the one hand and the tasks of fighting monsters, casting spells, and questing for treasure on the other.[15] Such romance tropes in SFF fiction, film, television, and video games require immediate investigation by medievalists, not only because they are interesting but also because they may help medieval studies to articulate a new political mission that counteracts the field's complicity with imperialism and white supremacy.[16] Such a mission may also contribute to the similar efforts by scholars of gaming like Amanda Phillips, Shira Chess, and Kishonna Gray to describe and confront the gender-, race-, and class-based violence in gaming communities[17]—widely publicized around the #Gamergate controversy.[18] It may also contribute to the work by scholars like Chun, Ruha Benjamin, Safaiya Umoja Noble, Charlton McIlwain, Shaka McGlotten, and Lisa Nakamura, which demonstrates how digital algorithms and social media re-encode systemic violence whose origins can be traced to the clerical culture of the medieval period at least.[19] In brief, then, there are many urgent reasons to better understand the intuition that the forms of medieval texts are uniquely expressive of the forms of digital culture, whose applications extend beyond the merely academic interest that this phenomenon may inspire. And though this collection of chapters by white, settler scholars may only go so far in doing the specific work of decolonization and anti-racism, it hopes to contribute by amplifying the activist voices cited above and by opening paths for new voices, not least by inaugurating a book series that is seeking to promote such voices.

Of course, neither "gamer" culture nor DH discourse is the first instance of a movement and period in the post-medieval world with an imaginative investment in European medievalism. Notably, English neogothicism sought to rescue "gothic" forms like romance from their relegation as feminized and backwardly Catholic things, unworthy of notice by eighteenth-century Enlightenment rationalists and connoisseurs.[20] In eighteenth-century England the term *gothic* became the preferred antiquarian synonym for *medieval*, based on the logic that "classical" Rome ended with the conquest of the city by Alaric "the Goth."[21] In this same period Horace Walpole wrote the first gothic novel, *Castle of Otranto*, which he published anonymously—claiming it was a translation of a medieval text—in 1764. This "romance" features a gigantic supernatural knight in plate armour, a melting heroine pursued by a black villain intent on destroying her honour, a secret passageway between church and castle, and all manner of Catholic superstitions. Walpole's spectacular gothic mansion, Strawberry Hill in Twickenham, with its campy suit of armour and outrageous papier mâché ceilings, was begun in 1747. Strawberry Hill was also (among other things) a repository for Walpole's antiquarian collections, which included many medieval artifacts.[22] In Walpole's interweaving of artistic and archival practices, then, we see how already in the eighteenth century modern memories of the medieval period constructed it as a residual, countercultural past whose material remnants were in dialectical tension with the dominant, "enlightened" forces that faced towards the future.

In the nineteenth and twentieth centuries, the Gothic Revival continued to push back against Enlightenment neoclassicism and rationalist and minimalist forms.[23] Artists like William Morris and John Ruskin studied and theorized the medieval and gothic as they created in its style.[24] Building projects as diverse as the Palace of Westminster (1836) in London and the Cathedral of Learning (1926) in Pittsburgh deployed neogothic style to communicate stateliness and permanence.[25] All of these projects have had their detractors, and all of these artists their counterparts. The modernist architect Frank Lloyd Wright, for example, scoffed at the Cathedral of Learning and called it "the largest keep-off-the-grass-sign" in the world.[26] Nonetheless, the very existence of such controversies about the "gothic" marks its importance to post-Enlightenment aesthetics, in contemporary popular culture as in eighteenth-century England.

This importance is underscored by the survival of the term *gothic* in the present, in both popular and technical meanings. Since the 1980s, black-wearing "goths" have diverged from a fairly consistent (if campy) DIY-inspired post-punk subculture into splinter identities, including "industrial" and "cybergoth," which rely on dark, beat-driven synthesized music.[27] Meanwhile in academia, disciplines like art history, book history, and architecture persist in using "gothic" as a descriptive category.[28]

The challenge of defining with any consistency the (technical, historical, pop-, and sub-cultural, medievalizing) term *gothic* instantiates the larger methodological challenges to medieval studies as it attempts to build connections to cognate disciplines. A closer engagement with the discourse of media studies can help to address this challenge.

The chapters in this volume deploy paradigms based on those developed by scholars like Lisa Gitelman, Bonnie Mak, and David Edgerton—whose counternarratives of persistence and continuity over historical epochs challenge the teleological progress narratives of modernity—and by media archaeologists like Wolfgang Ernst, Jussi Parikka, and Sigfried Zielinski, who challenge the same narratives through their engagement with the materiality of archival memory.[29] Each study in this volume helps to untangle the conflation of medieval and media "concepts," as described below. Media histories have always occupied the interstices of technology, philosophy, and historical and cultural production, and they have always required that we identify a common, "middle" space between their methodologies and terminologies. So medieval studies is also at its best when its investigations do the same.

In the remainder of this introduction to the media histories of the "Middle Ages" collected below, we will briefly describe challenges to the development of new frameworks, as to clarify the goals towards which the chapters are directed. We will argue that the seemingly technical and local concerns of medieval studies have always been part of a larger conversation about media technology, extending beyond the debates in our own academic disciplines and beginning long before medievalism became a defining aspect of "geek" identity. In the brief history of medievalism in digital culture and the long history of the gothic in the English-speaking world we may see how the notion of media as a problem for communication—what John Guillory calls the "media concept"—is commonly thought in modern European intellectual contexts with specific reference to memories of specifically medieval communications technology. In the rest of this introduction, then, we will justify this starting premise, in order to frame the (more local) interventions of the chapters collected below. This justification will begin in the next section with a more robust definition of "medievalism," as this concept will play a crucial role in our analysis.

Period Troubles

It is hardly an innovative reading of the "mediating ages" of the medieval period to suggest that their figuration in official and popular histories is contradictory and unstable. It might better reorganize and resist the order of things.[30] Indeed, as Bruno Latour suggests in his influential exploration of these issues, *We Have Never Been Modern*, modernity defines *instability itself* by analogy to its construction and rejection of the hybridized medieval past: this periodization precedes and shapes the conceptual framework that would justify its demarcations.[31] On the one hand, the "middle," "dark" ages of European history are remembered as ages of disorder in the textual and cultural transmission of classical Greek and Latin texts via the medieval scriptoria of monasteries and the first universities. If the establishment of a new order in these traditions marked the end of the medieval period and the rise of humanism and Enlightenment, it also coded medieval people as not only "dark" but also as monstrous, abject, and irrational.[32] In one well-known example, ever since *Pulp Fiction* (1994) we "get medieval" whenever we take violent or aggressive measures in interpersonal situations.[33] And the adjective *medieval* in popular culture commonly evoked notions of excess, violence, and superstition, which have reinforced the notion that the medieval period was a backward and/or childlike age.

On the other hand, "childlike" opens up space for positive valences to the medieval concept. When the medieval period is presented as a sort of adolescent approach towards modernity, it may be coded instead as a time that was relatively simple and (often racially as well as morally) "pure," so that the medieval may become the object of a nostalgic desire for return.[34] Hence modern imitations of medieval literature— most famously Disney's animated fairy tales and the novels of J. R. R.

Tolkien—are so commonly coded as "family entertainment" and "children's literature."[35] Moreover, there is an association of popular medievalism with games and play, which has contributed to the tendency to erase labour from popularly imagined medieval worlds.[36] For all their contradictions, then, both nostalgic and derogatory views of the medieval period implicitly accept the premise that the medieval period is a time we *must* leave behind and a phase we *must* outgrow, whether we wish to or not.

The consequences of this construction for popular medievalism may be demonstrated with reference to what is perhaps the best-known example of a ludic recreation of the medieval past, the gaming system Dungeons & Dragons (D&D).[37] In D&D, we see how the contradictions of the medieval concept described above may transform medieval settings into enormously potent imaginary spaces, as the medieval is often figured not as a period antecedent to modern history but as a heterotopic and non-modern space that exists outside of history itself.[38] D&D has gone through five major editions, excluding minor revisions and optional extensions, but it has remained a rigorous and carefully constructed framework for assessing the likely outcomes of actions chosen under conditions generated by the synthesis of disparate fantasies and mythologies. So, for example, players may simulate what would happen if a barbarian like Conan teamed up with a ranger like Aragorn to fight monsters from the Lovecraft mythos while wielding Thor's hammer and Apollo's Greatbow respectively.

The basis for the medieval fantasy setting of D&D was Gary Gygax's Fantasy Supplement to his medieval war game *Chainmail*, which drew upon the tropes of "sword and sorcery" fiction to supplement game rules developed in imitation of the known factors that determined the tactics of actual medieval historical battles.[39] In this sense, D&D is born from the combination of two clashing reconstructions of the medieval past, wherein each pushed the other towards a looser, more contingent practice of conjectural simulation. A good example of the principles at play is the fireball spell of *Chainmail*, later incorporated into D&D. Tresca has described how fireballs in *Chainmail* function like cannons in the rule systems of cognate Napoleonic war games, and so the historical fact that medieval people believed in "magic" justifies the otherwise anachronistic integration of eighteenth-century technology into a medieval battle simulation.[40] In this sense, then, the extraordinary openness of the D&D gaming system to assimilating heterogenous content from any number of heterotopic fantasies and histories appears to reflect the defining contradictions encoded into *Chainmail*'s medieval setting. In the popular conception, "anachronism" and "superstition" are rampant in medieval romance, and hence the deployment of anachronistic and/or magical elements in simulations of medieval life is paradoxically consistent with popular notions of historical accuracy about the period.

In this way, D&D instantiates the larger phenomenon whereby modern refusals to contemplate the impact of medieval history on the present can lead to the re-eruption of ahistorical medievalism in popular culture, particularly in conceptual and ahistorical secondary worlds of ludic possibility.[41] Just as "cyberspace" effaces the material conditions of digital networks in Chun's analysis cited above, the virtual space of the (neo)medieval game effaces the material preconditions of modernity, especially evidence for the origins of modernity in medieval learning and clerical culture.[42] Erased medieval histories and emergent medieval fantasies reinforce the bare, "modern" idea described by Latour, that time only moves in one direction and effaces the past in its wake.

As several scholars cited above have already suggested, such constructions and erasures of the medieval past have provided moral justification for the colonization, subjugation, and enslavement of nominally primitive or "underdeveloped" peoples.[43] Such callous Whiggery makes it crucial to construct alternative histories that undermine notions of race rooted in assumptions about medievalism. And yet—as progressive medievalists have complained for decades—post-colonialists, queer theorists, and feminists often base their critical methodologies in the historical conditions of the very modernity they aim to undermine, tacitly accepting the premise they otherwise challenge, that such conditions are the only ones in which something like true social justice might be thinkable.[44] We will attempt to contribute to those efforts to address the political concerns of these philosophically informed discourses by tracing the origins of medievalism's "medieval concept" back to the moment in the history of philosophy where Guillory identifies the emergence of his "media concept." In particular, we will argue that the necessary reliance of early-modern philosophers on medieval manuscripts of foundational works by thinkers like Plato and Aristotle contained and sublimated the larger contradictions that accompanied the construction of European modernity. The problem of specifically medieval media became the test case for imagining the problem of media themselves, and the modern study of medieval thought became circumscribed by questions of how medieval authors mediated the cultural products of earlier eras. In brief, we hold that the medieval and the media concepts are the historical and epistemological dimensions respectively of the same construct. We will continue our explanation of this claim in the next section with Guillory's description of the media concept's emergence.

The Media Concept

There is an assumption in media studies that in the medieval and early-modern periods, the material and technological conditions of communications media were invisible to writers and thinkers, so the interrelation of medium and message was not properly theorized until after technologies like radio, film, and eventually television and computers made the importance of media visible.[45] We see this assumption, for example, in Kittler's famous, that "Discourse Network 1900" replaced the older circuit—leading from the mother's voice to internally voiced silent reading—with an awareness of phonographic sound as disjointed from time and space.[46] We build here on the important steps taken in John Guillory's influential article "The Genesis of the Media Concept" towards challenging such inferences, as he traced alongside the philological record of the words "media" and "mediation" in English a narrative of how the evolution of media technology has occasioned larger changes in the discourses of human self-conception.[47]

Guillory's study of the "media concept" surveys a number of works, starting with Francis Bacon's *New Organon*, to trace a prehistory of media that begins before the OED's first attestations of the term *media* itself. By coincidence, this work by Bacon *does* use the Latin word *media* in the phrase *media tempora* (mediating times), which is also one of the earliest attested occurrences in England of the modern historical term *medieval* (from *media æva*, "mediating ages").[48] Hence while Bacon may not use the word *media* to describe communications technology directly, he does use it while articulating his dim view of the historical periods that mediate its three "great" eras of writing and knowledge production—ancient Greece, ancient Rome, and his own early-modern period. In the next two sections we will unpack the implications of this term *media tempora* in Bacon's writing for Guillory's argument, and so contextualize more precisely the encounters between the discourses of medieval and media studies that will occur in the chapters that follow.

Guillory's essay begins by positing that the concept of a medium of communication was absent but wanted for the several centuries prior to its appearance, and so it was a lacuna in the philosophical tradition that exerted pressure, as if from the future, on early efforts to theorize communication.[49] In the course of fleshing out his claim, Guillory characterizes this pressure as a desire for transparency and communication among and between humans, which will ultimately replace the emphasis in classical rhetoric on concealing one's thoughts and manipulating one's audience.[50] *Media* in these terms are the means through which communication is attempted, and so also by the same fact they are physical reminders that true transparency is impossible and perhaps even undesirable. For Guillory, then, the emergence of the term *media* for *communication technology* in the twentieth century may be described as the articulation of an older problem of communication, which had become so severe it required the establishment of a new conceptual framework for addressing it.

Guillory suggests that the *media concept* preceding the coinage of *media* first emerged in the early-modern period out of a historical process of remediation.[51] Following in McLuhan's footsteps, Guillory focuses specifically on the early-modern emergence of "print culture" as the larger, civilization-wide remediation that led to the first glimmers of the media concept.[52] This means Guillory's narrative is predicated upon the notion that the invention of print was a revolution that led more or less directly to the political and cultural formations of early modernity.

Guillory's discussion of the Middle Ages in this article is confined to a single footnote. He begins his narrative with the opening section of Aristotle's *Poetics*, which identifies the parts of the mimetic artwork as roughly analogous to the positions of the matter, form, and substance of an object. The translators of this passage consistently refer to the "matter" element of this triad as the "media" or "medium" of an artwork, though the Greek is more precisely translated as the artwork's status of being "in different things."[53] Guillory writes, "After briefly commenting on the different media of imitation, [Aristotle] devotes the remainder of the *Poetics* to the other two subjects: the objects and modes of imitation. He sets the question of medium aside, *where it remained for two millennia.*"[54]

Guillory's footnote, which cites no medieval text, cites instead the late-antique author Martianus Capella to observe that the visual arts are not included in the schema of the seven liberal arts. He concludes on this basis that the concept of artistic medium was not a subject of serious scholarly debate between the fall of Rome and the voyage of Columbus.[55] When his narrative picks up two millennia after Aristotle, it does so with Francis Bacon's *New Organon*. Specifically Guillory discusses the passage where Bacon observes that movable type seems latent in the original technology of alphabetic script, as it is only a refinement of writing's original division of speech into a small number of repeated graphic units for the purposes of dissemination.[56]

As we have said, Bacon's *New Organon* provides a useful basis for demonstrating how the history of the modern medieval concept described above intersects with Guillory's history of a media concept, as is indicated most obviously by Bacon's own use of the Latin adjective *media*. However, it will be necessary to provide some context to ground this point. The title of Bacon's work alludes to the "old" *Organon*, which is to say Aristotle's six works on logic as classified by the Peripatetics. As the title of his work makes clear, Bacon self-consciously breaks with both Aristotle and the entire intervening tradition of commentary on the *Organon* as he knew it, following especially after the "rediscovery" of Aristotle by Latin Christian Europe in the later medieval period. As we shall see, Bacon was certainly aware of the widely attested and influential Aristotelian traditions from medieval Christendom and Islam in the same period, but he explicitly rejects their usefulness as a model for his own work or, indeed, for any purpose related to learning.[57]

One pertinent example of these medieval Aristotelian traditions is that of the *Poetics* itself. After a long hiatus following the fall of the western Roman Empire, the *Poetics* was reintroduced to medieval Europe by Hermannus Alemannus in the middle of the thirteenth century, in the form of a Latin translation that incorporated elements of a commentary by the major Arabic philosopher Ibn Rushd (Averroes), and also fragments from Ibn Sīnā (Avicenna) and Abū al-Naṣr al-Fārābī.[58] Following these thinkers, Hermannus considered the *Poetics* to be part of Aristotle's original *Organon* and hence a work of logic, which moreover could be positioned in continuity with Aristotelian ethics. For example, Aristotle's remarks about praise and blame in relation to tragedy and comedy are understood in this medieval tradition to describe how poetry either promotes or dissuades readers from certain kinds of behaviour.

It is not unreasonable for Guillory to suggest that, in a *Poetics* configured thus, mimesis falls by the wayside and with it Aristotle's nascent notion of an artistic medium.[59] Still, the absence of mimesis from the vocabulary of medieval thought would hardly mean that the medieval discourse of art and poetry "sets the question of medium aside." Hermannus's emphasis on embodied, ethical responses to art may raise the question of medium in a different context and focus on different implications, but the question itself persists.

It seems, then, that Bacon's gesture towards the nascent media concept does not so much *invent* a set of questions about media as it *explicitly rejects* an alternative set of questions about media, developed and circulated among Aristotle's medieval Persian, Middle Eastern, Andalusian, and (eventually) Christian European readers. This is made particularly clear in the *New Organon*'s denigration of the "middle ages" in favour of the learning from the modern and classical periods: "For only three revolutions and periods of learning may truly be counted. First, among the Greeks; second, among the Romans; last, among us, the nations of Western Europe, and to each of these scarcely two centuries can be assigned correctly. *The mediate ages of the world*, in respect of any rich or flourishing growth of the sciences, were unproductive. *For there is no need to mention either the Arabians or the scholastics*, who *throughout the mediating times* rather crushed the sciences with a multitude of treatises than added to their heft."[60]

As this passage reveals, Bacon explicitly refuses to engage with the intellectual tradition that preserved and commented upon the *Organon* in the centuries that passed between Aristotle's death and the start of Bacon's own career. In particular Bacon conflates "Arabians"—which is to say the authors who wrote in Arabic like Ibn Rushd and Ibn Sīnā—with the medieval "scholastic" philosophers who were so profoundly influenced by these thinkers, in the wake of Hermannus Alemannus and the other Latin authors who brought Arabic and Muslim learning to the European mainstream. Bacon accuses these authors of generating texts that have no intellectual content and function only as matter, as they "crush" with their "heft" the very sciences they pretend to facilitate. In the next section, we will return to Guillory's analysis to demonstrate how this passage reveals that the question of material media was not "picked up" by Bacon from Aristotle. Rather, it was a novel formulation by Bacon to help him justify his radical (and explicitly racialized) break with medieval Aristotelianism. Specifically, the nascent media concept was itself useful for Bacon's claim that medieval manuscripts contribute nothing "useful" to the communication of important ideas.

The Medieval Concept

We may now return to Guillory's argument, to see how Bacon's phrase *media tempora* provides crucial context for assessing his early articulation of a media concept in the passage about printing from book 1, chapter 110. Here, Bacon first asserts that "the technique of printing certainly contains nothing which is not open and almost obvious," and then addresses the attending question of why it took so long for printing to be the dominant mode for reproducing texts.[61] Bacon speculates that medieval scribes must have known that the cost of writing by hand was cheaper than the costs associated with rearranging letters, but that they lacked enough foresight to recognize that once a book was typeset, "innumerable impressions" could be pulled. It seems, then, that the fault was in the individual choices made by generations of medieval scribes, who consistently chose to perpetuate what was expedient instead of disrupting book production to enable greater efficiency and productivity.

In light of his other complaints about "mediating ages," then, it seems that Bacon's point is not so much that print is transparent as it is that medieval manuscripts are unnecessarily opaque, in a manner that reflects the obstinate commitment to opacity he sees in the medieval scholastic learning. In this passage, then, Bacon is not just (as Guillory asserts) "moving away from speech in order to affirm the greater utility of writing for transferring thoughts."[62] He is emphatically rejecting the perceived heterogeneity, disorder, and material excess of the medieval manuscript, whose irrational construction and meaningless, Arabic-influenced contents embody both the pre-imperial European past that

Bacon's early modernity sought to abandon and the non-white peoples whose humanity that modernity sought to efface.[63]

One of the most insightful passages in Guillory's essay observes that "we see that whether communication fails ... or is deliberately frustrated ..., the effect is to bring the medium into greater visibility."[64] So also is Bacon's early glimpse of the media concept clearly related to his irritation about the frustrating opacity of late-medieval scribal culture, with print technology serving as his material evidence that such abominations have no part in his own era of human achievement. In this, Bacon's framing of print and manuscripts indeed anticipates the modern concept of media qua media, as Guillory suggests. Both Bacon's disparagements (and Guillory's own elisions) instantiate a modern "medieval concept" closely related to the "media concept," which has (mis-)used the historical example of medieval textuality to affirm the utility and virtue of (modern) order, consistency, proportion, and continuity in communications technology. Hence we may expand Guillory's claims to propose that the persistence of this "medieval/media concept"—which, we should emphasize, was only nominally derived from the criticism of actual medieval media—has both inspired and frustrated modern efforts to understand the material attributes of media from all periods, and to catalogue and contextualize their disorders, inconsistencies, excesses, and ruptures.

By implication, there is more at stake in this volume than just the better understanding of medieval artifacts that may be gained by applying media studies paradigms and methodologies to medieval evidence. The application also intervenes in the philosophical underpinnings of those paradigms and methodologies, and forces them to attend to evidence that, since their very foundation, they have elided and effaced. Because of the particular role played by medieval media in the modern formulation of the media concept, a deeper understanding of medieval media will enable us to reframe and so clarify the philosophical problem of mediation itself, as it pertains to the apparatus of learning that would facilitate the projects of colonialism and empire. This new framing will lend new insight into the phenomenon with which we began, that digital and medieval media have so commonly provided each other with a symbolic vocabulary useful for describing their forms.

Against Epochs

As we have demonstrated in the last section, *The New Organon* instantiates the larger truth that medieval manuscripts have generated some of the more fruitful and generative frustrations in the history of Western civilization. In particular, gaps and ambiguities in the medieval corpus of classical texts have arguably been just as important to the development of modern ideologies as have been faithful and accurate records. As we have also suggested above, the uses of medievalism to interrogate modern identities serve in this way to expose the historical dimension of mediality itself, both as it has been practised and as it is thought by modern and postmodern philosophy. In this section, we will conclude this introduction's survey of the scope of the problem with a few brief thoughts about current trends and potential directions forward, as prelude to our summary of the chapters that follow.

As scholars working in different periods, we editors bring together approaches that cross what are often understood by analogy to geology as medial "epochs."[65] Media, as John Durham Peters sees it, are the stuff beneath the culture, what culture grows in and on, as on agar in a petri dish.[66] The cloud for Peters exemplifies the amorphous and banal nature of media, which spans both nature and culture, storing and sustaining our collected experiences as much in DNA as in books or external hard drives.[67] Re-situating medieval, modern, and digital media epochs in relation to each other enables us to counteract the teleological sensibilities of a bookish Enlightenment, for which the computer network is radically other so analogous to other, earlier others. In fact, the cultish fealty to print that Bacon fomented would prove to be as hostile to the digital as it was to "primitive" orality, and to the disordered medieval manuscript.[68] But as we explain below—and indeed throughout this volume—there are many other ways to stage the affinity between digital and pre-modern frameworks for communications, beyond their mere negations of the modernity that divides them.

As we have already observed, the perceived affinity between the digital and the scribal has led to new forms of editing, which, in the early days of digital networking, were quite commonly spearheaded by medievalists. For example, in the subfield of medieval English literature, Kevin Kiernan, Hoyt Duggan, and Peter Robinson have each justified the expense and difficulty of producing his respective digital edition of *Beowulf*, *Piers Plowman*, and *The Canterbury Tales* by arguing that the dynamism of digital texts make the medium well-suited to overcome what Duggan calls the "limitations of print."[69] Perhaps predictably, the benefits of digital editing outlined by editors of medieval manuscripts migrated through fields most preoccupied with textual studies. Notably The William Blake Archive, launched in 1996, harnessed the early internet such that anyone with a connection could compare the minutest differences in versions of Blake's illuminated books, the originals of which were locked up in collections thousands of miles apart. While the limitations of print have been apparent to the editors of manuscript (or in Blake's case, manuscript-*like*) texts well before the digital age, they have also been lamented in DH circles by scholars best in a position to make changes to our practices of knowledge production as well as to use digital tools to change the scale of the objects we study.[70] In this way DH has led to the development of an architecture that Alan Liu has described as the "digital humanities archive, corpus, or network" that aims to supplant the individual text as the object of analysis.[71]

One result of the shift in scale is a shift in scholarly language, from the high-stakes politics of "culture" into a more politically neutral engagement with "data." Liu notes that such models are consistent with programs of post-1968 cultural criticism, which have argued that the best way to challenge the academic hegemony of patriarchal, heteronormative, colonial white supremacy is to promote methodologies that facilitate true intersectional exchange between multiple, embodied, contradictory voices, both in published scholarship and in the world that scholarship aims to describe. Certainly, too, a heterogenous flattening is implicit in Peters's subject/object–nature/culture intermedial cloud. Information, after all, is a ghostly non-being until it is made material *as media*.

It is our position here that media are implicitly political, and that accordingly medieval studies now finds itself faced with a unique opportunity and challenge in relation to DH. We maintain that medieval texts recorded multiple, embodied, and contradictory voices, but that the radical potentials of the medieval manuscript were strangled by a hegemonic narrative about the dominance and superiority of print. For too long, the media concept and the medieval concept have shared space, and this has obscured our understanding of both the resistances and facilitations of matter to communication, and also the history and culture of Europe in the period of its recorded history where it was least relevant to global geopolitics. This book calls for a new, intermedial regime that breaks down the monolithic epochs of the oral, manuscript, print, and digital "ages," and so creates the space for new modes of politicized historical imaginings. If, as Sisken and Warner argue, the Enlightenment is nothing more than an event in the history of mediation, this change in our thinking will enable us to better contextualize that event and understand its ramifications.[72] As much as a digital corpus may help us to scale up our object in order to break down the boundaries of literary and historical periods, a thoroughgoing rethinking of media history will show the continuities, reversals, and overlaps are more compelling than revolutions or epochs, as they help us both to better understand what the artifacts of the past have to teach us and to better respond to the contingencies of our own historical moment.

Recently, the Americanist Patricia Jane Roylance has argued that digital manuscript reproductions can offer a fuller picture of the *trans*-medial histories and temporalities implicit in different modes of editing.[73] For Roylance, the *desire to conserve* through textual reproduction may be similar across time and media, but the sense of temporality differs drastically in a diary written in the seventeenth century and printed book with the same content edited by an antiquarian in nineteenth-century Massachusetts. Similarly a current-day digitizer aspires to save for posterity through text, but her "guesses about the future" are inscribed into both medium and message.[74] In finding the affinities between technologies of digital mediation and remediation and technologies of the medieval period, we too wish to respect the temporalities and situated nature of afforded to each. Since Adrian Johns's landmark *The Nature of the Book*, we have been aware that the authority of the printed word comes not from the machine but from compositors and press workers, who *worked* to render the marks of their hands less visible than the marks left by their wonderous machine.[75] If textual transmitters, editors, and mediators are joined by our desire to conserve, we are also joined in the labour it takes to do so. Our hope with this volume is to expose these connections to view, and to bind them more tightly together.

The Chapters

The chapters in the first section, "Long Durations," conduct their investigations in tension with periodizations of medieval and modern histories, and the practice of periodization itself. These chapters make interventions that take two forms. First, they construct narratives of transmission and practice that span centuries, and in so doing they demonstrate how the frameworks of periodization designed to elucidate the evidence from the past are often at odds with that evidence. Second, they model how studies of medieval media may borrow more from and contribute more to the theoretical and methodological paradigms of media studies more generally, breaking down the boundaries of periodization and so challenging the entrenched power structures that such boundaries preserve.

The chapters in the second section, "Affective Affordances," are less concerned with narratives than they are with juxtapositions, wherein we see affective and material markers in medieval media that have closer analogues in digital media than they do in print. These markers are not new to medieval studies scholarship, and indeed these studies are quite closely aligned with the traditional interests of the discipline. The tags, glosses, letters, and commentaries that are the subjects of these chapters encode "official" medieval Christianity, in more than one sense, and so their modern readers often elide—like those students of digital networks described by Patrick Jagoda—the "microlevels of affect and effect" that characterize the experience of the subjects who inhabit their structures.[76] Each of these studies underscores the basic point that, ultimately, clerical authority was a practised technics, whose haptic negotiations between embodied subjects and emergent institutions are the true matter of many medieval manuscripts. Thus the volume moves from the studies in its first section, which engage directly with the questions that already concern media studies and DH, towards studies in its second section that demonstrate the unique affective affordances of medieval artifacts, our chapters offering more and more resistance as we go along to the analogies between contemporary and medieval media cultures with which we began, in order to open up new possible questions in the studies of contemporary and digital media.

In the first chapter, "Genesis of the Digital Concept," Brandon Hawk historicizes the dualism between "digital" and "analogue" in relation to the terminology of medieval computation. The Latin word *digitalis* refers to the digits, and in particular the fingers, that were used to make mathematical calculations. There is, then, a conceptual connection between digital computation and manual labour, which is particularly significant in the context of medieval monasteries, which were centres of mathematical learning and also places where the practice of labour had spiritual significance. Hawk traces the implications of this earlier dualism, *digital/manual*, for the later dualism of *digital/analogue*, reading in this way across media epochs and so challenging the periodizations implicit in media studies as a whole.

In the second chapter, "Protocol and Regulation: Controlling Media Histories," Stephen M. Yeager identifies a formal distinction in histories of control between protocols, which control systems by allowing only certain choices of actors, and regulations, which control systems by forbidding certain outcomes of actions. Though in fact protocols and regulations are interrelated and mutually generative control strategies, there is a tendency in histories of control to distinguish between the two control strategies, discernible both in official narratives of control systems' histories and in plans for future action that apply the lessons of those narratives. The heuristic is therefore helpful for describing the origins and dissemination of the "medieval concept," as it has been described above, and also for situating that concept in relation to other political uses of historical archives.

The third and final chapter in the "Long Durations" section, Kathleen E. Kennedy's "The Coconut Cup as Material and Media: Extended Ecologies," pushes at the (racialized and gendered) boundaries of what constitutes media history with a study of the history of the coconut cup. For 700 years coconuts were synonymous with luxury housewares. Kennedy traces the global ecologies in which coconut cups functioned as both material and media for artisans and drinkers. The coconut cup models how media histories that transcend inherited period boundaries and notions of "media" can expose the gendered and racialized nature of those boundaries and notions. In this way it transitions from the first section's more direct engagement with research questions in media studies into the second section's more indirect modelling of how medieval studies can serve as the basis for new research questions in its more presentist cognate disciplines.

In the first chapter in the second section, "Multimedia Verse," Fiona Somerset examines the tagging schemae of anonymous mnemonic verse tags to demonstrate how we might view their textual remains as the artifacts of a culture of abstract thought within and beyond the schools in which easily altered condensations of key ideas move fluidly among written, oral, and performance media and discourses. Learning in these artifacts was plastic, protean, and transmissible, memorized and voiced to achieve rehearsed effects. Accordingly, it passed between different institutional and disciplinary contexts, in a process we see preserved when mnemonic tags scattered across a variety of written genres and linguistic settings. The chapter's preliminary examination of tagging and of codification in a few specific medieval scholastic intellectual traditions illustrates the urgent need to reimagine the critical vocabulary for describing the functions of tagging and coding in contemporary programming, and for interrogating the possible sites of continuity between such practices. The digital cannot be prioritized over the medieval in these interrogations, nor vice versa: the two must share equal footing.

In the second chapter, "Ex Illo Tempore: Time, Meditation, and the *Ars Dictaminis* in Letter 65 by Peter the Venerable," Jonathan M. Newman engages with epistolarity and the ways in which the authority of the letter relates to the authority of face-to-face conversation. This chapter begins with a striking letter by Peter the Venerable, abbot of Cluny and one of the most notable letter-writers of the Middle Ages, which articulates with particular clarity a "double logic of remediation" (as Bolter and Grusin call it) that discloses how readers and writers of letters in the twelfth century conceptualized the relationships between time, "immediacy," and textual mediation.[77] In particular, the letter illustrates how the affective expressions of longing for presence in conventional medieval letter-writing were directly implicated in the administrative, record-keeping functions of letters and letter collections. Hence this chapter not only serves to reveal the mediality of the medieval epistle, but also how medieval epistularity may continue to shed light on contemporary notions of mediation.

The final chapter in the volume is Alice Hutton's Sharp's "The *Gloss* on Genesis and Authority in the Cathedral Schools." This chapter analyzes the early history of the *glossa ordinaria* of the Bible. The books of the *Gloss* are now often interpreted as a way of replacing teachers with books, and the decentralized, charismatic authority of individual luminaries with the regulated, official authority of the institutional church. This chapter demonstrates how the glosses are in fact far more complex, as they perform aspirations to authority by compilers who were the students of master teachers and wished to replicate their acumen. With reference to the manuscripts of the *Gloss* on Genesis, which survives in two distinct stages that reveal the methods of its compilation, Sharp argues that the content of the *Gloss* was shaped by the formatting of the manuscript page, and that the expansion of the text was made possible with innovation in scribal techniques. Given the technical challenges inherent in producing the *Gloss* format, Sharp then analyzes the role of the manuscript format in the use of the book as a symbol of teachers' participation in a magisterial authority, an authority that was performed in the lecture hall and passed on in an exegetical tradition to their students, thus training the students to embody that authoritative tradition.

Taken together, these six chapters point to a new way of theorizing the "medieval concept" that rejects assumptions that have been in operation since the Enlightenment. Certainly there are productive analogies between digital codes and manuscript codices, and between social media and medieval societies. The studies in this volume offer many examples of these. But such analogies must be contextualized in relation to detailed analyses of actual medieval media, and of their actual functions and concerns. We write and publish this book in a media environment of extraordinary complexity, when the advent of virtual and augmented reality technology leads us to believe that human lives may become even more heavily mediated in the future. Many of the forms that make up that media environment may still be traced back to medieval media, even despite the efforts of modern thinkers and writers to obscure this history through master narratives of empire and oppression. The studies in this volume bring media and medieval studies into closer alignment, as a way to uncover a history of media and of the medieval period that might overcome its historical complicity in such efforts.

PART I

Long Durations

CHAPTER I

Genesis of the Digital Concept

Brandon W. Hawk

> Our impulse to store and access data through
> coded languages predates computers by
> thousands of years, and that's really all magic is.
> —*G. Willow Wilson*

In his history of the word *digital* for the *Oxford English Dictionary Online*, Richard Holden writes that this lexeme "underwent an explosion in usage and in meaning in the twentieth century as a direct result of the development of modern computing."[1] While acknowledging the long history of the term in English, he also claims that "for most of its history, *digital* was a relatively unimportant term: it wasn't until the early to mid-twentieth century that the word became more significant and widespread."[2] This chapter will demonstrate how attention to the early lexical history of the term *digital* has significant implications for how the word has come to be used. The medieval evidence surveyed in this chapter links lexical terms and attendant concepts surrounding *digital* (pertaining to the digits and computation) and the closely related term *manual* (pertaining to the labour of the hand) in order to trouble distinctions between digital and other forms of media in contemporary discourse. Our "digital age" follows on the invention of a distinction between the "analogue" and the "digital" that replaced the older interconnected model of the "manual" and the "digital." The development of our digital concept provides crucial context for the emergence of digital media and its relation to computation.

In this chapter, I examine evidence surviving in British texts from the premodern period, composed in both Latin and English, building on similar examinations of medieval and early modern media to inform contemporary examinations of these topics.[3] In particular, Kathleen E. Kennedy has demonstrated the underlying connections between medieval scribal culture and modern computer hackers, even in lexical associations, showing how such concepts travel across time.[4] Similarly, the evidence of medieval texts demonstrates long-standing correlations between the word *digital* and mathematical computation that should be taken into account when considering the term's lexical and conceptual history. "Digital" technologies for computation are very old indeed, as people have not only counted but done advanced mathematics on their fingers for a very long time. We know from major works of cultural criticism like Raymond Williams's *Keywords: A Vocabulary of Culture and Society* that there is much to learn from critically interrogating such terms beyond contemporary semantics.[5] This is especially true of terms that develop not in the modern period, but that have much older histories. In line with the Foucauldian notion of telling alternate histories that underpins much of cultural studies and media archaeology (and influenced Williams), I offer a survey of the digital concept for the medieval period, as a contribution toward a more general history that has yet to be written.

In the OED, multiple sense definitions of the term *digital* include notes about how it is "typically contrasted with *analogue*."[6] Though recent conceptualizations in media studies seek to complicate and even challenge this division, an emphasis on the differences remains prevalent in popular discourses about computational media.[7] The basic distinction is that between continuous analogue signals, like radio waves, and discontinuous digital signals, which in binary code alternate between ones (i.e., signals) and zeroes (i.e., interruptions). The binary between them is present already in foundational works on digital computation like Alan Turing's famous article "Computing Machinery and Intelligence."[8] We also see its popular conception in the social media response to the comments of former United States Senator Ted Stevens, whose 2006 statement that the internet is "a series of tubes" gave rise to the humorous malapropism of "intertubes."[9] The joke of "intertubes" is that "digital" technology must be juxtaposed to "analogue" technology if it is to be intelligible to non-specialists, but that such analogies are ultimately confusing and misleading. In this chapter, I interrogate the division underlying this presumption by demonstrating how it replaces an older model of computation from the premodern period.

The present chapter draws on John Guillory's "Genesis of the Media Concept" in both theory and argument.[10] Guillory charts how the "media concept," or discourses of communication theories, preceded the coinage of the term *media* as a word for "communication technology" in the nineteenth century. He argues that "the concept of a medium of communication was absent but *wanted* for the several centuries prior to its appearance."[11] In a parallel manner, I suggest that the premodern digital concept comprised computational correlations that remained part of its ideational history until twentieth-century culture made them explicit. This argument does not make a teleological claim urged on by presentism rewriting the past; rather, it insists on the significance of underlying currents across the *longue durée* of media and digital concepts.

There are major distinctions between the history Guillory presents for *media* and the conceptual history of *digital* that I present in this study. While Guillory demonstrates that there was no specific language for the *media* concept in discourse about communication from Aristotle to the late nineteenth century, the *digital* concept was part of computational discourses for centuries with an underlying semantic potential presaging its later popularity as a prominent cultural keyword. In order to survey the premodern digital concept and its semantic associations, I take up a methodology similar to Guillory's, through "a series of philological annotations on a linked set of evolving terms,"[12] in English, Latin, and Anglo-Latin, including *digitus, digiti, digit, digitaliter, manus*, and *manual*.[13] Each of these lexemes contributes to the semantic range surrounding the digital concept, spanning from premodernity to our own pervasive uses of the term. Particularly important is the easy slippage between the digits of the fingers (*digitus*, *digiti*, *digital*) and the uses of the hand (*manus*, *manual*) as ways of doing and understanding the labour of computation. The *digital* concept continually evokes the physical ways that algorithms are relayed through these extremities, as it roots the mathematical in the material context of computation. In this way, the following account of the lexical history of *digital* shows that medieval conceptions of mathematics were linked with systems of manual labour. It will also show how computation, key to the digital concept in the medieval period, goes somewhat dormant in the early modern period until it re-emerges in the mid-twentieth century.

In his influential book *Virtually Anglo-Saxon*, Martin K. Foys rightly notes the difficulty for modern people imagining how medieval, manual mathematics works for large-scale calculations and points toward connections between physical and computer-aided systems of calculation. "Most of our ability to calculate," Foys writes, "has successively developed through a series of technologies, beginning with Arabic writing and culminating (for now) with microchip processing."[14] He further connects medieval finger reckoning (to be discussed) with mechanical technologies by way of the eighteenth-century German engineer Jacob Leupold (1674–1727). Leupold had created plans for a mechanical calculating machine (though he never built it) and printed an image titled *Der Alten Finger-Rechnung* (1727) depicting the system "as an indicator of both the historical foundation and the technological progress of the mechanics of calculation."[15] Later, Foys again draws a connection across time by noting that both early medieval and modern computer technologies "do the same thing—execute algorithms—but they now stand just about as far removed from each other on the functional and historical registers as possible." Yet the associations of numerical computation surrounding the digital concept from this earlier period may help us to reconcile such distance conceptually.[16] We continue to manually use our digits to bring together computistical algorithms and labour in our own communication technologies. Just as in the medieval period, the use of computers today is still largely through typing and clicking with fingers.

The medieval examples remind us that digital computation is a physically constituted code for embodied action, representing mathematical calculations through manual labour. The following examples demonstrate the long history of interplay between what we now consider the distinctive realms of "analogue" and "digital" computation in sources about finger-counting and the development of advanced mathematical systems. The medieval digital concept has much to offer to contemporary discussions of both computers and the long history of media. The present chapter points the way forward with some key examples that instantiate the sort of evidence that must be taken into account in the future.

Putting a Finger on the Digital

My starting point is the lexical history of the word *digital* before its appearance in the English language. According to the *Oxford English Dictionary* and *Middle English Dictionary*, the earliest extant attestations (to which I will return) of English *digit* and *digital*, derived from Latin *digitus*, appear around the turn of the fifteenth century.[17] Yet the Latin *digitus* and related terms have roots stretching back to well before the medieval period. My goal here is to highlight certain developments in specifically early medieval England that presage later uses regarding computer technologies, but I must acknowledge at the beginning that these in turn derive from the digital computational practices of the classical and late antique periods.[18] Developments in the classical period are of course important to the much longer history of digital computation, not least because of the Greco-Latin system known as *computus digitorum* in which fingers are used to calculate advanced mathematics.

In this chapter, I begin with the major changes to these practices first attested in the Middle Ages, as these are the most significant for the present study.

The first major attestation of medieval computation is in the *Etymologiae* of Isidore of Seville (ca. 560–636), an encyclopedic collection of classical learning that influenced many later thinkers.[19] This work was a "bestseller" of the medieval period, in educational settings and elsewhere, with over a thousand whole or fragmentary manuscript copies surviving—an extraordinary number matched by only a handful of major works from the period.[20] As the title advertises, Isidore collects and organizes classical knowledge around his etymologies of key terms. While he does not follow modern philological methods, Isidore explains his approach most clearly in a section "On Etymologies" (*De etymologia*): "Etymologies of words are furnished either from their given cause ... or from their origin ... or from the contrary.... Some are created by derivation from other words ... some from sound ... some are derived from Greek etymology and have a Latin declension."[21] He aims, then, to offer conceptual explanations of words through received semantic and cultural meanings.

Isidore's most explicit discussion of *digitus* and received thinking about the term appears in *Etymologiae* 10.1.70, among his comments on "Human beings and their parts" (*De homine et partibus eius*). In this section, he claims, "The fingers are so called, either because there are ten [*decem*] of them, or because they are connected handsomely [*decenter*]. For they combine in themselves both the perfect number and the most appropriate order [*decentissimum*]."[22] Modern linguistic theories remain inconclusive about whether Isidore is correct to argue that *digitus* and *decem* are related: the precise etymological origin of *digitus* is not altogether clear. It is noteworthy, however, that *decem* and *dextra* share the same root (**dek-*).[23] In his etymological wordplay, Isidore hints at the numerical properties of the word *digitus*. Regardless of the accuracy of his etymological claims about *digitus* and *decem*, the associations between fingers and numbers persisted throughout the medieval period, not only for lexical similarities but also for practical, mathematical practices.

The first British author to use Latin *digitus* in the computational sense is Bede (673/4–735), and the word is particularly well-attested in his work *De temporum ratione*.[24] Bede's main aim in this treatise is to lay out a proper system for calculating dates, especially Easter, which is most important for Bede's conception of time within a Christian framework of both narrative world history (what has happened before) and cyclical, liturgical worship (what is celebrated annually). Within Christian theology, with Easter at the centre, the need for correct calculations of feast days across time was pre-eminent. Amid contemporary controversies about the date of the world, calculations of the proper times to celebrate Easter, and even speculations about calculating the end of the world, Bede undertook a major feat to systematize mathematics and the uses for Christian science. *De temporum ratione* became a highly influential work on calculating dates and Easter, and later authors concerned with mathematics could scarcely ignore it. Indeed, like Isidore's *Etymologiae*, Bede's treatise became a standard in educational settings during the Middle Ages, and it survives in whole or in part in 240 copies across Western Europe.[25]

Most pertinent is Bede's discussion at the start of *De temporum ratione* of a system of mathematical computation represented by a type of numerical sign language with fingers, in a section titled "On Calculating or Speaking with the Fingers" (*De Computo uel Loquela Digitorum*). As a foundation for Bede's later sections, this part was necessary for establishing the necessary means of mathematics for understanding and calculating calendrical dates like Easter. In this section, Bede relies on the classical tradition of *computus digitorum* for his calculations.[26] This type of computation is now known as finger reckoning. For example, Bede instructs readers to count to one as follows: "So when you say 'one,' bend the little finger of the left hand and fix it on the middle of the palm."[27] He continues by explaining how to represent numbers in this way up to ten; he then explains the tens from twenty up to ninety;

moving to the right hand, he explains one hundred, followed by the consecutive hundreds, one thousand, followed by the consecutive thousands; and he ends by explaining, "When you say 'one million,' cross your two hands, linking your thumbs together."[28] By incorporating the same system that Isidore discusses (since he surely knew the *Etymologiae*) and putting it to use for practical mathematics, Bede's discussion demonstrates the role of mathematical systems with digital subjects that have come to rest at the heart of algorithmic culture in the "digital age." The key point for our present discussion is that this system for counting became more generally a system for mathematics and computation.

Bede's comments demonstrate close links between the digital concept and several issues that appear throughout premodern sources. In this context, *digital* and *manual* retain their most literal senses, since the mathematical work Bede lays out is done with fingers and hands. There is also a clear aspect of labour to this work, which is not merely mental but physical. Working with one's hands carries an important symbolism in a monastic context like Bede's. The core tenets of Benedictine monasticism were "ora et labora" (pray and work), as enshrined in the *Rule of Saint Benedict* that rested at the heart of early medieval monasticism. The ritualized, repetitive speech and motions of counting to one million codes Bede's system of finger reckoning as a devotional ritual, combining mental and physical rigour, as indeed was ideally the case for all work and prayer in the regulated environment of the monastery.

In other words, Bede's system for using fingers and hands for numerical reckoning as he describes mediates abstract computational notions into physical embodiment.[29] Even more, this materiality of computation relates to the moral life of monasticism and its tenets (pray and work). We are reminded, then, of Bede's basic impetus for writing his treatise, to demonstrate the proper, moral means of calculating Easter, which he upholds against those he views as unorthodox and heretical. Finger reckoning in this context is a material medium for not only communicating mathematics but also promoting Christian morality. Digital computation for Bede and other medieval thinkers is an embodied form for mediating mathematical concepts, which is a holy practice that elevates and purifies the community, for example, by making sure that they celebrate Easter at the appropriate time. What is "mediated," therefore, is communication with the divine, God's purpose for humanity, and focus on salvation in the Easter season, all wrapped up in mathematical calculations enacted with the body.

Already we see many avenues for approaching links between mathematics, hands, and medieval labour. For present purposes, I single out only a few useful avenues for study and reflection. First, images of fingers and hands (in visual art and ekphrastic descriptions) feature heavily in medieval mnemonics, such as the musical chart known as the Guidonian Hand, which was employed in the later medieval period for both theoretical and practical uses.[30] Another similar example is a vision in which a monk is taught to recite prayers to the Virgin Mary using his knuckles as a mnemonic device (perhaps akin to use of the rosary).[31] Combining memory and communication is the Cluniac system of monastic sign language, translated into Old English in the eleventh century.[32] We might also examine medieval hand gestures, in visual media as well as textual narratives: for just a few sacred examples, we might consider doubting Thomas, the Godhead's three-fingered Trinitarian indicator, or other gestures toward, from, or evoking the divine.[33] In all of these examples, we see issues of encoding, decoding, and meaning-making that offer useful thematic analogies between medieval and modern "digital" cultures.

Surely there is much to be gained from extended reflections on hands elsewhere in medieval culture. Not least of these is the handwritten "manuscript," named because of the Latin terms for handwriting *manus* (hand) and *scriptus* (written). Though the term was largely propagated in the early modern period to indicate distinctions with print,[34] manuscripts are fundamentally works of manual labour (Latin *manualis*).[35] And when we consider how this category extends into the labour of farms, trades, crafts, and beyond (within and without monasteries), we find new meaning in Proverbs 12:24: "The hand of the valiant shall bear rule: but that which is slothful shall be under tribute."[36] The remainder of this chapter will set the stage for such "valiant" endeavours by focusing in particular on the trajectory of the word and concept *digital*.

Remediating Bede

Bede's manual system of digital computation was taken over by a number of medieval authors as it solidified a place in Western European mathematical traditions. At the same time, the general trajectory of this intellectual history demonstrates the continuation of mathematical associations in British Latin sources up to the first appearances of *digit* and *digital* in English language texts.[37] As mathematical methods multiplied, so did adaptations of Bede's system through expansions, visualizations, and cross-language translations. Each of these constitutes a mediation of finger reckoning—already mediated from physical practice to verbal description—into practical application. Each subsequent author takes Bede's own mediation of abstract mathematics in *De temporum ratione* and translates it into a new form of communication, such as expanded explication, tabular representation, or application to algorithmic problems at hand. In this sense, as the mathematical system is represented in different ways, old media and old theories mingle with new media and new theories across time.

The first British author to discuss computation fully after Bede was Byrhtferth of Ramsey (fl. ca. 986–ca. 1016), in his *Enchiridion*.[38] This bilingual manual (some parts written in Old English, others in Latin, often code-switching), covers topics related to mathematical, scientific, and calendrical material, encompassing many of the same topics in Bede's educational works and drawing heavily from them.[39] Byrhtferth also draws on and synthesizes the works of the French monk Abbo of Fleury (ca. 945–1004), who had adapted and expanded Bede's system in the tenth century.[40] Eighteen instances of Latin *digitus* appear in the *Enchiridion*, all in section 4.1, in contrast to only two instances of Old English *finger*-related terms, including "beginning of the forefinger" (*scytefingres anginne*) and "the nail of the little finger" (*þæs læstan fingres nægle*) in 2.2.[41] A few examples demonstrate Byrhtferth's uses and how he both draws on and extends Bede's earlier work.

Byrhtferth's discussions of the numbers thirty and one hundred represent his reliance on Bede and correlations between fingers (sign-language) and numerical signification. In the first instance, he writes, "In the number thirty, finger is joined to finger.... In thirty, you join the nails of the index finger and thumb in a gentle embrace; in sixty, you carefully surround the curved thumb with your index finger from the front."[42] Soon after this passage, Byrhtferth also claims, "The perfection of the number 100 is shown in the sign-language of fingers, since it goes from the left hand to the right, inscribing an arc in the form of a crown, thus exhibiting 'a never fading crown of glory.'"[43] As in Bede, both sign language and fingers play a key role in the system of calculation in this text, and Byrhtferth's comments point toward the complex, moral processes involved in mastering advanced algorithms with finger reckoning.

Most of Byrhtferth's uses of *digitus* (especially in singular dative form of *digito*, as a direct object) appear in a later section of part 4.1, on the multiplication of units. For example, "si multiplicauerus singularem numerum per decenum, dabis uniquique digito .x. et omni articulo .c." (If you wish to multiply any number by 10, you assign 10 to each finger and 100 to each joint); he uses the same formula ("si multiplicaueris ... dabis unicuique digito ... et omni articulo") for subsequent multiples.[44] In these cases, he continues to rely on Bede's manual method of computation, as expanded by Abbo. In the progression of this system from Bede, through Abbo's work, and taken up by Byrhtferth, we see the adaptation of the digital computational system into new explanations and new forms, which lend to the increasing complexity of representing mathematics by way of and associated with Latin *digitus*. Byrhtferth presents not only a description but also further moralization and theoretical application, extending the finger counting from *De temporum ratione* into more advanced uses and allegorized explanations.

As a compendium of medieval mathematical knowledge, Byrhtferth's *Enchiridion* also demonstrates a latent connection between the digital concept and code. In book 3, the treatise includes a convenient collection of charts, which adapt Bede's system and portray their evolution into a full system of visuals for encyclopedic knowledge. One example to demonstrate this point is a set of tables listing Latin, Greek, and Hebrew alphabets along with numerical values for Latin and Greek letters.[45] The first table in this sequence lists the Latin alphabet along with the meanings of various letters now known as Roman numerals: *I* for one, *V* for five, and so on. In the next table of this sequence, numerical values accompany letters of the Greek alphabet: *alpha* (*α*) for one (I), *beta* (*β*) for two (II), and so on. These charts speak to the encoding of numbers with language in a way that links computation with fingers to signs on the page. Furthermore, these charts point toward the dual nature of semiotic forms on the page, which may be inscribed and understood simultaneously as technology for linguistic or mathematical communication as well as numerological interpretations. Language and computation—the same computation enacted digitally, with finger reckoning—are bound together in a manner that foreshadows encoded mediation of communication with the development of twentieth-century computers. At the same time, these charts also draw together notions of mediation and physical labour with language and encoding.

The twelfth-century renaissance brought further developments as scientific knowledge increased in Western Europe. This period brought an influx of works from the Arabic world, the rise of the university, and new methods in scientific learning. In his *Regunculae super abacum*, in a section on multiplication, Thurkill Compotista (fl. 1115) discusses the means of creating a multiplication table.[46] Exploring the basics first, Thurkill then describes how to determine the types of numbers involved: "Considera tunc et caute delibera, utrum prolatus numerus sic ex caracterum duplacione confectus digitus sit an articulus, uel uterque simul" (Then consider and carefully decide whether the number thus brought forth from the duplication of characters made together is a digit or an article, or both together); the rest of the calculation rests on this basis.[47] Here we find computational connections with *digitus* and *articulus* (a division, or joint in the finger—again signalling physical embodiment in the hand) alluding to the older system of finger reckoning as expounded in the works of Bede and Byrhtferth, as well as the foundations of a new system of calculation. Thurkill's notions move mathematical practices further away from manual computation with the fingers, increasing the reliance on and sophistication of visual tables and coded information.

Twelfth-century and later explications of multiplication continue to move beyond finger reckoning, while at the same time using the same vocabulary and concepts of *digitus* and *articulus*. For example, Adelard of Bath (born in or before 1080, died in or after 1150) explicates the process of multiplication in his *De eodem et diuerso* (ca. 1109): "Hence, if any product arises from multiplication on the countable digits and *articuli* of the abacus, the correctness of the calculation can be proved by the division of the same product."[48] Similarly, Robert of Ketton (fl. 1141–57) expresses the same ideas in his *Liber restaurationis et oppositionis numeri* (a Latin translation of the Arabic *Algebra* of al-Khwarizmi): "Since the multiplication of a composite number by a composite number is the same as the multiplication of each part of the one composite by each part of the other, so it follows that the multiplication is fourfold, namely article by article, digit by article, then article by digit, and fourthly digit by digit."[49] In the thirteenth century, Bartholomaeus Anglicus (b. before 1203, d. 1272) writes about such numbers in his *De proprietatibus rerum* 19.123, "De denario" (On money), citing Bede and stating that "numerorum alius est digitus, alius articulus, alius compositus" (among numbers is the digit, another the article, another the composite).[50] In this account, he relies on an earlier treatise by John of Sacrobosco (John of Holywood, d. ca. 1236), *De arte numerandi*, with the exact same wording.[51] Bartholomaeus continues by defining each term, first relating, "Digitus continet numeros simplices ab uno usque ad decem" (Digit contains simple numerals from one up to ten) and continuing from that point. This overview of major texts charts the continued tradition of associations between calculation and physical mathematical practices through the digital concept.

The first known extant recorded instance of *digitus* in English appears in John Trevisa's translation of Bartholomaeus's *De proprietatibus rerum* (ca. 1398), in which he renders the previously quoted sentences: "Herof it followeþ þat som nombre is *digitus*, and some *articularis*, and somme *compositus*. Euerich simple nombre byneþe ten is *digitus*."[52] From around the same time or shortly thereafter, the English forms *digitus*, *digyt*, and *digit* pervade in vernacular mathematical treatises, as in *The Craft of Numbering* (ca. 1400–ca. 1425) and *The Art of Numbering* (ca. 1450).[53] Both the OED and MED record the earliest English attestation of *digital* in *The Craft of Numbering*, although it does not actually appear in this text. It does, however, appear in the near-contemporary text *The Art of Numbering*, with the meaning of a number or numerical unit of less than ten. For example, the first use relates a definition of the noun form: "Of nombres, that one is clepede digitalle, that othere Article, Another a nombre componede oþer myxt. Another digitalle is a nombre with-in .10.";[54] in a later instance, we find the adjectival form "a digitalle nombre."[55] Again, the influence of earlier treatises is apparent, and it is clear that these Middle English texts are indebted to the longer tradition of computing already charted.

The earlier Anglo-Latin examples help to situate these later Middle English texts, since the vernacular treatises draw on the same scientific knowledge circulating at the time. Thus, *The Art of Numbering* is a translation of John of Sacrobosco's treatise, while *The Craft of Numbering* is an adaptive translation of glosses on the Latin *Carmen de algorismo* by the French teacher and poet Alexander of Villedieu (d. 1240 or 1250).[56] As already noted about sources, Bartholomaeus relied on John

of Sacrobosco's treatise, which was, in turn, based on the longer tradition of computing from Bede through to the thirteenth century.

In such influences, we are able to see the interconnected network of
ideas, texts, and authors that take part in this history. Setting Middle
English examples alongside Anglo-Latin sources also demonstrates
the increasing use of the vernacular for scientific writings in the late
fourteenth and early fifteenth centuries.[57] Various texts that accompany
these sources in surviving manuscripts highlight these trends. All three
Middle English texts appear alongside other scientific works: *The Craft
of Numbering* in London, British Library, Egerton 2622 (s. xv$^{1/4}$) is accompanied by works in Latin (like Alexander of Villedieu's *Carmen*)
and English (like Geoffrey Chaucer's *Treatise on the Astrolabe*);[58] and
The Art of Numbering in Oxford, Bodleian Library, Ashmole 396 (s.
xv) is one part of a compilation of scientific texts in English (like a
translation of the *Secretum secretorum*) as well as mathematical and
astrological tables.[59] All of this amounts to a veritable web of related
materials in the fifteenth century.

Middle English texts and the general lexical history presented in this
study further cause us to confront the interplay of multilingualism in
medieval Britain. As recent reassessments reveal, the history of premodern English (and subsequent periods) is not centred on a single,
monolithic language but characterized by dynamic, mutual relations between the diverse varieties of languages in England as they mingled and
influenced each other.[60] In many cases, histories of English vocabulary
focus on one-way influences such as the adoption of loanwords, especially from Latin and French. Yet the particulars are not so simple. Uses
of *digitus*, *digit*, and *digital* in Middle English texts cannot be easily
demarcated from precursors in Latin; and, in this sense, no clear date
emerges for the adoption of these terms into English. Instead, these
instances demonstrate the fluidity of multilingualism and how lexemes
crossed linguistic boundaries as part of that flexibility. Most authors and
scribes translating, writing, and copying English mathematical treatises

were capable of reading, writing, and comprehending Latin, English, and likely French—attested by the sources used and the appearance of texts in multiple languages together in manuscript collections. The history of the digital concept is part of this multilingual heritage.

Within the multilingual contexts of late medieval England, we might also expect substantial evidence from Anglo-Norman literature. Unfortunately, the major lexicographic resources fail to include the term *digital*, likely because most of the attestations from this time and place are in Latin.[61] As already seen, the term is both enigmatic and elusive for the way it crosses linguistic boundaries and retains its semantic potential as a mathematical concept. It is likely that the same connections may be found in Anglo-Norman sources, but more work in this area is needed.

To illustrate the multilingual and semantic interplay discussed so far, we may turn to one other case from the late fourteenth century: the use of adverbial *digitaliter* ("with the finger, by pointing") in a theological treatise attributed to John Wyclif (ca. 1320–84), titled *Determinatio contra Kylingham Carmelitam*, composed around 1372.[62] Discussing John the Baptist in the line of prophets, Wyclif contests his opponent's beliefs about the essences of things: "But truly he says that he is not a prophet, nor a false prophet, per se, in species or kind, just as he says also that John is not a prophet, while pointing [showing with the finger] toward the Messiah, about whom there are prophecies."[63] Wyclif's use of *digitaliter* fits into the general pattern of adjectival word formation in the late medieval period,[64] with the use of suffix *-alis*, a common feature in medieval Latin that supplied both practical loanwords in the Middle English period as well as a model for parallel formations in late Middle English vocabulary with the suffix *-al*.[65]

Even more, this instance of the Latin term *digitaliter* in Wyclif's treatise foreshadows later adverbial uses of *digitally* "by means of the fingers (and thumbs)."[66] According to the OED, the earliest recorded attestation in English appears in 1832, in Oliver Yorke's editorial disclaimer to an article published in *Fraser's Magazine for Town and Country*: "The present paper ... is not by the same hand that indited [*sic*] the other. We have had nothing to do, digitally speaking, with either. The views of our two friends are in direct opposition."[67] In other words, the two works mentioned are not composed (*digitally*) by the editors, nor by the same authors. By the late twentieth century, this usage had come to overlap with the adverbial meaning "by means of numerical digits; in digital form; by means of digital or computer technology," as computer-aided mathematics via finger-driven machines emerged as a significant technological development. This is evident in the first recorded instance with this meaning in 1946 by physicist John W. Mauchly: "It is then obvious that we might store ... information digitally" with what he calls a "digital or arithmetic device."[68] In this usage, the semantics of the digital concept converge again, through the common associations with computation that the history of *digits* has handed down through mathematical technologies.

Where Fingers Meet Hand: Digital, Manual, Analogue

Comparing the medieval uses of *digital* surveyed above to the word's contemporary semantic range brings to light the associative contrast between the latter and contemporary notions of *manual* technologies, despite the etymological, historical, and conceptual usages that would otherwise bring the two words together. As I have stated above, *digital* relates to *manual* as closely as fingers relate to hands. In this section I dwell on the implications of this history to the terms, in order to clarify the nature of the "digital concept" as it has evolved. Semantically, both *digital* and *manual* derive from Latin anatomical lexis and signify a relation to the embodied human. Grammatically, both words are formed with the same adjectival suffix *-alis*. Finally, like *digital*, the English term *manual* is etymologically derived from Latin *manus* (hand) and *manualis* (with the hand),[69] via Anglo-Norman *manuel* and *manual*.[70] These terms are also closely connected beyond these semantic, grammatical, and etymological aspects, as they play out further considerations for the digital concept across time.

Surveying some instances of the numerous medieval uses of *manus*, *manualis*, and related terms in both Latin and English demonstrates the close links with physical labour, especially through crafts. In Isidore's *Etymologiae*, he claims, "The hand [*manus*] is so called because it is in the service [*munus*] of the whole body, for it serves food to the mouth and it operates everything and manages it; with its help we receive and we give. With strained usage, *manus* also means either a craft or a craftsman—whence we also derive the word for wages [*manupretium*]."[71] This section (which goes on to explain the right and left hands) appears just before Isidore's discussion of fingers (*digiti*), creating a logical connection both anatomically and thematically, reminding us again of the materiality of hands, fingers, and the embodied work that they perform physically and conceptually. In Isidore's *Etymologiae*, we are also reminded of the close connections between *manus* and *dexter* ("on the right hand, propitious, skilful")—leading to the English term *dexterous*, with further associations between what is done with hands and the skill of crafts.[72]

Notions that actions of the hands denote particular craftiness carry over into the medieval period. Representative of Latin associations are uses of the terms *manualis* and *manu artifex* by Roger Bacon (ca. 1214–92) in his *Opus tertium* 75 (1267). Here he discusses how music (*musicus*) is made by playing a cithara (*cytharizare*) "by operating with the hand" (*manualis operatur*). Directly following, Bacon attributes this skill (*artem*) to a *manu artifex*, "one who works with hands," "craftsman," or "performer."[73] The first known extant attestation of *manual* in written English, by Thomas Hoccleve (ca. 1368–1426) in *La Male Regle* (ca. 1405–6), makes the connection to physical work strikingly apparent. The poet provides a mock-penitential view of his youth, at one point writing, "And of thy manuel labour, as I weene, / Thy lucre is swich þat it vnnethe is seene / Ne felt."[74] No doubt Hoccleve nods toward a play on the multiple meanings of *manuel* and *labour* as he tries to imagine a middle way between his youthful dalliances (lacking in *manuel labour*), his life of debt and poverty, and his work to earn wages as a poet (*manuel*, by hand). Most instances of *manual* throughout the fifteenth century indicate its medical significance, as represented by the definition of "surgerie" as "a manuel operacioun" in the Middle English translation (ca. 1475) of the *Chirurgia* of Henri de Mondeville (ca. 1260–1316).[75] Medieval manual labour was every bit as technical and specialized as medieval digital computation, and for this reason it seems that the early association between the digital and the manual persisted into the early-modern period at least.

In this lexical history, we see a key type of interplay between ways of thinking about the *digital* and the *manual* that presage nineteenth- and twentieth-century developments in analogue and digital computing.[76] In analogue computers, we have a means based on physical forms for data; while in digital computers (later on the scene), we have a means based on symbolic representation of values—but both rely on the long-standing desire *to compute* in more advanced ways. This is the same urge behind Bede's own digital strategy, a means of representing advanced calculations by showing one's work in the process of calculation. This is also the same impetus behind later developments during the medieval period: numerical charts and other mathematical pursuits that rely on the digital concept for computation. These examples are all thoroughly *digital* and *manual* in the technical senses, and in this way they frustrate later distinctions between "digital" and "analogue" technologies.

It is, of course, well known that analogue computers are very old. We might consider the Chinese south-pointing chariot used for navigation, from around the first millennium BCE, or the Greek Antikythera mechanism used for astronomy, from ca. 150–ca. 100 BCE. Well before either of these, the abacus had appeared in Mesopotamia between about 2700 and 2300 BCE as one of the earliest computing technologies. In contrast, digital computing is often seen as the younger, more modern means of calculating, which took dominance in the twentieth century and led to all of its many outgrowths as we see in our own "Internet of Things."[77]

But, as media archaeology shows, history often suffers from presentism and teleology, and the narrative of analogue losers and digital winners in the nineteenth and twentieth centuries obscures alternative histories and conceptual correlations. After all, analogue computing continues even now as part of our own technological subculture.[78] Indeed, the emergence of the Internet of Things reminds us of complex, tangible links between the digital and the physical. The *digital* concept in the medieval period, and the many associations discussed here, show that, from a certain point of view, digital and analogue computing were not so far removed from each other in their long history. It might be no surprise that the first adoptions of the term *digit* into the English language in the fifteenth century occurred within decades of Chaucer's own commentary on an analogue computer in his *Treatise on the Astrolabe* (1391).[79] The early fifteenth century also brought about the adoption of the noun *computation* (*computacioun*) into the English language, from Latin (*computatio*) via French (*computation*).[80] Tracing the digital concept through the Middle Ages reminds us of the haptic element in the history of computing: we insist on touch, physicality, embodiment, the manual nature of labour, as that labour is mediated through our digits typing data into our computers. There is, then, a little of the analogue in all of our computing, from a time before Bede's finger reckoning to our own "digital age." This chapter is a prelude to those investigations that will further historicize and trouble these concepts.

Q̄m inuenīri possit courrentes 7 data cuīlibet anni per manum.
Scribo t̄ lecere mirandu calculandi copendiu. copendiosi q̄de q̄ ornari sz leui
quia breui. Hon loq̄r ornare loq̄r au sub breuicace. Ee laboro breue. plus
tam ee leui. Primo itaq; sciendū ÷ q̄ cerrentes 7 q̄ data simul crere so
leanr. Hoc au subiecta

G	A	B	C	D	E	F
VII	VI	V	IIII	III	II	I

Hnc q̄ expedit: ecc̄li solarem
fiǵa docebit et usus: cū concurrenrib; 7 datis 7 bissertū
i man̄ siniste: i sinist̄ a radice idicii inchoa. 7 singloy digntoy articlos cū su
mitatib; copitando ependens: eunde ecc̄lū i sūmitate medii dexre consumabit.

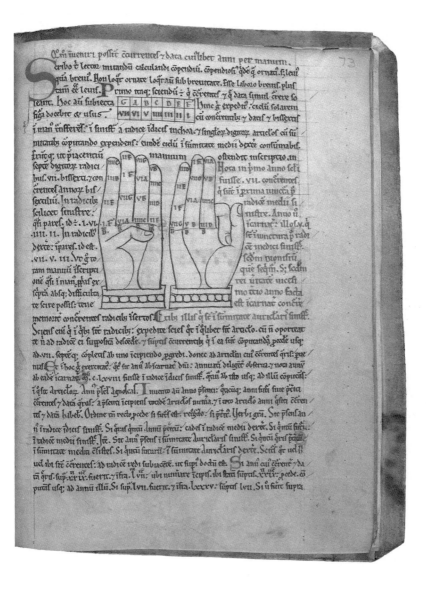

Siniq; ut placentiū manuum ostendit inscriptio. in
sepe digntoy radici
bus. vii. bisserta. 7 con
crentes annoy bis
sextiliū. In radicib;
scilicet sinistre:
q̄si pares. id ÷. 1. vi.
.iiii. ii. Jn radicib;
dexre: ipares. id est.
.vii. v. iii. Vt q̄ ro
tam manuū iscripti
one est i man̄; q̄as es
septū absq; difficulta
te scire possit: ue
memorie concurrentes radicib; isertos
Hora in p̄mo anno scti
fuisse. vii. concurrentes
q̄ sut i p̄ima iunctura p
radice medii si
nistre. Anno u
icarnat: illosy q̄
se iunctura p radi
ce medici sinist.
sedm monstru
q̄e sedm. S; sedm
rei uritate uicesi
mo tcio anno facta
est icarnat concep

Exrb: illis q̄ se i sūmitate auriclaris sinist.
Scient eni q̄ i q̄bi sut radicib; expedire scies q̄ i q̄liber sut articlo. cū n oporteat
te n ad radice et supposita descede. 7 supias occurrentes q̄ i ea sut copitandi. pcede usq;
ad. vii. sepe q̄; copleas ab uno icipiendo pgredi. donec ad articlm cui cerrentes q̄ris: pue
nias. Et i hoc q̄ exercitas: q̄ sir anni ab icarnat dni: annuati diligent obseria. 7 noa anni
ab eade icarnat. q̄. c. lxvii. finisse i radice idicii sinist. q̄n u ab ipso usq; ad illū copitas:
i q̄ sir articloy anni p̄set agnoscas. Inueno au anno p̄seni: q̄acūq; anni siti siue p̄sti
cerrentes 7 data q̄ras: a p̄seni icipiens uade articlos numia. 7 uero articlo anni ister cerren
tes 7 data habeb. Ordine tū recto. pcede si fuer it: retigio. si p̄st. Uerbi gra. Sic p̄seni an
ni i radice idicii sinist. Si q̄ras q̄ui anni p̄teriti: cadet i radice medii dexre. Si q̄ui sucu:
i radice medii sinist. Sic anni p̄seni i sūmitate auriclaris sinist. Si q̄uti q̄ris p̄teri:
i sūmitate medii est iste. Si q̄ui sucurit: i sūmitate auriclaris dexre. Scisf q̄ uel si
uel ibi sir cerrentes: Ad radice redi sub uicece. ut supi docui est. Si anni cui cerren 7 da
tū q̄ras: sup. cc. vii. fuerit. 7 ista. Lui: ubi nuniate scripsi. ibi stati supias. cc. vii: pcede. co
purtū usq; ad annū illū. Si sup. lvii. fuer it. 7 ista. lxxxv: supias. lvii. Si u fuere supta

Anonymous, *De Computus manualis*, diagram of hands in brown ink with numbers in red and green, 11–12th Century, British Library, London, Egerton 3314 (f. 73r)

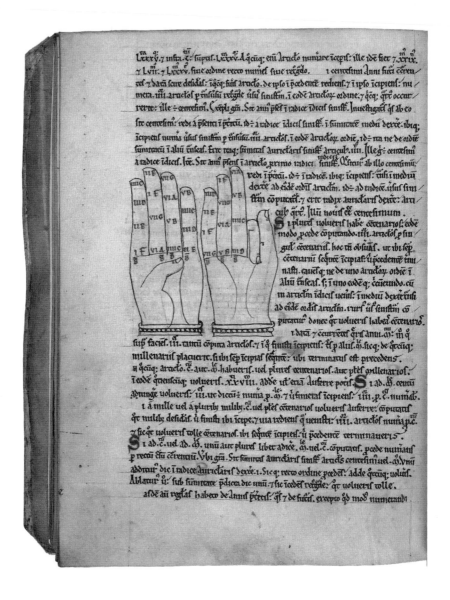

Anonymous, *De Computus manualis*, diagram of hands in brown ink with numbers in red and green, British Library, London, L, Egerton 3314 (f. 73v)

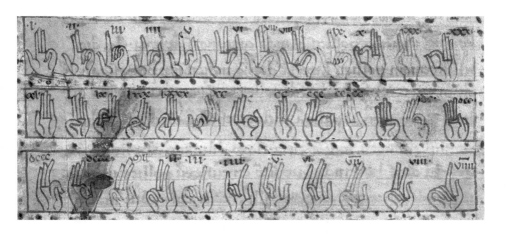

Bede, *De temporum ratione*, Table of the figure calculations of the Computus (detail), France north or central, fourteenth century, British Library, London, Royal 13 A XI (f. 33v)

CHAPTER 2

Protocol and Regulation

Controlling Media Histories

Stephen M. Yeager

Besides its broadly influential popular reception, McLuhan's *Gutenberg Galaxy* (1962) had a major impact on the discourse defining the boundaries of medieval studies, as it popularized a new materialist framing for the period distinction that the terms "medieval" and "modern" apply to European history between the fourteenth and sixteenth centuries.[1] In contrast to the older debates interrogating and defending a distinction between the "Renaissance man" and "his" medieval counterparts, McLuhan's focus on the spread of the printing press helped reframe the debate as a fluid but still period-defining distinction between medieval "manuscript culture" and modern "print culture."[2] This reframing tied the periodization of European history to a new major question: Can we argue that Gutenberg's famous printed Bible began a revolution that broke radically with manuscript culture, given that these Bibles were identical to contemporary manuscripts in their layout and formatting, and were even illuminated by hand? Though scholars began almost immediately to qualify McLuhan's confident assertions that indeed we may hold this to be true, his periodization of medieval and early-modern media history has nonetheless become a crux in any number of political and aesthetic debates about the forms of culture that have become possible, probable, and/or desirable after the invention of mass media, and especially after the internet. This chapter, then, will propose a heuristic for describing how periodizations like McLuhan's can work to limit and control the potential political implications of debates about history, as a contribution towards the vital task of unpacking the features of this particular crux and its implication for our own historical moment.

The core of my heuristic is an opposition between *protocol* and *regulation*. These terms will be used to name contrary, opposed forms of documented, disseminated control, which justify their contrary, opposed "protocological" and "regulatory" philosophies of responsibility and punishment by contrary, opposed organizational schemae for arranging and using the archive. In brief, this chapter uses the opposition between protocol and regulation to identify formal patterns in the use of historical evidence that govern the evolution of dominant ideologies in continuity with the past and in response to the present. Such patterns cut perpendicularly across (explicitly periodized) political divisions like "conservative" and "progressive," "reactionary" and "revolutionary," and so their description exposes more clearly to critical view the social function of periodization itself, as a strategy for enabling political and cultural changes while also perpetuating continuities.

It bears stressing moreover that the term "ideology" is used here in its Althusserian sense, to refer to the inherited *material* conditions that delineate what is thinkable and what is not, and so limit the disruptive potential of political resistance.[3] Because historical media are not only inherited material objects but are also the objects through which we consider our relations to our historical inheritances, they are necessarily central to both the original construction of ideology itself and to any critique that would seek to be self-aware about the fact of ideology as an aspect of previous historical moments. This chapter aims to identify some of the structures that pattern both ideological critiques and critiques of ideology in the specific discourse of media history.

In the decades since *The Gutenberg Galaxy*, Elizabeth Eisenstein and others have complicated but ultimately affirmed McLuhan's main point, that the ways in which texts are put together in printed books determined and were determined by the larger forms of social and political organization in the contexts where commercial printing was first developed.[4] In their recent summary of and intervention into such arguments, Johnston and Van Dussen have defended the usefulness of a period distinction between manuscript and print cultures, which they frame in terms of the decentralization of authority in the former relative to the centralization of authority in the latter.[5] This framing is representative of the common view that both manuscript and digital cultures were relatively reliant on protocols, while "modern" print culture was relatively regulated. Hence, for reasons that will be explained below, protocological readings of media history tend to emphasize continuity over the *longue durée* while regulatory ones tend rather to see discontinuity and, in recent decades, devolution. The result of such framings has been that debates about the history of the book have become hopelessly intertwined with debates about the future of the internet, and specifically about whether digital authority ought to be decentralized (as it is held to have been in manuscript culture) or re-centralized (as it is held to have been in high print culture).

It is worth emphasizing that this framing of such a broad, disparate, but densely interrelated set of issues and arguments cannot and should not be considered independently of the political context of the early twenty-first century, nor especially of my own personal political and social identities. Nonetheless, it seems productive to describe the political investments of historians and critics like myself formally, especially when those engagements tend to find repetitive patterns in history that have consistently been promoted and accepted by the field and by the public in the service of presentist—and, more strikingly, contradictory—agendas. I hope that in the future, the descriptive vocabulary provided here might serve as a taxonomy for organizing cross-disciplinary conversations on their shared tendencies. For now, however, I will focus my discussion on the particular problem of how or whether we ought to periodize the history of communications in Western Europe before, during, and after the age of empire. I will begin in the next section by defining my terms more precisely.

Protocol and Regulation: Definitions

A *protocol*, in the terms used here, is a branching narrative that identifies a series of circumstances in which actions might be required, and then lists appropriate choices for actors in response to those circumstances. A *regulation*, in contrast, imagines consequences of possible actions and disallows them, typically by attaching them to penalties, which are not typically features of protocols. In brief, protocol is an immanent law that cultivates an actor's virtue and eliminates the need for discipline, while regulation is a transcendent law that disciplines actors but otherwise allows them subjective freedom.

The relation between these laws and the study of historical media is illustrated by the history of the word *protocol* itself. The oldest sense of *protocol* refers to the outermost part of the papyrus roll, or *protokollon* ("first glue" or "first page").[6] In the Byzantine period the officials in charge of papyrus production began to write information on these protocols as a way to control production of this writing material, requiring all official records to leave the protocols attached if they were to be valid.[7] As the formal study of Roman civil law spread throughout Europe in the medieval period, the term became a metonym for authenticating paratexts attached to documents and for documented records themselves, and in particular for documented agreements.[8] From here the term migrated into the sphere of diplomacy, where it came to refer to not only the documents recording negotiations but also to the procedures for the conduct of negotiations. This procedural protocol is the kind practised in and between digital networks, and its dictates are constantly revised by the addition of new nodes and loss of old ones, the invention of new technologies and the disappearance of obsolescent ones, the emergence of new ISPs and the conglomeration of their competitors, and so on.

In this way, the word *protocol* evolved from a name for material records of transactions into a name for the procedures governing transactions, which in turn generated new records that led to the refinement and/or abandonment of older procedures, in a feedback loop of self-critical analysis. This method for storing and applying the records of the past is central not only to the methods governing the operation of computer networks, but also to the encoding of the bureaucratic systems of archival organization that computer networks perpetuate. On the basis of this history, then, I define protocol in my heuristic as an attempt to control actors by limiting their choices to only the sorts of actions that history has proven effective, as must be demonstrated with reference to an archival record of some sort.

It is crucial to note that the obsession of protocol with such records by no means implies a reverence for them, or even for the past they record. On the contrary, the records are constantly called into question for their accuracy and their applicability, serving as the occasion for and a distraction from arguments about embodied action in the present and future. As I have argued elsewhere, such criticisms of historical documents can be founded only on an intimate knowledge of them, and indeed there are worse measures of the "literacy" and dependence of a set of actors on a storage medium than the detailed intensity with which those actors critique the technical shortcomings of that medium.[9] In protocols, the authority of the past is always subordinate to the needs of the present, not least because the former is always mediated and the latter is, in theory at least, immediate. Next time something will be different, and the protocol must be ready to adapt to the emergent data. But at the same time, the subordinate past is fundamentally constitutive of the protocol. Without a documented historical basis for the organizing principles that govern its provisions, a "protocol" would be just an improvised plan.

With this basic definition of protocol established, we may now describe more precisely the obverse control method of regulation. Regulations are defined here as control diagrams that theoretically allow actors the freedom to choose any actions they wish, but disallow possible results by attaching them to penalties. Where a protocol extrapolates principles of action from its practitioners' analysis of archival evidence, regulation authorizes itself by claiming that it was introduced to a system by a central sovereign authority through some force like divine intervention, reasoned consideration, an apparatus for state-sanctioned violence, a rapid change in economic conditions, or some other agent of (re)constitution. Like protocol, regulation is occasioned by a literate and familiar distrust of the archival technologies of the past, but rather than correct old mistakes it seeks to break with that past and build a new control system from scratch. The great irony noted above, that protocol's very claims of continuity with the past lead to a flattening of history and a conceptual emphasis on the eternal present of political and ethical action, is mirrored by the similar irony that regulation's claims of discontinuity with the past divide history into a sequence of discreet moments and so leads to a structural obsession with historical narratives of progress, decadence, and/or cyclical alternation between the two trajectories.

A final term I will use in this discussion is *revolution*, a concept that is crucial to the periodization of history. The fact that the Latin word from which *revolution* derives may mean "revolve," "turn around," "turn back," "unroll a scroll," or "open a book" in medieval British sources nicely illustrates the true nature of such debates, as always concerned primarily with identifying hidden patterns that may shape the structure of memory and hence, materially, with (re-)organizing the archive.[10] Following on its seventeenth-century applications to regime changes, the term *revolution* has long coded tumultuous events as positive instances of progress, as, for example, the Glorious Revolution and the Industrial Revolution were so called while they were still in progress by the proponents of the historical changes that the terms still name.[11] Here, I will proceed from Latour's account of "revolution" in his work *We Were Never Modern* to define the term as a designation for a historical moment claiming that progress occurred at that moment, so rapidly and with so many simultaneous moving parts that it is in the final instance impossible to instrumentalize as a pattern for future improvements to protocol, though at the same time its radical break with tradition marks it as a point of origin for new regulations.[12] McLuhan's print revolution is one example of such a moment, and the debate about continuities and discontinuities between manuscript and print cultures that has followed his intervention demonstrates the cultural work that may be done by either affirming and denying the idea that a given revolution has taken place at a given historical juncture.

In the next section of this chapter I will turn to a historical example to ground my thesis that such debates about revolutions are common sites of conflict between protocological and regulatory philosophies of control. As Kathleen Davis has compellingly argued, the term *periodization* "does not refer to a mere back-description that divides history into segments, but to a fundamental political technique—a way to moderate, divide, and regulate—always rendering its services *now*" (her emphasis).[13] My specific historical example will proceed from her work, in which she suggests that political debates about the laws that would govern the English Empire and historical debates about the origins of the English constitution were deeply intertwined, as politics determined which aspects of the records of early English history were worthy of analysis and which were not, and the early records determined the ideological positions taken in the political debate. Specifically, I will proceed from her work to argue that the periodization of medieval English "feudalism" around the arrival of William the Conqueror in 1066 illustrates how the dualism of protocol and regulation can shape the study of historical media. It is no coincidence, I believe, that in the most recent debates about the revolutionary aspects of William's reign, the Domesday Book looms as large as Gutenberg's Bible does in the discussion about feudalism's end.[14] The more fraught such divisions become, the more dependent becomes the debate on the description of specific media objects as a way of articulating the various positions.

In the next section I will build on Davis's work to demonstrate how the dualism of protocol and regulation help to contain political debate and lend it an arbitrary coherence, by framing it as an organizational question about historical evidence. Identities based on common histories appear to be rooted in the unspoken set of starting points for debate that participants in those identities share, and one common starting point has been the presumption that events from the past ought to be privileged as especially useful indicators of the sorts of events that might happen in the future, over and above conjectures that find no historical analogue. Under these conditions, political arguments are most communicable when they conform to spectrums of acceptable theories about what "actually" happened in the past that, in turn, unfold along axes defined by the agreed-upon features of the evidence cited to support our understandings of events. It is in this sense that the archive has come to serve as a fundamental precondition for even violent political communication between the entities who share it. Common histories provide the occasions for and serve as the media of such struggles.

Periodization and Control

As I have said above, McLuhan's account of a print revolution is only one version of the received historical narratives of "Western" civilization, whereby modernity emerged in a period that has long been called the "Renaissance." There are many complaints by medievalists about the uses and abuses of the term *medieval* to describe the period immediately antecedent to this alleged rebirth.[15] Among the more recent and sophisticated analyses of the question is Kathleen Davis's *Periodization and Sovereignty: How Ideas of Feudalism and Secularization Govern the Politics of Time.* As the subtitle indicates, her study is focused on the conjoined ideas that, first, European "feudalism" was a more or less coherent economic system that was slowly replaced in the modern period by capitalism, and second that "secularization" slowly undermined and supplanted the "religious" governing apparatus of European Christianity. In brief, she describes how the *historical* question of whether a feudal, Christian, and medieval Europe was transformed by revolution into a proto-capitalist, secular, and modern seat of global civilization has long been subsumed by a *political* question about the legacy of European imperialism, and by extension about the sorts of reparations that might best contend with that legacy.

Particularly relevant for our purposes is Davis's statement that "periodization, if it is to have a historical legacy, results from a *double* movement: the first, a contestatory process of identification *with* an epoch, the categories of which it simultaneously constitutes ... and the second a rejection of that epoch identified in this reduced, condensed form" (her emphasis).[16] As I will argue below, these two elements of a single movement are tied to the control strategies of protocol and regulation respectively. In brief, the contestatory identification with earlier epochs is the dominant impulse in protocological agendas, which advocate for control systems that emphasize the personal responsibilities of actors to choose from prescribed lists of actions, while regulatory agendas tend to reject the models of earlier epochs and to sequester them off using narratives of revolution and rupture. In this way, tracing Davis's double movement will set the stage for the fuller definitions of protocol and regulation outlined in the next section below.

Davis's double movement is exemplified in her study by her reading of opposed, politicized periodizations of feudal history, discernible in the work of the early-modern historians Henry Spelman and John Selden. In the sixteenth and seventeenth centuries, the question of whether to divide the English Middle Ages at 1066 had important implications for the struggle between the king and Parliament that culminated in the English Civil War. In brief, "a history of feudal law beginning with the Anglo-Saxons would strengthen the argument for an 'ancient constitution,' while a history of feudal law as introduced by William I, and thus by conquest, would favour the king."[17] Selden's view was that

English feudal law originated well before 1066, and in this way his account favoured the notion of a prehistoric constitution, which Magna Carta only articulated and reiterated.[18] Spelman, meanwhile, argued forcefully that English feudal precedent traced back only to the revolutionary action of William of Normandy, who made English land and title (i.e. "feuds") hereditary.[19] By implication, the king decides the law, and so Magna Carta matters only because a later king signed it.

In the terms of this chapter, Selden's argument about procedural continuity extending before and after 1066 is an example of a protocological reading of history, which is to say that it posits a continuity of practice between protocols in the past and protocols in the present, which lends the present protocols authority. Specifically, Selden imagines the true source of sovereignty in England to be rooted in the parliamentary protocols of law-making that have been practised, revised, recorded, and so continuously renewed by the English since time immemorial. By suggesting that there is continuity between the earliest recorded English history and his own day, he implies that subjects of English law in the present ought to respect and protect this continuity for future generations.

Spelman's history, in contrast, is a regulatory reading that seeks rather moments of rupture that undermine protocological continuity and so authorize frameworks of regulation. In his account, the Norman Conquest was a break that introduced discontinuity into the protocols of law-making. For that reason, his account uses the Norman Conquest as precedent for the principle that ultimately the person of the king (Latin *rex*, which shares its root with *regula*) is endowed with the centralized and sovereign authority to (re)make and so revolutionize the institutions of government as he sees fit.[20]

Though the theses of these historians have clear connections to the political context of the their own moment, they were also articulated through a discourse of historiography wherein truth claims had to be rooted in *proof*, which is to say in historical media whose formal features justified the determination that they were created in the period in question and so could be held to record information about it. The apparent "objectivity" of these media objects is the precise reason that descriptions of them may help to sway the views of the historians' intended audiences.

In this instance, theses like Selden's, which held there was an "ancient constitution" of English law, were long predicated on the conventional opening lines that may be found in many Old English legal pronouncements, alluding to the king's consultation of his *witan*; literally "wise men" or "smart people," but also more specifically his counsellors.[21] Indeed, the debate continues into the present as to whether the *witan* alluded to in these texts were an empowered, parliament-like entity (sometimes called the *witengemot*) or if they were a more informal assembly.[22] In the former case, the texts that tell us about the *witan* would document precedent for the Westminster parliamentary system, wherein authority is distributed across a non-hierarchical multiplicity of "peers" who exercise the rights attached to their title to pass laws and make decisions, as long as they follow the protocol that may, for example, require a quorum before a session can begin, or mandate procedures whereby bills are tabled and voted upon, or insist MPs save questions until the question period.

If a historian may use the archival evidence to convincingly argue that the *witangemot* constrained the conduct of its participants according to protocols similar to those constraining the actions of MPs in the present, then she could follow Selden to argue that there is protocological continuity in the English parliamentary system stretching back to the seventh century at least. As a result, republican arguments in favour of Parliament's sovereignty would carry the weight of precedent. Meanwhile if another historian could support Spelman's position and demonstrate that the parallels between the *witan* and the Westminster Parliament are coincidental, then it would mean the texts alluding to the *witan* are essentially irrelevant to legal history and provide no meaningful precedent for the later protocols of English parliamentary procedure.

In other words, the question of the "ancient constitution" of England determines not only the sovereignty of Parliament in later periods, but also the most basic organizing principles applied by medieval historians to the legal archive. Should Old English law codes be categorized as records of parliamentary history, or should they not? Do we mark them as merely pertinent to the study of another, earlier period, or do we claim that they are part of the history of the laws that persist until this day? Whatever the resolution to this question, the law codes are made pertinent to the history of Parliament by the very existence of the question itself, and so they become a part of the body of historical givens that shape the debate about the relative merits and demerits of republican protocols and royalist regulations. The archival-periodization questions and the political-sovereignty questions establish each other's starting conditions, and hence their evolution over time is tightly recursive.

The heuristic of protocol and regulation, then, is useful for describing how this recursivity serves to ensure stability and continuity of practice. Simply put, it is easier for England to survive internal conflicts over the massive social, political, economic, and legal changes accompanying its reinvention as a global imperial power if the English subjects who would wish to argue about those changes must first argue about the features of English "feudalism" instead. Medieval laws and legal records are particularly well-suited to this pragmatic purpose of misdirection and containment. On the one hand, they tantalizingly promise a possible connection to the past, of a sort that may finally resolve the conflict if the truth is uncovered. On the other, they create mediating distance from that past, and so the opposing sides may simply insist on interpreting the evidence differently forever. No matter how radically the conditions in the present evolve or how dramatically they reshape the landscapes of power, it will always be possible to project the various arguments onto unending disagreements about archived objects whose features never change, excepting of course when the occasional discovery is made. The stability, permanence, and—most importantly—*predictability* of such debates is manifest materially in the archive, which designates and preserves the historical evidence pertinent to these alternative periodizations to reify and so control conflicts that might otherwise spiral into chaos.

Perhaps the clearest sign of this heuristic's importance to societal stability is the fact that politicized narratives of history cannot allow equal weight to protocological and regulatory proscriptions, even when they acknowledge openly that protocol and regulation cannot exist independently of each other. Rather, arguments about history are politicized almost exclusively by the extent to which they either valorize the strict adherence to prescribed codes of conduct or the strict punishment of proscribed consequences. This is not to say that it is impossible to hold an intermediate position. One may argue, for example, that both the king and Parliament should together hold sovereignty in England. Indeed, this is roughly the structure of the English constitutional monarchy that emerged after the "Glorious Revolution." So also might one imagine the Norman Conquest to be revolutionary in some ways but not in others; the *witangemot* to be related to Parliament but not identical; the Old English law codes to be useful records of parliamentary history, but only somewhat useful; the systems of English government to have changed over time without being radically discontinuous; and the popularization of the printing press to be a major development, but not a "revolutionary" one. The paradox is that such conciliatory framings are consistently marked as apolitical, despite serving both as reasonable descriptions of historical reality and reasonable plans for future action, for the contradictory reasons that, firstly, they are accepted in theory as starting principles by all parties (even Cromwell saw the purpose of the Crown, hence his role as "Lord Protector"), though secondly they are rejected in practice by all parties as betrayals of their starting principles (Cromwell also refused to ever accept the title of "king"). The attending unfalsifiability of the protocol/regulation contrast suggests that the final goal of both protocological and regulatory framings of history is not to generate synthetic narratives that best describe the ambivalences of the evidence, but to instrumentalize those ambivalences in the service of an unending conflict between control philosophies that is itself a source of societal continuity and institutional stability. Protocological and regulatory readings of history collaborate to create a single, coherent, and irreconcilably oppositional spectrum of interpretations as a way of using the pre-existing archive of cultural production and human thought to limit possibilities for the future.

In the present instance, it is both striking and typical that the political motives informing the theses of Selden and Spelman had little if any bearing on their works' reception. As Davis explains, Spelman's *Feuds and Tenure*—now "the acclaimed foundation of English feudal historiography"—was conceived "in response to a court decision by which the crown seized colonial property in Ireland, and in which the court had rejected Spelman's interpretation of feudal history" to base its ruling on Selden's longer and more expansive view.[23] One consequence of tracing the origins of English law back to the earliest historical records is to lend greater credence to the earliest examples of English land claims, which are generally gifts from the Crown. If such claims are in fact the basis for land ownership in the seventeenth century, then this would imply that the king has the right to repossess the land bestowed by his predecessors, and hence also any land considered to be owned by England. Such was precisely the determination of the court when it rejected Spelman's view that feudalism in England began with the Norman Conquest to uphold Selden's view. And as Davis herself observes, there is an obvious irony to the fact that the Crown was able to benefit materially in such an extravagant way from an historical thesis that theoretically undermined the Crown's claims to absolute sovereignty.[24]

The key fact here is that when Spelman's account rose to prominence in the academy as an authoritative history and Selden's shaped legal precedent for the ownership of colonial possessions, both politicized arguments were assimilated into the same invisible neutrality of the archive. It may seem remarkable that contrary arguments, attached to contrary positions in one of the most divisive and bloody conflicts in English history, should both simply lose their political valences to be assimilated as transparent fact and accepted legal precedent in this manner. But such is typical of both protocological and regulatory instrumentalizations of historical evidence, which instrumentalize archival objects in order to assimilate novel social and political developments into the archive and so in the process develop new patterns for assimilating future novelties. As I will argue in the next section, we may see a similar process at work at the moment of this writing, in ongoing debates about the past and future of digital culture.

Protocol and Regulation in Internet History

A classic instance of the distinction between protocol and regulation in media history is that between the relatively protocol-based internet broadband networks and the relatively regulation-based telephony networks from which they evolved.[25] A brief summary of this evolution will clarify the basic formal distinction between protocological and regulated control, and also explain why I have chosen these particular terms for my heuristic. In this section's conclusion I will clarify the difference between the protocol/regulation dyad and the similar, earlier dyad of rhizome/tree taken from the works of Deleuze and Guattari, itself commonly deployed in media studies accounts of protocol and regulation in data networks. My hope is that this will then provide a useful starting point for reading across constructions and deconstructions of dominant media periodizations.

It is a commonplace of telecommunications history that for most of the twentieth century, telephony was a heavily regulated control system. Telephone communication relied on an apparatus of "circuit switching," wherein a central administrative authority designated a unique physical connection for each individual call. When one picked up the receiver and dialled a number, then a pathway of cables and wires was set up between receivers to transmit one's voice to the recipient of the call. Only when the call had concluded could the physical infrastructure of the connection be repurposed for another call. As a natural consequence of this centralized architecture, there arose a dominant belief in the tele-communications industry that quasi-public monopolies like the Bell Telephone Company ought to regulate phone calls. Centralization en-abled such monopolies to collect the data necessary to manage the com-plexity of managing thousands of individual phone calls over a single network, as these data helped them to predict traffic patterns and so ensure that the network could—with minimal redundancy—ensure that the network would not become overtaxed and so return busy signals when the phone on the other end was not in use. Bell was then regulated in turn by public commissions whose oversight ensured that the neces-sary infrastructure of cables and wires built on the basis of these data was maintained and deployed as efficiently, fairly, and cheaply as possible.

This centralized, regulated framework was the status quo in the United States until the division of Bell Telephone into regional companies, as part of a larger trend towards deregulation in telecommunications in the 1980s and 1990s. These same processes of deregulation led telecom-munications networks to adopt increasingly decentralized protocols of data transfer like TCP/IP, which used "packet-switching" methods based on those deployed by the early digital network ARPANET.[26] In packet switching, the message is reduced to data "packets" at their place of origin and then sent out over a decentralized network of routers, which were tasked with identifying the best pathway towards a given packet's destination and then with sending the packet forward to the next router along this route. The message was then reassembled when all the pack-ets reached the receiver. Because the adoption of TCP/IP enabled com-puters and routers to send information to each other without needing to reconfigure the physical wires and cables connecting them, its protocols contributed to the industry's belief that there was no longer a need for the monopolies and regulatory frameworks of traditional, centralized telecommunications.

Though both the regulation-based and the protocol-based network design philosophies described above sought to govern the same sorts of communication acts, there is an apparent formal contrast between their overarching strategies of control. Like any protocol, TCP/IP defines and encourages desired actions. Routers that follow TCP/IP must recognize packets when they arrive, check them for mistakes, identify the best route forward, and send the packets along that route. However, many of the specifics related to the implementation of these protocols are left to the individual routers, reflecting the principle that individual routers and connections may join and leave the network at any time. Even if a router deliberately flouts the standard protocol, there is no particular penalty beyond the resulting incompatibility issue. In fact, there is every likelihood that the protocols have already prepared the sending and receiving computers for managing such contingencies.

The same would not be said for an employee at Bell Telephone who refused to follow the company regulations that governed circuit switching. If customers began getting busy signals in their phone calls because of human choice or error, then the agent(s) responsible for managing those connections could expect to be chastised, fired, sued, or even sent to prison, depending on whether the regulation(s) she broke were company policy or law. Centralized and regulated systems of this kind have their advantages, as they are able to disincentivize many of the redundancies and inefficiencies that have always plagued the commercial internet. And yet telecommunications regulations hardly prevented inefficiency at the Bell Telephone company before the 1990s.

There is, then, considerable latitude for any individual investigating the media history of the commercial internet to determine whether or not the emergence of its network constituted an advance, a devolution, or simply another moment in the continuous history of telecommunications. The range of dominant viewpoints may be productively described with reference to the contrasting paranoias about the internet named in the title of Wendy Hui Kyong Chun's book *Control and Freedom*.[27] To the extent that a history of telecommunications argues the internet creates "freedom," by unshackling users from the hierarchical constraints of Bell Telephone's byzantine bureaucracy, then it implicitly favours protocol-based control systems over regulation-based systems and so it is in the terms laid out here "protocological." To the extent a history argues rather that the deregulation of telecommunications has unshackled the technology from effective public oversight and so turned the internet into an instrument of illegal surveillance and "control" (as Chun herself ultimately suggests),[28] then that history implicitly values regulation-based control systems over protocols, and so the account is "regulatory." Finally, a history that takes no position on the relative merits and demerits of regulations and protocols gives up its ability to argue for the future of telecommunications, and it serves only as a mere record of facts from the past that offers no coherent framework for putting those facts to use in the present.

It will be helpful to demonstrate the specific implications of this heuristic if we compare it to the similar dualism of the "rhizome" and the fascicular root of the "tree," which has long been commonplace in internet histories informed by the theoretical framework of media studies. Rhizomatic structure corresponds roughly to my protocological control as arboreal structure corresponds to my regulatory control, though there are important distinctions between the dualisms listed below. While the radical dualism of rhizome/tree originates in the formative articulation of Gilles Deleuze and Felix Guattari in their book *A Thousand Plateaus*, this context is of secondary usefulness here, as the dualism has itself spread across the disciplines in a rather rhizomatic fashion, abandoning its original status as ontology to become instead a framework for describing organizational strategies and design philosophies.[29]

In most of the dualism's occurrences, arboreal root systems are imagined to be centralized, sequentialized, and "organized" in the original sense of this term, which is to say they are divided into interdependent, specialized organs and so given structure. Meanwhile the rhizome is an "acentered, nonhierarchical, nonsignifying system without a General and without an organizing memory or central automation."[30] Rhizomatic elements are neither discreet nor non-discreet, they are semi-autonomous and so modular, and they have no necessary sequence, freely shifting their relative positions and so extending on a horizontal plane of reconfigurable simultaneity. Because such movements constantly frustrate all efforts at sequential narrative organization, Deleuze and Guattari say that the rhizome is therefore "antigenealogy" and "antimemory"—terms that nicely describe the paradoxical manner in which protocols perpetuate themselves through their very antagonism towards the records, genealogies, and memories that gave them form.[31]

As media theorists like Chun and Alexander Galloway have long recognized, it is not coincidental that the rhizome is also a fitting image for the ideal diagram of the protocol-based "distributed network" that the internet has aspired towards for decades, but has never quite become.[32] Indeed it seems quite likely that the success of Deleuze and Guattari's concept in such a wide variety of contemporary discourses is surely related to the amenability of the rhizome to the task of figuring the design logic of the most important technological, cultural, and archival development of our time.[33] In his own Deleuzian analysis of digital protocols, Galloway describes the internet as a dialectical tension between two "control machines," one of which centralizes and hierarchizes information into arboreal structures, and the other one of which distributes information into rhizomes.[34] And as becomes clear over the course of this analysis, Galloway imagines the latter forms of organization to ultimately transcend the former, and hence he suggests that the "true" control structure of the internet—and so the ideal form of internet activism—is rhizomatic.[35] Galloway envisions the internet's configuration of protocological control as a means towards the end of bringing the internet towards this ideal form, or at least for structuring resistance to the internet's abuses. We may see, then, in Galloway's writing one example of the widespread association between rhizomatic systems and the commercial internet described above, which positions these against the arborescent systems of traditional telephony and the private and public entities that regulate(d) it.

But while there are affinities between my protocol/regulation dualism and such deployments of the rhizome/tree dualism, there is at least one key difference. Protocol/regulation, as I use it here, is presupposed to be not only a contingent distinction but a *wholly false and misleading* one when it is applied to describe actual structures of any actual historical organization. No control system has ever been more or less protocol-based or regulation-based than has any other system. Each form of control leads directly into the other and derives entirely from the other. The dualism serves, rather, as a heuristic that describes a formal distinction between contrasting political arguments in the same milieu. In internet history in particular, protocols were just as central to the functioning of Bell Telephone networks as regulations are to the functioning of ISPs today, and there are many examples of configurations online like the domain name system (DNS) and virtual private networks (VPNs), which combine features of regulatory and protocological frameworks for data transfer. Hence insofar as readers of Deleuze and Guattari like Galloway apply their ontology to control structures and privilege the rhizomatic over the arboreal, their deployment of the rhizome/tree distinction is itself protocological in my terms, perhaps especially when they determine that an ideally rhizomatic system of organization is not an achievable political goal.[36]

There is, finally, a clear analogy between the emergent polarities in these debates about the history of control in telephony networks and the debates summarized above, about the history of control in the English constitution. Like Selden's republican history of feudalism, Alexander Galloway positions the autocratic Foucauldian sovereign as a historically specific aberration from more natural and rhizomatic forms of decentralized power relations—which we might call, in both instances, "peer-to-peer"—whose practices may be obscured by the sovereign's arbitrary power but whose basic desirability, it is posited, will always persist. Meanwhile, Chun's argument formally resembles Spelman's more royalist history, insofar as she martials data to demonstrate how the systems she studies are in fact iterative, processual, and so subject to considerable change over time, in a manner that makes historical claims for the persistence of ideal principles untenable. Again, such formal polarities in the politicization of historical lessons may be found throughout the historiographies of control that have emerged in many cultural and historical contexts, precisely because the polarities allow for conflict and disagreement without thereby threatening stability and continuity of practice.

It is, of course, hardly novel for me to propose that historical analyses will privilege some historical details over others, and that these details will be selected for ideological reasons. My more specific point is that the formal oppositions between protocological and regulatory analyses of history tend to hide how they nonetheless work in concert to privilege the same historical artifacts, either because these artifacts are conducive to their own narratives or because they are conducive to their opponents' and so require criticism. Because it is impossible to dispute that the various copies of the Gutenberg Bible *exist*, it is therefore possible to dispute forever whether or not this existence is important to the history of human culture and so to the politics of our moment. The more intractable the formal disagreement about control philosophy in a debate of this kind, the more stable the overarching control diagram it occupies, as agents who hate each other mortally and without reservation are condemned to argue forever about the same set of data points. These, then, are the argumentative constraints that perpetuate the analogies between digital and the medieval textuality with which we began, and that serve to limit the potential of that debate to intervene in the emergent historical developments it wishes to anticipate.

Below, I will briefly consider how we might envision a way out of this opposition, to imagine both medieval and digital textuality differently. It is vital that we do so, and not only so that we can construct more nuanced narratives of English legal history or of the origins of the internet. This chapter appears at a moment when the field of medieval studies has begun, belatedly, to reckon with its own historical complicity in violence and exploitation, as the colonial and imperial powers enabled by Selden and Spelman's historiography have informed the genealogies of medieval studies to this day.[37] I believe that a full, true reckoning with our disciplines' colonizing structures would require us to recognize the subtle challenges that face our efforts to construct alternative critical frameworks to those we have inherited, and that if we are to meet these challenges we must reconsider our methodologies for studying historical media. Below I will articulate some of the principles I believe we should use to apply the protocol/regulation heuristic to this task.

Beyond Protocol and Regulation

One way of summarizing the insights of Bernard Stiegler in his *Technics and Time* is to say that "the archive," in the broad Derridean sense, is a synonym for "technology."[38] Stiegler begins the first volume of his work with a survey of classical anthropology, in which he observes that this discipline's narrative of human evolution and of the development of cultures begins with technology.[39] In Stiegler's summary, the anthropological record of clay pots, burial mounds, and evidence of agriculture are the signs that tell us when humans became humans. And since the larger skulls of human remains that postdate the earliest of these remnants, it seems that human intelligence is itself a product of such tools and techniques, rather than the other way around. Insofar as any prehistoric tool conveys information to us about the people who made it and the culture in which they lived, each tool is a record of the past, which differs from a birth certificate or registered will only to the extent that it was not specifically designed to convey such information. Indeed, if we hold that the one function every tool shares is its ability to record, for example, the fact of its own usefulness and the clues about its operation that might enable one to reverse engineer it, we may even define this recording function as central to the category of "tool" itself. Not only is a record a sort of tool, but—more fundamentally—"tool" and "record" are different names for the same kind of thing. The "archive," then, is the name for the technological apparatus that structures and makes intelligible the interrelationships between the records and tools that surround and shape us, not dissimilar in this regard to the material apparatus of "ideology" with which I began.

It is, then, sensible to extend Stiegler's principal insight beyond his key statement that there is a third category of "technological" existence, mediating the known categories of animacy and inanimacy, to suggest further that the recognition of this third category may require that we abandon the original two. For Steigler it is the human that gives rise to the tool, just as the tool gives rise to the human. But what, finally, is the distinction between these elements of his system? What would it mean for an object existing in the world to *not* be a tool, if all a tool needs to do is record history—as, say, a ring in a tree trunk or a layer of sedimentary rock may tell us respectively about the length of a rainy season, or the date of a volcanic eruption? Alternatively, can we imagine an animacy that is more than just a composite image extrapolated from the evidence provided by such markers of past actions and historical events, or a human who is not herself a record of the life she remembers, and so also (among other things) a tool?

In this way, Stiegler's analysis suggests that claims about cultural origins, about human rights and responsibilities, and even about possible futures are invariably circumscribed by the arbitrary (but not reliably so) survivals of records and tools from the past, as indeed the abstractions "culture," "nature," "human," and even "future" are simply categories used to organize the material and technological records that surround us, shape us, and—most crucially for the present discussion—condition our plans for anticipated contingencies. In these terms, a "contingency" would be nothing more than a moment where new evidence is introduced into our accumulated records, occasioning a re-evaluation of the overarching organizational scheme. Thus the unending flow of successive contingencies must continuously increase the archive's organizational complexity by increasing orders of magnitude, as every new record's addition also creates new relations to every other record that the archive already possesses. This process of archival expansion—identical to historical time itself—necessarily generates near-infinite, ever-increasing possibilities to reshape the totality of the archive and of the world it constitutes, and hence for political change. If it is accepted that ongoing debates about the archive and the history it records serve to control this potentiality without eliminating it completely, these debates should become more and more polarized along the protocol/regulation axis as history progresses, and the production of more and more information requires stricter and stricter controls on the sorts of information that can be considered admissible in public political debate. Periodization has long been an important mechanism for maintaining this control, though it is beginning to show signs of strain.

It seems, then, that we ought not to limit or define types or periods of "media" as a starting point to our analysis of the evolving, ever-expanding body of evidence for human communication and record-keeping. Historical distinctions between the types of communication and the time frames of their use are themselves acts of containment and archival organization, and so they are properly imagined as the objects of analysis, not preconditions for it. In the specific instance with which I began, the media-historical hypothesis that print technology created a moment of "revolution" dividing European (and so colonial) history into discreet epochs continues to provoke a broad debate about the appropriateness of the divisions between medieval and modern, modern and post-modern, which debate has served as the underpinning structure that binds contrary programs for future action to the same set of archival givens. To equate the medieval with the protocological and the modern with the regulatory may enable certain kinds of useful analysis, but it cuts off other kinds at the knees, preventing our scholarship from figuring the ambivalences and contradictions of the past and our politics from effecting truly radical, transformative change.

To summarize, then, it is my contention that arguments about media history tend to fall into a spectrum between two poles, which encode contrary philosophies of control. The first pole is marked by a preference for centralized, hierarchical, and regulated systems of control that would place little if any constraints on the choices of actors, but that would rather forbid and punish certain outcomes of their actions. The second is marked by a preference for distributed, non-hierarchical, and protocological systems of control that would place the responsibilities of governance on individual actors and constrain them to a particular range of acceptable choices, thereby obviating the need for central authority and even for social organization itself. This second preference is linked to a tendency to express skepticism about the division of history into discreet epochs, along with a nostalgic desire to revive or retain in the present whatever admirable attributes of earlier periods remain possible. In contrast, the former preference has a revolutionary mania for such epochal divisions. In both cases, the material evidence of historical media is foundational both to the articulation and application of the control philosophy, as it contains the proof both for the benefits of their own views and for the dangers of their opponents'.

As I have suggested above, there is a tendency to connect print culture and modernity to regulatory control, and to connect both digital and manuscript culture to protocological control, with the result that medieval and post-modern cultural forms are treated as analogous by scholars, programmers, and activists alike. And as the introduction to this volume has surveyed, examples of this medievalism in digital culture are so common, and apparent in so many technical, social, academic, and pop-cultural forms, that the problem is not identifying examples but establishing some sort of rhyme or reason within them. The heuristic proposed above is intended to serve as a descriptive vocabulary that may help us to accomplish this task, and in so doing to find new ways to think about the histories we inherit and the futures we create.

CHAPTER 3

The Coconut Cup as Material and Medium

Extended Ecologies

Kathleen E. Kennedy

All but forgotten today, coconut cups, coconut shells harnessed into stemware, were valued and valuable everyday objects in households all over the world from at least the thirteenth century until World War II. Before the colonial period coconut cups mediated European craft traditions, replacing one medium (maplewood) with another (imported coconut shell). However, Europeans took coconut cups with them around the globe and there coconut cups came to mediate both European and indigenous cultures. Improbably, the coconut cup was such a successful media format that it adapted to a wide range of media climates and continued to reproduce and communicate cultures for nearly a thousand years. Much like plant species introduced from one ecology into another, the results of this mediation could be both positive and disastrous. The coconut cup might in some cases be viewed as an invasive media species, replacing indigenous media. At times, as an introduced species, coconut cups failed to thrive in their new environment, surviving only when deliberately nurtured. In yet other cases, culturally hybrid uses of coconut cups allowed indigenous practices to survive, albeit in altered form, when they might otherwise have been erased entirely by colonialism.

Perhaps only now that Moore's Law may be reaching its failure point can we see how older media theories limited our understanding of media ecology: in essence, the transistors at the heart of all microchips no longer get smaller, faster, and cheaper in a predictable fashion.[1] This study models the ways in which media studies may broaden its reach to consider understudied media objects across extended timelines and ecologies stretching into millennia. Below, I explore how these objects both enrich and challenge current orthodoxies within media studies. This revisioning of media studies resituates our current media environment on more complete foundations by including evidence that has hitherto been marginalized or unexamined. In coconut cups we can see complicated interplays between plant and person, between pre-colonial Europe and India, between colonizer and subaltern, between political patriarchy and women, and we can view these exchanges over a span of nearly a thousand years. The present chapter concentrates on several specific phases of these processes, considering benchmark media forms, how coconut cups came to compete with those forms, and how coconut cups adapted to new media ecologies as they spread through part of the Americas during the colonial period.

Media Ecology

Though it was Harold Innis who suggested that communication success or failure influenced the rise and fall of empires, it took Marshall McLuhan's media theories to create the necessary soil (or what gardeners might call the "medium") for the development of theories of media ecology.[2] Paul Levinson asserted that McLuhan was as vital to media ecology as oxygen and hydrogen are to water.[3] Levinson goes on to summarize McLuhan's approach as exploring the "soft power" of media to communicate, and therefore to influence, human culture.[4] McLuhan pioneered the argument that if history mattered, then the media through which people communicate mattered too, as communication enables the actions of human beings and cultures through time.[5] McLuhan saw media as influencing the messages people communicated, so that a culture might engage the same message sent through various media in different ways. As Neil Postman asserts, media ecological theory draws upon the metaphors of botany, biology, and chemistry used above, which are implicit in McLuhan's work and common in the discourse of communication studies that he founded.[6] For Postman, media ecology weds biology to technology: "A medium is a technology within which a culture grows; that is to say, it gives form to a culture's politics, social organization, and habitual ways of thinking."[7]

Postman's definition of media ecology as "the ways in which the interaction between media and human beings give a culture its character" rests, however, on Aristotelian notions of household maintenance.[8] Because it is founded on ancient Greek notions of the household, this classical media ecology has not been able to engage material culture—particularly material culture associated with women in the household, such as housewares—as technologies of communication. More recent explorations of media ecology emphasize instead "the way in which circuitries or assemblages of organic life, technological components, and other material and immaterial elements can become powerful and complex systems, often operating in conditions that are far from any stable environmental equilibrium and producing effects beyond both subjective human intentions and predetermined technological capacities."[9]

Recent, inclusive revisionism of media ecology is indebted to Félix Guattari's triple sense of ecology as material, social, and mental.[10] Consider eating with a pointed knife instead of a fork. At their most basic levels, pointed knife and fork require a different cast of thought. The material components seem only mildly dissimilar, and yet when engaged with organic life—from the food on the plate to the human wielding the utensils—the differences engender and influence a range of social practices, from table etiquette to hygiene to cuisine preferences, that can continue to be viewed in the two strategies of handling the fork seen in the United States and Europe to this day.[11] Moreover, widespread adoption of the fork in Western cultures took several hundred years, highlighting how incompletely human intention controlled this cultural change.

I suggest that material culture, specifically housewares such as knives, forks, and coconut cups, functions precisely as such assemblages. Given the androcentric nature of much media theory, I fear that that the historical and persistent association of housewares with women's work has occluded them from theorization by media critics. Such definitions can explain why a scholar like John Durham Peters, who is deeply interested in communication over time, and who carefully teases out the desperation for touch in long-distance communication technologies like the telephone and radio, claims that "of all the senses touch is the most resistant to being made into a medium of recording and transmission," and does not explore the potential of material culture itself to act as a communication medium.[12] As Peters admits, "No real [human] community endures without touch," but the media of touch and gesture are not so rare as Peters thought: they are as close as his own coffee cup.[13]

Our definitions of technology remain overwhelmingly presentist, a point on which even David Edgerton stumbles. His attempt to distinguish "things" from "technology" fails in the face of broader views of *techne*, of technology: Egerton's examples of "things" are all constructed, are all *techne*.[14] Historians such as Elly Truitt and Marcy Norton forcefully argue that technology is not simply a modern phenomenon.[15] In fact, Norton shows how notions of premodern technologies highlight the entangled relationships between indigenous and colonizing cultures in the early modern world, and this blend of cultures with technology fits well into recent media ecology theory.[16] Edgerton is not wrong that a use-based history can be global and nonlinear, but I would argue history of technology can be too.[17] Moreover, Edgerton's assertion that use-based history "gives us a history of technology engaged with all the world's population ... half female," grows wan when his study never actually considers women at any length and uses female pronouns only when discussing ships.[18] My argument considers media technologies used by half the world's population to which Edgerton alludes as well as men. Further, I would extend Truitt's and Norton's projects and argue that, for media ecology, examining the *longue durée* of material culture is necessary: ecologies can change quite rapidly, but they also develop slowly, over spans of centuries.

Mazers

Before we can understand how coconut cups functioned as media, we first need to consider the original environment of the European coconut cup. Already common in ecology, the notion of a benchmark species can be usefully imported into media ecology. In ecology, a benchmark species is identified and used to measure environmental change over time.[19] We must consider mazers as a benchmark medium for pre-coconut cup European media ecosystems. One of the most famous medieval allusions to mazers comes from Chaucer's Wife of Bath, who acknowledges that even the wealthiest eat off dishes made of tree, but characteristically temporizes concerning how luxurious some of this woodenware could be.[20]

Europeans set tables with mazers for everyday and festival use for hundreds of years, and the wood itself conveyed value. *Mazer* or *maple* referred to the use of the wood of maple burls to make fine drinking vessels. Different maples are native across Europe, and this results in local variations in the wood available for mazers. For example, to the east, the most common maple was the sycamore (*Acer pseudoplantanus*); however in England, the smaller field maple (*Acer campestre*) is the lone native maple. Each of these maples might hold different value in various parts of Europe. In the late 1470s or early 1480s the London goldsmiths guild enacted an ordinance that no guildsman was to keep tableware of sycamore (a tree the medieval English did not identify as maple), lest it be fraudulently sold as maple.[21] Moreover, mazers were at least occasionally imported into England on ships hauling Mediterranean cargo, suggesting that the grain of some of the Mediterranean maples (perhaps the *Acer opalus*) was also sought after.[22]

While wooden bowls can be quite simple, mazers were often embellished in ways that highlight their use as cultural media, conveying both

Anonymous, *Drinking Bowl*, The Cloisters Collection, Metropolitan Museum,
New York, 1955, 55.25

status and ethics. As early as we have regular probate and inventory records (the thirteenth century) we find wealthy people harnessing mazers
into metal structures, adding stems, feet, rims, and sometimes lids of
gold, silver, and gilded brass[23] (see figure 1), Many of these cups literally
spoke, with apotropeic inscriptions common around the metal rims.
"Who is eldest take this cup without strife" says one, and "How good it
is for him who knows who he can trust" another.[24] Other inscriptions

Old Media and the Medieval Concept

are in Latin, identifying owners, or calling down blessings on the drinker.[25] Ritual uses are suggested with names like "Pardoncuppe" and "God Morwe."[26] "God Morwe" contained a gallon measure, very large for a cup, and such a size and name hints at use in shared, ritual drinking such as wassailing and popular feast days, as might the paired cups "Bollocks" and "Bride."[27] With a touch of the lips to the words, drinkers interacted with this silent speech with every sip. The social, communal emphasis of many inscriptions is difficult to ignore, and some mazers must have been in heavy use during community feasts and festivals.

Mazers continued to be constructed and harnessed in fine metal throughout the Middle Ages, and it is not until the later fifteenth century that their numbers diminish enough in the documentation for one to suspect that their popularity began to wane.[28] Until that point, however, they were a normal fine houseware across northern Europe, and there is evidence that they continued to be manufactured at least occasionally, and older cups preserved and used, throughout the early modern era.[29] Thus, as a media form, mazers grew up at the intersection of organic and metal, between daily life and public feasting, and existed as both material and textual culture. In Europe, mazers continue to successfully transmit culture until 1500, and for some time after that in a diminished capacity.

Medieval European Coconut Cups

Once we identify mazers as benchmark media, we can begin to understand medieval coconut cups and what they meant before the global colonial era. Coconuts are genetically native to the Maldives, and were already an Indian export by the Roman period.[30] We have no reason to believe that coconuts ceased to be exported from India to the Middle East at any point thereafter. Indeed, insofar as England and parts of Europe were Roman, and therefore part of Roman trade networks, coconuts are likely to have reached northern Europe very early, and their regular importation ceased only as part of the general trade disruption of late antiquity and the early Middle Ages as Roman infrastructure disintegrated and long distance trade became more sporadic and dangerous.

In the more stable eastern and southern portions of the former Roman Empire, coconuts continued to be used without break.[31] The fruit appears to have been cultivated to a limited degree in eastern Africa and Yemen by the Middle Ages, but the market outstripped supply, necessitating additional imported nuts. As long-distance trade rebounded in the high Middle Ages (1100–1300), this tropical medicine began to make its way again into northern European markets, known as the *nux indica*, or "nut of India." (The name *coconut* is early modern in origin.)[32] Only this time something new happened.

The coconut shell has unique affordances: as a pit shell, it is a hardwood, is water-tight, and is naturally large enough to use as a cup, among other things. Globally, humans have employed coconut shells as cups and containers for thousands of years. This utility makes it that much more surprising that I know of no evidence that coconut shells were used as metal-harnessed goblets until the Middle Ages, and then only in Europe. This, then, is a fundamental mediation that coconut cups witnessed—that of one medium for another. Northern European artisans and customers enjoyed the rich, speckled grain of burlwood maple so much that they polished it and set it in precious metals. This tradition appears to have been adapted for coconuts, which feature dark, speckled shells not unlike maplewood. European artisans began harnessing coconut shells as they had mazers by the thirteenth century at the latest.

Even more than mazers, medieval coconut cups were profoundly hybrid objects, and their cultural weight differed from that of mazers. The coconuts had travelled from as far away as India, and the metals used in their construction might also have been mined far from where the cups were manufactured. Like mazers, coconut cups appear to have been enjoyed by a wide range of classes, in part because simply drinking out of the shell was believed to have therapeutic effects.[33] Germans went further and made some coconut cups into reliquaries capable of infusing their contents with both herbal and divine healing power.[34] In England,

Anonymous, *Coconut Cup and Cover*, Royal Ontario Museum, Toronto,
1.960.9.7.a-b

coconut cups turn up regularly in wills, suggesting financial value on par with that of mazers.[35] This value also explains their presence among the gifts of plate donated to Oxford and Cambridge colleges during the later Middle Ages.[36] The London goldsmiths' guild records show their care to maintain metal quality and manufacturing transparency. From these records we can also discover that some non-precious coconut cups were made of gilded brass and silvered lead.[37] It seems equally likely that customers knew about such practices as it does that they were being misled, and this may suggest that there was also a market for coconut cups outside the wealthiest classes.[38] For all their similarities, however, coconut cups could not fully accomplish the cultural work of mazers. While mazers might be shared and passed around a table on festival occasions, it seems that coconut cups were more individually employed. At the same time, coconut cups seem to have functioned more exclusively ceremonially than mazers. While coconut cups were frequently identified as "mine," there is no evidence that anyone ever identified a coconut cup as "the one I drink [from]" as was done with mazers.[39]

Europe's relationship with its coconut cups changed less than we might think as the Portuguese introduced coconuts to the west coast of Africa, and even after Vasco da Gama opened up a direct route to the Indian supply. Although coconuts were more readily available in Europe than ever, this does not appear to have diminished their popularity. Instead we find coconut cups undergoing aesthetic changes to suit sixteenth- and seventeenth-century tastes.

From carving to metalwork, early modern European coconut cups illustrate cultural changes, some of which may relate to Europe's widening media footprint as these nations developed into colonial powers. Rabia Gregory suggests that a sixteenth-century interest in carving biblical scenes onto cups redeployed the coconut shell's tropical associations toward evangelical ends: the European Bible, like European coconut cups, was spreading into tropical zones in the early global colonial period.[40] The multiplication of the forms of coconut cups, especially into zoomorphic vessels in the shape of ostriches may indicate an increased interest in the flora and fauna of equatorial regions as more and more European nations became colonial powers.[41] Indigenous peoples of the Americas were occasionally depicted on European-style coconut cups, and a few show a caryatid form in which a native American warrior–African warrior hybrid figure serves as the stem.[42]

American Benchmark Media and the Introduced Coconut

We have seen how the European benchmark species was the mazer, and how coconuts were introduced and came to compete with mazers, but did not replace them. Coconut cups remained an introduced media species, and while they competed successfully against the benchmark, they never outperformed the native media tradition. When Europeans took coconuts west to the Americas they quite literally planted them into new soil, and the cultural mediations made by these coconut goblets were complicated further by the colonial cultures established in the Americas.[43] In some places coconut cups thrived, and in others they did not.

When Columbus's voyage began the Spanish colonial era in the Americas, coconuts were along for the ride. Coconuts had already arrived along the western shores of Central and South America, however, so they were not entirely unknown.[44] Yet coconuts had not captivated Americans as they had Europeans, perhaps because of limited distribution, as even in the later sixteenth century they were not yet cultivated beyond their original extent: beach areas along the coastlines of Costa Rica, Panama, and Colombia.[45] In addition, on either coast, coconuts were still relative newcomers and had arrived after local traditions were already ancient.

In pre-Columbian America, the benchmark medium was the *jícara*, a dried squash or tree gourd omnipresent as a medium for containers and cups. Just as Europeans developed the mazer as a houseware made of local products, pre-Columbian American cultures used *jícaras* as housewares. From these gourds, Americans drank indigenous beverages such as yerba maté and chocolate, often in ceremonial ways. As a benchmark medium, *jícaras* highlight the ways in which a cultural medium involves specific technological interactions of organic, metal, and cultural parts. As Matthew Fuller reminds us, the "dynamism" of notions of media ecologies "arises out of concrete conditions," and this is notably true of *jícaras*, as individual gourd species have different physical and cultural affordances, and grow in different environments.[46]

The most common gourd species used for containers, worldwide, is the bottle gourd (*Lagenaria siceraria*), a vine calabash that serves as a truly epochal benchmark medium. Especially convenient for transporting water, the bottle gourd has been used as a container for liquids and as cups since prehistoric times. Natural and human activity spread bottle gourds around the world in the paleolithic era.[47] The Spanish were not surprised to see bottle gourds when they arrived in the New World.

However, the Americas also offered a range of gourds not found in the Old World—tree calabashes (*Crescentia cujete* and *Crescentia alata*)—and each of these species also lends itself to use as *jícaras*. *Crescentia cujete* grows quite widely in Central and South America. *Crescentia alata*, however, had a restricted habitat when the Spanish arrived. *C. alata* appears to have evolved for seed dispersal by megafauna, including early horses.[48] When Central America lost most of its megafauna in the early Holocene, the range of *C. alata* shrank. The Spanish arrival with horses, cattle, and pigs, all of which quickly developed (in some cases enormous) feral populations, led to a boom in *C. alata* dispersal and spread. Both *C. cujete* and *C. alata* were made into *jícaras* before and during the colonial period. However, thanks to the renewed large mammal populations, *C. alata* would have been more available during the colonial period than at any time since the early Holocene. As we shall see, *C. alata*'s similarity to coconut shell may also have made it a more desirable material for cups in some places than *jícaras* of *C. cujete* or *Lagenaria siceraria*.

The Spanish divided their enormous land claim into roughly two administrative regions, the Viceroyalties of New Spain and Peru (though the names and boundaries shift over time), and each of these areas already enjoyed its own distinct foodways. Upon their arrival, the Spanish immediately saw that chocolate was drunk as a ceremonial beverage, particularly by elites, widely throughout the empire of the Mexica and its far-flung tributary states.[49] Famously, chocolate was so central a symbol of the Mexica that the beans were a significant part of the empire's tribute levies. Further south, however, tropical chocolate became less important where it simply could not grow. In more temperate zones, yerba, a tea-like infusion made from a shrub, featured in pre-Columbian foodways, particularly as a medicine. Both yerba and chocolate were vital to their respective cultures, and the Spanish spread both further under colonial rule. However, the social status of each beverage was different, stemming from their original cultural uses. Such differences influenced how each drink was adopted by the Spanish, and by developing mestizo cultures. We can see these differences in how each culture adopted, or failed to adopt, the European coconut cup.

Coconut Cups Cross the Atlantic: Yerba Maté

Just as the viceroyalties changed names and shapes over time, so too does the vocabulary of yerba maté. Literally meaning "a cup of herbs," depending on what scholarship you read, in English or Spanish, yerba maté can be referred to as either "yerba" or "maté."[50] "Maté" can literally denote the cup or be used as a shorthand for the beverage. Since the present investigation concerns cups, a "maté cup" could be a redundant term. Likewise, a *jicara* can also mean a generic cup, made of gourd, rather than one specifically associated with drinking yerba.[51] In an attempt to avoid confusion in English I will discuss "yerba cups" to generically refer to any cup used to drink yerba. I will use the term *jicaras* to refer to yerba cups made of gourd. No less so than using overly general terms like the "Viceroyalty of Peru" these terms only imperfectly reflect a dynamic, hybrid houseware and cannot consistently reflect any one period's or location's usage.

Though additives to the tea and the implements themselves might indicate social status, yerba and its *jícaras* serve as the heart of a profoundly social, communal foodway, and one in which women had a guiding hand to a greater degree than they did in coconut cup rituals in Europe.[52] By the second half of the sixteenth century, yerba-drinking customs were clear: in Paraguayan culture, yerba was mixed in a pot and then poured into a *jícara* that was passed around a circle as everyone took a sip.[53] Often a woman, the host kept the *jícara* filled so that the sharing could continue without pause.[54] As cultural media, then, the implements of yerba-drinking communicate this comparatively egalitarian custom, and coconut cups simply could not transmit such equity.

Yerba maté offers an excellent comparison to chocolate, and its cups allow us to consider how media objects physically reflect and to an extent direct one pre-Columbian culture's development into a colonial culture. The Spanish popularized yerba widely outside of its native Paraguay and surrounding regions because it served as a colonial cash crop in areas without precious mineral deposits.[55] Indeed, yerba continued to be a vital crop for Paraguay long after the colonial period ended and in nearby regions into the twentieth century.[56] Europeans took yerba back to Europe with them, making repeated, periodic attempts to develop a European market for it.[57] Nevertheless, yerba did not successfully translate outside of South America, and unlike chocolate, it never developed any popularity in Europe.

Some yerba gourds came to be harnessed like Europe's own benchmark medium, the mazer, showing a direct blending of the two houseware traditions that underscores a similarity in use: like the yerba gourd, the festival mazer was shared among a group. Yerba continues to be drunk out of *jícaras*, sometimes harnessed, to this day. The structure of the metal fittings may suggest changes in the gestures of the yerba ritual over time. Though yerba may have begun by being passed hand-to-hand, harnessed yerba *jícaras* suggest a shift to a seated affair at a table. The mouths of yerba gourds tend to be narrow, perhaps to prevent

Anonymous, *Mate Cup*, South American (unknown origin). Silver. 15.5 × 7.8 × 2.7 cm. Museum of Fine Arts, Boston, 41.402

splashing when passed between people, and perhaps to keep the *bombilla*, the strainer-straw, from falling out of the container. Silver feet in a pedestal or tripod design may also have developed in order to stabilize the straw, eventually made of silver, in the lighter-weight cup when set down on a surface. Argentine documents refer to such bases, apparently separated from their cups, as *pie de maté*, and this play on words is often seen in existing tripod cups, in which each of the three feet is hooved or shaped like a bird's claw clutching a sphere.[58] A famous engraving of the early nineteenth-century Paraguayan ruler José Gaspar Francia shows him grasping a pedestal-style yerba cup by the stem.[59] However, some pedestal-style substructures were affixed to saucer-like bases called *salvilla* in the Argentine documents, and were not fixed to the gourds.[60] All such substructures might allow one to share the cup and set it down too, enabling a lightly harnessed gourd to be easily passed from person to person, and then, when set into a *pie* or *salvilla* also be securely set down on a tabletop. Certain localities made use of long-necked gourds and left the necks as convenient handles for the cup; sometimes these handles too were harnessed in silver. Such silver garnish so far from the centre of gravity of the cup necessitated a significant base for any cup that was to be set down, offering further clues to how the gestures of this everyday ritual evolved. The early modern women managing yerba rituals took the yerba service very seriously, and so we must understand that the hostess valued each aesthetic aspect of any given yerba cup for its ability to flatter her guests and reflect as much honour on her household as financially possible.[61]

Coconut-shell yerba cups from the eighteenth and nineteenth centuries exist in essentially the same forms as harnessed *jícaras* but remain novelties in comparison.[62] Ecology may be partly to blame. The geography of yerba's original production and use does not lend itself to coconuts. In general, Paraguay's climate is variable, and it gets both too cold and too dry for coconut palms to thrive widely. (The Paraguayan coconut, *Acrocomia aculeata*, is a different species.) Thus coconuts would have remained uncommon in the heartland of yerba culture and cultivation. Coconut yerba cups may therefore be localizable to parts of Brazil or Peru that could support wider-scale coconut growth and fruiting, or to trade with these areas, and, indeed, the great essayist of yerba culture Amaro Villanueva claimed that coconut yerba cups were characteristic of Brazil and occasionally imported into Argentina.[63] Yet ecology is not sufficient to explain coconut's failure as a medium of yerba culture. If yerba had been a high-status beverage, perhaps imported cups would have added to that cultural lustre, but instead, yerba was proudly commonplace. The very shared nature of yerba-drinking may have made the individual coconut cup impractical to adopt, especially as a status-marker. The few coconut yerba cups that do exist mark an essential failure of the European coconut cup to adapt to American media soils: the coconut cup never transmitted yerba culture well, and yerba only infrequently adapted to European coconut cup culture. At the same time, lively production of harnessed yerba *jícaras* illustrate the continued transmission of indigenous yerba culture into the colonial period in a mestizo medium, both indigenous and Spanish.

Coconuts Cross the Atlantic: Chocolate

Chocolate contrasts with yerba maté in almost every way. Rather than commonly shared, pre-Columbian chocolate was traditionally reserved for nobility and ceremonial occasions, and its preparation and pouring into *jícaras* were strictly prescribed activities. Chocolate *jícaras* were not shared, but deeply embedded in these rituals that reinforced social hierarchies even as they promoted bonding among members of the same rank.[64] However, just as the Spanish popularized yerba maté widely across the Viceroyalty of Peru, they popularized chocolate widely throughout New Spain, including present-day California, Texas, and Florida, and south to the northern parts of Peru, including present-day Venezuela.[65] Yet it took several hundred years for chocolate to fully shed its pre-Columbian air of exclusivity. Europeans took both beverages back to Europe with them in the sixteenth century, and in contrast to yerba, chocolate exploded in popularity across Europe in the seventeenth century.[66] For a century and more, in the Americas and in Europe, chocolate was king, losing ground to coffee and tea only in the eighteenth century. Though chocolate continued in use as a break-fast beverage into the nineteenth century, evidence suggests that coffee was beginning to replace chocolate as a ceremonial beverage by the later eighteenth century.[67]

As with yerba, there are terminological difficulties in working with both primary and secondary sources on chocolate. *Jícara* might be used as a generic term for chocolate cup, and be made of porcelain or other pottery rather than gourd: Norton says that *jícara* was "a Hispanized pre-Columbian term used for chocolate vessels."[68] In English primary sources, *cocoa* might refer to either chocolate or coconut, and a *cocoa nut* might refer to either a cacao pod or a coconut. Likewise a *coco* in Spanish documents refers to a coconut-shell chocolate cup and serves as a commonly understood short form of *coco chocolatero*, or a coconut cup of a European design modified for drinking chocolate.

Like yerba, the benchmark medium continued in use throughout this period. Chocolate drinkers continued to make use of gourd *jícaras*, sometimes harnessed in metalware just like European coconut cups and mazers. Currently, more material evidence of this practice remains for yerba than for chocolate, but documentary sources shore up missing physical traces. Archaeologists have simply not been looking for organic housewares. As Graham and Skowronek put it, "The widespread presence of *jícaras* in the account books is another challenge to archaeologists to consider fragments of perishable items like gourds as more than botan-ical evidence. Research makes it clear that gourds were used extensively as drinking vessels and containers."[69] Documentary evidence shows that chocolate was being exported back to Spain, along with *jícaras* painted in the traditional manner, or gilded in a Spanish-American hybrid, by the first quarter of the seventeenth century.[70] *Jícaras* continued to be used across New Spain and were imported into border areas along with

Anonymous, *Coconut-Shell Cup (Coco chocolatero)*, Los Angeles County Museum of Art, Los Angeles, M.2015.69.3

chocolate and chocolate-making utensils.[71] However unlike yerba, chocolate was enjoyed widely in areas with long tropical coastlines and prime coconut-growing ecologies. Therefore while we have extant examples of harnessed chocolate *jícaras*, these may have been specializations of certain localities, such as Guatemalan use of *morro* (*C. alata*), and therefore viewed as worthy of preservation.[72]

Like harnessed yerba *jícaras*, *cocos chocolateros* offer an exceptional example of a changing media ecology and show successful competition with the hybridized benchmark medium of the harnessed chocolate gourd *jícaras*. First, coconut cups were adapted for chocolate very quickly. What were already called *cocos chocolateros* by the late sixteenth century were standard throughout much of New Spain, and today remain in far greater numbers than coconut yerba cups.[73] Second, together with archival documentation, extant *cocos* allow us to begin to reconstruct the ways in which the coconut blended with the pre-existing foodway and altered it to fit the developing mestizo culture.[74] Spanish stemware was quite low, compared with elsewhere in Europe, and both harnessed chocolate gourds and *cocos chocolateros* generally follow this model.[75] Venezuelan *cocos* often sit on flat metal lacework bases, fixed to the cup with a bract-like metal fitting.[76] Mexican *cocos* stand on very short stems or tall bases.[77] Unlike eighteenth-century European coconut cups, in the Spanish Americas the nutshells were often carved in delicate geometric or organic tracery, or with folk art–style flowers or birds.[78] Also unlike European cups, there is evidence that some *cocos* were inlaid with mother of pearl, and others might have had their tracery embellished with paint or paste inlay.[79]

Cocos chocolateros show physical changes that mark their adaptation from European coconut cup to American chocolate cup to facilitate communicating a new, hybrid culture. *Cocos* are frequently smaller than their European forebears, and bear small ear-like handles. These changes demonstrate how alterations in foodways affect housewares. Moulds used to cast the handles appear to have themselves been copied and circulated, as many existing handles share a strong resemblance, often bearing the Spanish armorial lion.[80] (This is another difference with harnessed yerba *jícaras*, as one sees much less design repetition in their silver work.) The addition of handles must relate to the change in beverage. European coconut cups were designed for alcohols drunk at room or cellar temperature. Like yerba, chocolate was warm or hot, making a bit of distance between the hand and the shell useful, perhaps. Likewise, the vessel volume changed, as alcohol was served in larger quantities than warmer chocolate. Even *jícaras* tend to be smaller vessels, and artisans making *cocos* quickly followed suit, apparently deliberately selecting small nuts for *cocos*.

The handles and feet may have aided *cocos* in communicating class standing and refinement, as in early modern Europe the gestures used with stemware were strictly circumscribed. Etiquette manuals and art illustrate that stemmed wineglasses were correctly grasped by the foot.[81] Such a gesture, when steadied with an additional finger or hand resting on the small handle, might be imagined for *cocos*. Nevertheless, at least one contemporary depiction shows the handles going unused, while the cup is lifted by the base, exactly like a European wineglass. The frontispiece of Philippe Sylvestre Dufour's *Traitez Nouveaux et Curieux de Café du Thé et du Chocolate* (1685) shows a Native American holding a steaming *coco chocolatero* by the foot and short stem. This *coco* is garnished with a silver rim, characteristic handles, short stem, and foot. A Turkish man holds a coffee cup and a Chinese man holds a teacup, but neither vessel shows substantial alteration from its indigenous forms. The *coco* visibly demonstrates its hybridity through this metal garnishing and its manner of being held. Gesture etiquette surrounding European wineglasses was explicitly a way of signalling class standing, and chocolate drinking had been limited (in theory) to specific pre-Columbian classes. We know the Spanish adopted chocolate in part thanks to its class associations, and they may well have adapted their own gesture etiquette to the beverage as well. Particularly in borderlands where tableware and etiquette might be all that distinguished one home's status from another's, a *coco* and its ritual gestures may have been vital to the communication of social class.[82]

For several hundred years, *cocos chocolateros* served as one of many media communicating the "two overlapping strains of creole patriotism: one that emphasized ancient greatness and another that praised the glories of Indo-Christian New Spain."[83] Moreover, women controlled the medium of the chocolate service to a unique degree, as chocolate might be kept under lock and key, to be opened only at the order of the mistress of the house.[84] This gave women a special means to engage these twinned strands of developing nationalism. Though *cocos* continued to be constructed in the nineteenth century, their primacy was eclipsed by further environmental and ecological changes: coffee, porcelain, and political disruption. Coffee displaced chocolate as the welcoming, ceremonial beverage of choice. Chocolate continued as an important breakfast beverage, but its cachet declined, and the social reasons to drink from *cocos* faded away. Thanks to the galleon trade between New Spain and the Philippines, porcelain had been available in New Spain quite early. Though pre-Columbian America had a robust ceramic tradition of its own, after the Conquest, porcelain coffee and chocolate services eventually displaced fine hybrid housewares such as harnessed *jicaras* and *cocos*. Finally, the old viceroyalty ceased to exist as independence movements spread throughout the old colony. These political upheavals shook up social classes and upended many traditions, allowing new customs to take root. Though *cocos* continued to be made throughout the nineteenth century, after mid-century many were deliberately nostalgic, and even politically symbolic of earlier eras.[85]

Conclusion

Residing as they do at the confluence of material, social, and mental, housewares register the entanglement of culture and technology in especially poignant ways and communicate culture through space and time using touch. The medieval European coconut cup could not transmit the same cultural information on the western side of the Atlantic as it did on European shores, and American harnessed yerba cups and *cocos chocolateros* emerge from within the rupture of colonization. Materially, socially, and mentally, *cocos chocolateros* reflect a new media ecology when compared to medieval European coconut cups. Both medieval European coconut cups and colonial *cocos chocolateros* could be treasured objects that were employed to cement bonds between members of a household and their guests. The form of the cup suggests that colonial Americans thought about chocolate in a manner similar to the way that Peninsular Spanish thought about alcohol. At the same time, the different beverages mattered: *cocos* communicated the social importance of American chocolate, rather than European alcohol. *Cocos* also demonstrated gendered authority to a different degree than European coconut cups. Thanks to their use during chocolate rituals, *cocos* were more tightly controlled by women in American culture than coconut cups were in Europe.

Harnessed yerba cups dramatically reflect the material, social, and mental traumas of colonization, even as coconuts failed to adapt as a medium for yerba culture. While yerba might continue to be shared from a simple *jícara* and straw, following colonization, whenever possible, hostesses added elaborate silver harnesses to the gourd itself, as well as accessories like the *pie* and *salvilla*. These material modifications communicated the social and mental changes required of an American foodway blended with European table manners. While the medieval European mazer and coconut cup may have provided formal models for harnessing *jícaras*, coconuts themselves failed to communicate yerba culture, even in its colonial, modified form, and were rarely employed as yerba cups.

Cocos chocolateros and harnessed yerba *jícaras* remind us of the powerful ways in which media ecologies enable traces of indigenous cultures to persist in the face of colonization and even modify the imposed culture of the colonizers. The history of chocolate and yerba utensils demands that media studies take into account women and household technologies. Despite their success as chocolate cups, the failure of coconuts to be widely adopted as yerba cups demonstrates the instability of ecologies, dependent on environmental factors well outside human control. Whether serving alcohol, chocolate, or yerba, the coconut cup is an example of a houseware whose invention, shifting meanings, and adaptations reflect the history of global trade networks. More media ecology projects should similarly consider objects overlooked as gendered and too frequently overlooked as historical curiosities because they are gendered, and treat them as seriously as earlier critics treated paper, print, and digital media.

PART 2

Affective Affordances

CHAPTER 4

Multimedia Verse

Fiona Somerset

Anonymous mnemonic verses have received very little attention among medievalists. Literary scholars disparage their meter, while legal and intellectual historians see in them the oversimplification of concepts better suited to prose exposition. Instead, though, we might view their textual remains as the artifacts of a culture of abstract thought within and beyond the schools in which easily altered condensations of key ideas move fluidly between written, oral, and performance media and discourses. Learning was not only sedimented in highly crafted and formalized writings such as encyclopedic compendiae, summae on various topics, penitential writings, sermons, commentaries on the Bible or on canon law, or "literary" texts such as narrative or lyric poetry. It was also plastic, protean, transmissible. Learning was not only formally copied and circulated between learned clerics, and sometimes also their patrons, in texts designed for silent or group reading. It was memorized and voiced: deployed to achieve rehearsed effects. It passed between different institutional and disciplinary contexts, through a variety of written genres, and between languages and registers. Short verses are not merely a way of stating accepted truths within a cohesive community that agrees on right and wrong. Instead verses of this kind seem to be a way of contesting accepted truths or their applicability in specific cases. Attending to mnemonic verse affords us an opportunity to examine how abstract thought is shaped by media technology, and transformed in the course of its cultural contestation.

Consider, for example, the verse embedded among the layers of glossing on a page of the Cambridge, Gonville and Caius College MS 253/497
copy of the *Decretals*, an early collection of papal decrees about points
of law accompanied by extensive commentary (appendix A).[1] The standard gloss accompanying the two columns of text is crowded by layers of
additional glossing added wherever they will fit: interlinear glosses, marginal glosses, a lengthy note at the foot of the page, and among them,
two-thirds of the way down the left margin in a sprawling, later hand in
darker ink, a verse, labelled "versus": "consentit, negligit, suadet, iuuat
atque tuetur/ hic minus hicque minus luit, hic equaliter, hic plus." The
verse looks like a random jotting, but it is not: it is a common annotation for this particular decretal. Another version appears as part of the
standard gloss in a 1582 printed edition.[2] Related consent verses that
assign differing levels of culpability to various sorts of action appear in a
number of manuscripts: in a display copy rather than a working copy of
the *Decretals*, the Smithfield *Decretals*, in which the verse is incorporated into the standard gloss;[3] on the lower margin of a polemical tract
by Wyclif, *De novis ordinibus*, in Prague, National Library XI.E.3, fol.
13v, where it appears to have been added by the scribe;[4] and incorporated into the prose text, in a Middle English commentary on the Ten
Commandments for lay readers extant in a single copy (though there
are many related commentaries) in Oxford, Bodleian Library MS Bodley
789, fol. 115r. These accreted artifacts of spoken and remembered verse
make differing claims about who is guilty of a sin because their actions
constitute consent to it; they are widely distributed geographically; and
they reinforce claims made in widely disparate kinds of accompanying prose.

As this example illustrates, verses are easy to remember and to alter.
What is more, verses of any kind and any length could be a means of
transport for shorter tags and phrases commonly deployed in argument.
While in recent years tagging as a mode of creating a network of associations has usually been associated with hypertext, we could think of

digital tagging as only the latest mechanism (albeit an extraordinarily efficient one) for a much older technology of association.[5] For example, any reader of medieval religious texts is very familiar with the way that short biblical quotations strongly associated with a given argument or mode of expression, deployed within prose as well as verse, have the sort of memorative portability and malleability of interpretation I have been describing. We might even suggest that they operate rather like memes in social media.[6]

One example would be "quis dabit capiti meo aquam" from Jeremiah 9:1, used at the opening of many verse complaints on a variety of topics to establish the mood of the poem and incite empathy for its lyric voice.[7] Another is "crescite et multiplicamini," God's directive to go forth and multiply, repeated several times in the opening books of Genesis.[8] In the *Book of Margery Kempe* a "gret clerke" asks Margery how she interprets this phrase, apparently in hope of eliciting some unorthodox statement on sexuality, but she satisfies him of her orthodoxy with the conventional explanation that it refers to spiritual works as well as the "begetyng of chyldren bodily."[9]

Legal tags, which can be as short as a word or phrase or else a longer verse, have a similar kind of portable force to them. Chaucer's Summoner provides us with a well-known example: an imagined scenario that lets us speculate how tags might have been used in the oral interchange of the courtroom. When he drunkenly cries out, "Questio quid iuris!" he is using learned language to challenge the authority of a legal argument, even if he does not have the legal acumen to judge the effectiveness of a reply.[10] In this case, the relative uselessness of the legal tag is Chaucer's point: it's just for show. But the author of the early fifteenth century alliterative dream vision in the *Piers Plowman* tradition known as *Mum and the Sothsegger* is making a rather different point about the efficacy with which legal tags might be deployed by widely differing types of people, when he claims, "Qui tacet consentire videtur"—the only Latin legal tag copied directly into his English poem rather than into the margins of the single extant copy—is common speech in the country as well as the language of learned clerks:

> And also in cuntrey hit is a comune speche
> And is ywrite in Latyne, lerne hit who-so wil:
> The reson is "qui tacet consentire videtur."
> And who-so hath in-sight of silde-couthe thingz,
> Of synne or of shame or of shonde outher,
> And luste not to lette hit, but leteth hit forth passe,
> As clerkz doon construe that knowen alle bokes,
> He shal be demyd doer of the same deede.[11]

Someone who remains silent seems to consent, when he or she knows about sin and does nothing to prevent it, and will be judged as the doer of the same deed: this knowledge is common speech in the country, written in Latin but accessible for anyone to learn, as well as an interpretation made by clerks with extensive book-learning. Citing this legal tag as common speech in the country draws on the conventional rhetoric of proverbial statement: that everyone says this proves that the speaker is right.[12] However, as is often the case with proverbs, the meaning of the statement and its application to the situation at hand is less than transparent. As is also the case for the Summoner's citation, the tag calls into question any straightforward linkage of voicing and meaning.

We can find mnemonic tags and short verses of all these kinds scattered across not only *Mum and the Sothsegger* and its margins, but *Piers Plowman* and other works in its tradition, and also political verse in both Anglo-French and Anglo-Latin as well as mixtures of all three.[13] From court records and narrative sources we know that legal tags were used in oral argument as well.[14] As our opening example of the consent verse has shown, verses and phrases are embedded in homiletic, penitential, or polemical prose works; perhaps the most fertile interface for their cultural transmission is the margins of canon law manuscripts. There, legal verses move from place to place, growing and changing form in response to shifts in legal thought, sometimes only adventitiously connected with the accompanying text, sometimes attaching themselves to a standard gloss so firmly that they come to be copied with it as a matter of course, and even incorporated into the gloss rather than standing alongside.

One way to trace the movement of verses and appreciate its range is to track similar verses across genres in a survey of the discursive terrain, as in the examples I have already given. Another method I want to experiment with here would instead take a kind of deep core sample, by investigating in depth the annotations to a single, heavily annotated manuscript used extensively in an institutional setting. I will examine the annotations to Royal MS 10 E ii, British Library, London, an early fourteenth-century copy of Gratian's *Decretum* heavily used at Oxford in the fourteenth and fifteenth centuries, and at one point owned by John Wyclif. Any given manuscript I might choose as a core sample can inform us about the community that surrounds the text; but equally, any knowledge we might have about the community that surrounded the text can inform our understanding of the evidence it presents to us. This has been a point brought home to me by Rachel Koopmans's *Wonderful to Relate*, in which she reconstructs the oral community in which miracle stories were circulated on the basis of extant written miracle collections together with a variety of other sources.[15] I have borne this complementarity of evidence in mind in choosing for my core sample a manuscript produced and used in a community whose writings I have been studying for over twenty years, and whose lives and social situation are reasonably well known to me. What sorts of materials passed through this reading situation and are found sedimented upon one of its most-read books? And how might this method lead to a different sort of insight into the living use of verse, beyond the written evidence that remains to us?

The ways in which the reforming interests of Wyclif and his colleagues and followers were influenced by their reading of canon law have been comparatively little studied, and are the focus of my current research.[16] But this is not my only reason for selecting a canon law textbook for this experiment, rather than any other manuscript copied or used in Wyclif's circle in the late fourteenth century. As many as half of the university students in late medieval Oxford were engaged in studying canon law, even if many of them went on to other careers.[17] Most churchmen had some familiarity with it, if only from their encounters (like the Summoner) with the ecclesiastical courts. Canon law was the accumulated legal tradition of the Roman church. It drew on a variety of written sources for its authority, including, for example, scripture, early medieval writers such as Jerome and Augustine, local statutes, the decrees of church councils, and papal letters. And it interpreted and reinterpreted these authorities in the light of changing circumstances and new rulings over time.[18] While there were many collections of legal writings before the twelfth century, the work traditionally known as Gratian's *Decretum* was the first attempt to create a systematic teaching tool for legal study in the form of a compilation of discordant canons organized as problems to be analyzed, or distinctions, under a succession of broad topics.[19] The *Decretum* appears to have been reorganized and augmented repeatedly in the course of its early use in Bologna, where it came to form a counterpart to the increased systematization in the renewed teaching of Roman civil law in the twelfth century.[20] With the spread of legal teaching across Europe it became a standard textbook throughout the medieval period, progressively augmented by glosses that were organized into a standard gloss (the *Glossa ordinaria*, which was then itself revised) then barnacled with yet more added commentary of the sort we saw on the appendix. The *Decretum* was succeeded, but not superseded, by a series of later collections known as the *Decretals*, *Liber Sextus*, and *Clementines*.[21]

The complexity of this legal tradition, and the succession of pressing social and political issues it was marshalled to address, ensured that many writers were hotly engaged in contesting the meaning of its key topics and phrases over a long period of time. The accretive annotation and ongoing commentary found on many canon law manuscript pages reflects this ferment of ideas; while far less ephemeral, its passionate level of engagement can resemble that of an online comments forum. As in Bible manuscripts, and as we saw in A.1, commentary often quite literally surrounds the text: the text is copied in a large hand in double columns in a small text block in the centre of a large page, then surrounded with the *Glossa ordinaria* developed from a compilation of early commentaries. Interlinear glosses and an extensive layer of secondary glossing added around the margins of the standard gloss would then proliferate to fill every square inch of some pages. These are not books designed for continuous reading, but for intensive topical study accomplished through cross-referencing and tangential engagement. Thus, again as in Bible manuscripts, it is common rather than unusual for canon law manuscripts to include a variety of finding aids and commentary and summary material in additional to the authoritative text they surround, and even to include seemingly irrelevant or unrelated content alongside these ancillary materials. As in Bible manuscripts, too, not every canon law manuscript includes the entire text as printed in early modern editions that collect all of the principal canon law collections together. Instead, it is common to see the *Decretum*, *Decretals*, *Liber Sextus*, and *Clementines* compiled or excerpted within a single volume, together with commentary and summary and indices of topics, or indices of other collections not included in the manuscript.

Royal 10 E ii exhibits several of these accretive tendencies. Copied in the earlier part of the fourteenth century, it includes the revised *Glossa ordinaria* on the *Decretum* by Bartholomew of Brescia, and also nearly all the *paleae*, that is, the added materials accreted to the *Decretum* as it was used in legal teaching in Bologna. The opening pages contain an index that cross-references the *Decretum* with passages cited in the various successive collections of decretals, thus making it possible to navigate rapidly between the *Decretum* and these later canon law collections and their commentaries (fols. 2v–3r). There are several layers of marginal glossing, including both the standard gloss and further, less standardized glosses and explanations. Additional materials copied into the manuscript include a purported papal letter, some longer poems, and a miracle story (fols. 340r, 5v, 286v, 338v). Most interesting for my purposes here, the margins and fly-leaves are replete with short verses of many kinds, many of them mnemonic; and also cross references and *notae* on canon law and other topics.[22]

Some of this material gives us further clues to the manuscript's provenance and use. Most significantly, there are two late fourteenth-century pledges to Oxford loan-chests that place the manuscript directly in the circle around John Wyclif (fol. 340v). The first is from John Hugate, master of Balliol College in 1366, who pledged the book in 1372, in the Warwick chest, the oldest loan chest in Oxford. The second pledge is from Wyclif himself, who pledged it to the Vaughan and Hussey chest along with four other masters (one of them Robert Alyngton, Wyclif's younger associate at Queen's College) in October 1381. Wyclif was forced to leave Oxford in May 1382, so it seems unlikely that this loan was redeemed. These pledges suggest that except when residing temporarily in loan-chests, the book remained in circulation in Oxford as a textbook and reference work throughout the second half of the fourteenth and first quarter of the fifteenth centuries.[23] Kathryn Kerby-Fulton has suggested that it was often unfashionable or out-of-date books that were pledged to loan-chests.[24] However, the very extensive annotations on Royal 10 E ii suggest that this was not the case for this book: rather, it was heavily used in the circles in which it moved, and that one of these was the circle around Wyclif. For someone familiar with Wyclif's and lollard writings about divine and human law, the verses and notes on this book seem uncannily like a guide to key elements of Wycliffite thought. Wycliffism sprang, of course, from the broader seedbed of reform-minded thought in and around Oxford over the previous century and a half, and interest in Wyclif's ideas at Oxford persisted through the early fifteenth century despite a series of attempts to suppress them.[25] So it is unsurprising that such ideas should be preserved in a standard textbook in ongoing active use.

For the purposes of this survey I have not traced where and how often legal verses are incorporated into the gloss as part of the commentary, and whether they are modified, instead focusing on the marginal verses and annotations to try to get a sense of their proportion and distribution. The prose and verse annotations to this manuscript cover a wide range of topics: not only legal verses, but verses about biblical interpretation and translation, a large number of general moralizing verses about features of clerical life, and even parts of well-known satiric verses copied from other sources. Some annotations cleave fairly closely to the content of the law and its standard gloss, noting topics of interest or steering their interpretation in Wycliffite directions. Thus, jottings on the pastedown in the front cover of the manuscript list various clerical abuses (fol. iv); and in the opening thirty folios we find notes on speaking the truth (fol. 9r), on who commands the English church (fol. 12v), on accord with the law of scripture (fol. 12r), on simony (fols. 13v, 27v), on whether a council of clerics can convene without papal authorization (fols. 18rv), and on whether the king or the pope has higher authority (fol. 19v). There are verses on legal and theological points scattered throughout the manuscript, as for example a verse on *latria* and *dulia* (fol. 323r), a distinction much cited by Wycliffites, between the veneration appropriate to God as opposed to that appropriate to objects or images designed to foster devotion.[26]

The annotations about biblical interpretation and translation (fol. 9r), on what books count as apocrypha (fols. 16rv), and on the relationship between laws found in scripture as opposed to human laws (e.g., fols. 197r, 219r, 270r, 307r, 234v) are more unusual in a canon law manuscript. They are characteristically Wycliffite: they would not be out of place in one of the biblical prefaces or summaries associated with the movement, or else in the *Thirty-Seven Conclusions*, which make heavy use of canon law and discuss how to reconcile that law with God's law as found in scripture.[27]

But these annotations do not simply pull in their own direction, independent from the text of Gratian. Several appear in the opening pages of the manuscript, in the margins of Gratian's first twenty distinctions, which are also known as his *Treatise on Laws*.[28] Here, Gratian similarly discusses the foundation of human law in scripture, and while he does not address this topic at length, the materials he compiles throughout the *Decretum* do put this stated principle into practice by citing scripture heavily and pervasively. Some of the verses deployed in the course of this sequence of annotations are highly conventional: *"littera gesta docet"* makes an appearance, to explain types of biblical interpretation and their utility, for example (fol. 7r).[28] Similarly, there is a mnemonic on the ten plagues of Egypt (fol. 239v).[30] Others seem more original, such as a distich that combines the adage that the new does not always destroy the old with the juristic principle that laws should be in concord (fol. 29v).[31] This principle is of course fundamental to the *Decretum*'s mode of exposition, and the foundation of the medieval study of canon law on which all subsequent commentary on the *Decretum* and successive compilations builds, in that each distinction or question proceeds by quoting and resolving the discrepancies between discordant canons. By comparing an oblique reference to the relationship of the old and new laws with the principle of concord, this verse too implicitly asserts that scriptural and human law should be compatible.

By far the bulk of the verses in the margins of this manuscript, however, are moralizing verses, many aimed at clerical life. These verses are loosely attached, if at all, to the canon law text that is their neighbour. Hardly any injunctions of this general kind are given in prose, in contrast with the other types of annotation we have canvassed. We might wonder why there is so much of what might look like anodyne boilerplate moralizing, in a canon law manuscript that belonged to Wyclif of all places. Our core sample experiment here may prompt us to reconsider what role commonplace moralizing might have in legal thought, and perhaps especially for complaint or for reformist thought. If *Mum and the Sothsegger* could present a Latin legal tag derived from Roman law as proverbial discourse, the common speech of the countryside, then perhaps, conversely, the common speech of the country, or moralizing speech that represents itself this way, may have a certain force in learned legal disputation.

The use of the *Distichs of Cato* for elementary instruction in Latin ensured that verse aphorisms were basic to how educated people thought about stating moral truths, regardless of their area of expertise.[32] However, while we may be accustomed to thinking of moralizing verses as generalized and largely unhelpful advice of the kind a Polonius might deliver, a number of the moralizing verses included in the margins of Royal 10 E ii are more topical than they look. Some are of obvious relevance to reform-minded clerics, and even to Wyclif in particular. For example, the well-known distich "Quanto dignior es aut per genus aut per honores / In te tanto res viciose sunt grauiores" (fol. 20v) matches up quite precisely with the advice Wyclif gives the king in *De Officio Regis*: that his rank, and the power over others' lives that it confers, make any vices he may indulge more serious in their consequences.[33] Literary scholars have been aware for some time that when Chaucer, Langland, Gower, or their imitators deploy moralizing quotations of this kind, they typically aim to complicate their surface meaning in the service of their larger narrative and argument, rather than simply rely on their wisdom.[34] But we may not have thought about how this sort of moralizing might be less simple than it looks in legal contexts, as well. As well as considering the social context and ownership of a specific manuscript, we might consider the context of these verses on the page itself. Some may simply be jotted in convenient blank spaces, so that their pointed relevance to discussions taking place around them needs to be reconstructed by reading other texts; but others may refer quite directly to neighbouring discussions in the text or standard gloss.

Similarly, the proverbial wisdom in moralizing verses themselves has not typically been thought of as subject to controversy or prone to modification. But variance among these verses suggests otherwise. For example, the advice to members of religious orders expressed in "Nunc lege nunc ora nunc cum fervore labora / Sic erit ora breuis et labor iste leuis" (Now read, now pray, now work with zeal / Thus the hour will be brief and the labour light)—that is the standard wording—seems to have been actively modified in the late fourteenth and early fifteenth centuries in England by those seeking a different kind of advice about how to divide their time in other walks of life.[35] This shift in emphasis is congruent with the Wycliffite contention that life in the world is a better means to pursue holiness than life in a religious order, especially considering the religious orders' abuse of their resources.[36] But it would also find broader sympathy among a wide range of religious writings that seek to make religious aspiration accessible to lay readers.[37] The single line "nunc lege, nunc ora, nunc disce, nuncque labora" appears on its own in the manuscript of the *Castle of Perseverance*, for example: "nunc disce" (now study) has been added in place of "cum fervore" (with zeal)."[38] Similarly, in Royal 10 E ii, the distich appears with the first line "Nunc lege, nunc ora, nunc instrue [now instruct], nuncque labora" (fols. 192r, 192v). Each of these versions places a new emphasis on learning, though only Royal 10 E ii exhorts readers to teach, at the same time that it attaches the benefits promised for religious to a broadened audience. This verse is copied twice on adjacent pages, as if for emphasis.

This core sampling of a single legal manuscript has suggested ways that we might complicate our understanding of how short mnemonic verses helped medieval people think about law. Rather than simply facilitating memory or restating accepted truths, these verses and the various media they travel through and stitch together may provide sites upon which truth and memory can be renegotiated. Rather than emerging from learned culture and filtering only unevenly through to vernacular verse, they may circulate between languages and contexts in ways that their sedimentation in various written forms can only partly record. In Royal 10 E ii in particular, moralizing verses seem to be a way of thinking about law in verse that may not have always seemed distinct, for this manuscript's users, from the verse annotations and legal tags that had emerged more directly from the context of legal teaching and commentary—the ones that ordinarily accompany the canon law gloss and are commonly incorporated into its text. Any of these verses, regardless of provenance, might be modified and redeployed in new contexts—and any of them, no matter how recondite its origins, might be remembered and repeated often enough that it might come to seem like common speech.

Raymond of Pennafort, *Liber Extra*, a folio to illustrate typical glossing and layout, Cambridge, Gonville and Caius College 253/497

CHAPTER 5

Ex Illo Tempore

Time, Mediation, and the *Ars Dictaminis* in Letter 65 by Peter the Venerable

Jonathan M. Newman

Introduction

The epistolary form was central to the religious and institutional life of the Latin West during the Middle Ages. In particular, the twelfth century is often regarded as a golden age of medieval epistolarity, and few of its correspondents are more celebrated than Peter the Venerable, Abbot of Cluny (1092–1156). Peter wrote well over a hundred letters to prominent figures across Latin Christian Europe, and their style epitomizes the development of letters written according to the *ars dictaminis*, the medieval art of letter-writing, into an artful form of diplomatic prose that combines personal and institutional communication.[1] This chapter will examine how a letter from Peter to Bernard of Clairvaux in request of a reply offers a model for understanding how the conventions of medieval epistolography informed and metonymically reproduced the church's corporate self-understanding, particularly during the twelfth century. This letter is particularly revelatory inasmuch as it uses its own focuses on the *mediality* of letters to express both the church's idealized self-understanding in its apocalyptic mission of salvation and the vexing experiences of institutionality and factionalization. My reading will apply terms and concepts taken from media theory to identify some of the causes and implications of the role letters played in authorizing the apparatus of ecclesiastical institutional authority. In particular, I will demonstrate how this letter's representation of mediality can clarify the role of epistolary texts and objects in the literature and documentation of this period, and in this way advance our understanding of this crucial literary and documentary genre.

It bears emphasizing from the start that when I refer to the mediality of letters, I mean the discursive protocols of composition as much as the material conveyances.[2] In Peter the Venerable's time, the first half of the twelfth century, the conventional formulas of medieval letters were continuously elaborated and codified in letter-writing handbooks that realized the church's structure through formulas of address and self-representation determined by institutional ranks and roles.[3] The institutional needs that drove the production of these conventions existed in tension with the affective, personal discourse of the conventions themselves, which often express the sender's desire for the recipient's presence and lament the relative insufficiency of the letter in comparison to face-to-face speech. Medieval letters thus demonstrate a tension between the letter's status as a situated (personal) event and as a (institutional) record of that event; letters are both instances of transmission and of storage media, expressions of desire in the present and documents of transactions in the imagined future.

The letter in question is letter 65 of Peter the Venerable to Bernard of Clairvaux from the 1140s, which expresses a preference for letters over messengers.[4] These two correspondents are suitably representative figures of the period's ecclesiastical elites. As abbots, authors, and reformers, they represent and articulate divergent and contrary views about monastic purpose and practice, but they do so in a shared medium and network.[5] As my reading below will show, Peter's letter is a particularly useful example of how the two related tensions identified above—between personal and institutional communication, between utterance and record—could give individual letters an indefinite temporality by which they could ascribe to themselves *as media and objects* a kind of charismatic authority previously identified with the body of the charismatic master or holy person.[6]

In particular, I will argue that letters had a pervasive role as the most important medium for public communication at a distance between individuals and institutions in the Middle Ages, and shared with face-to-face interactions a set of ceremonial qualities that expressed ranks and relationships.[7] Consequently, the way that medieval letters reflected on their similarities to and differences from face-to-face speech is inseparable from their social discourse. Various tensions attend the mediality of the medieval letter—tensions arising from a discourse on and in letters that articulate distinctions between absence and presence, or, conceived more precisely in terms of temporality, between present and not-present. Around this distinction comes a cluster of related contrasts—between spontaneous speech and the codified dictaminal letter, between institutional role and subjective desire (or "public and private"), and between the time and place of writing and the time and place of reading, the very difference upon which mediation rests. In order to map these contrasts and demonstrate their usefulness for reading the epistles of the twelfth century, I begin in the next section with my reading of the specific letter that is the occasion for my analysis.

Epistolary Mediation and Work of Association

In letter 65, addressed to Bernard of Clairvaux, Peter asks specifically for a letter in preference to the more "authentic" physical presence:

> Since that time [*ex illo tempore*], there does remain in me constantly, even as I hope [*utinam*] it does in you, the love which began together between us on account of Christ—And while I have enclosed this love in my heart and concealed it in that treasury as something more dear than any gold and more brilliant than every gem, I wonder that in so much time

I have not received the kinds of evidence of this love for my safekeeping as I might wish from you. I do give thanks that, since you have often sent greetings through someone or other, you have expressed that you have not completely forgotten your friend. But I complain that to this point you have not given more certain signs of this love through letters. More certain, I say, because the written page does not know how to change its discourse, while the tongue of speakers may too often alter the truth with which it is charged by addition or subtraction.[8]

Peter, comparing the relative value of the written word to the messenger who conveys a message by memory, asserts that the written letter is a surer and more reliable sign of the sender's love than the words of a messenger.[9] This discourse contrasting the alternatives for communicating at a distance demonstrates that "self-reflection of texts and artifacts on their own media-ness" in which Markus Stock and Anne-Marie Rasmussen see cause for examining medieval culture through the lens of present-day media studies.[10] And for Peter, the material medium of writing has a meaning apart from, but potentially consonant with the "message": the immutable sequence of a written letter would signify the permanence of Bernard's love, and therefore be a more appropriate medium for communicating it.

Medieval historians have long been aware of the anxiety about mediation expressed in Peter's letter here, which is indeed widely attested. Horst Wenzel, for example, has written about the way that an oral message and a written letter might be combined to verify one another, and how this implies that the reliability of either on its own might fail in some way.[11] So also in his short monograph *Letters and Letter Collections*, which remains an important touchstone on the subject, Giles Constable adduced this passage: "Sometimes an author relied on his style as a proof of authenticity, either because his seal was not to hand, as with the letters of St. Bernard mentioned above, or because the matter was so secret or so compromising to the writer that he hesitated to attach his name or seal."[12] Constable brings up as well the example of Petrarch, who states in one of his letters written sine nomine, "You recognize the voice of the speaker."[13] Clearly, then, the relation between speech and writing in medieval letter-writing is far more complex than a simple distinction between immediacy and mediation respectively.

In each of these examples, the presence of the speaker is understood to be mediated not by an indexical sign through contiguous attachment of the author's body to the material letter, but by an iconic sign, since the style of the language reproduces the sender's voice through its resemblance.[14] This emphasis on style as authenticating voice acknowledges the supplementary nature of the indexical sign—the seal or subscript—for the purpose of eliciting a sense of authenticated presence for the recipient.[15] The mutual supplementarity of body, seal, signature, voice, and style illuminates the interrelation of bodily presence, social authority, and literary style in the epistolary culture of central Middle Ages: "For medieval culture, the co-presence of bodies and the representation of absent people are fundamentally important categories of politically relevant communication. As research in the fields of medieval history, cultural studies, and literary studies has shown, the performative acts of people co-present in shared spaces are foundational for aristocratic practices."[16] The continuous attention that medieval letters pay to bodies in space, along with their ceremonious elaboration of forms of address, suggests that such letters serve not only to mediate verbal messages, but "performative acts" predicated on "the co-presence of bodies."

It is therefore remarkable that Peter's request for a verbal message argues that a written message will make the communication of Bernard's presence *less* attenuated than the spoken message of an oral messenger.[17] This request comes near the beginning, in the *exordium* of the letter, sometimes called the *captatio benevolentiae*—the effort to obtain the audience or reader's goodwill; the same request will be repeated later in the *petitio*. According to the protocols of the *ars dictaminis*, every letter contained five parts: *salutatio*, *exordium* (a rhetorical effort to gain the goodwill of the listener), a *narratio* (the "information" that the letter had to convey), a *petitio* or request, and a *conclusio*. These were compulsory elements of all dictaminal letters, which make up the overwhelming majority of letters written in the central and later Middle Ages.

From our experience of how letters, memos, and emails function in present-day organizational culture, we might view the *petitio* as the "business end" of the letter, the part that contains the "actual" message, and correspondingly view the letter's other parts—*salutatio, exordium, narratio, conclusio*—as filler, ceremonial face-work, or "phatic communion."[18] In fact, letters were a means by which organizational and individual associations were maintained remotely, so that such ceremonial face-work was often the entire point of the letter. Then as now, it was vitally important to ensure that everyone knew in every interaction who was in charge and who was subordinate, who made decisions and who enacted them, in theory and in practice. As a compulsory element, therefore, the *petitio* aligned senders with receivers in a culture of reciprocity (shared by ecclesiastical and lay elites) that ratified the respective institutional roles and relationships obtaining between senders and recipients.[19] Peter the Venerable's request for a letter in preference to live speech must be read in light of this function letters performed, as (re)productions of the training and practice that shaped the church into a corporate body that transcended times and place.

Given the putative logocentrism of Western culture, the notion that a letter may be a superior mode of communication to spoken words might seem surprising. In fact, this counterintuitive idea speaks to a tension between competing concepts of communication articulated by Hans Ulrich Gumbrecht: on the one hand, the communication of bodily presence, and on the other hand, the communication of a meaning above and beyond bodily presence for which bodies must be understood as mere vehicles.[20] This tension is expressed in the passage quoted above, and it is crucial to understanding medieval letters as a discursive practice coordinating social identities and institutions through specific texts.[21] Peter's both/and resolution to the contradiction between the letter form's mediality as a textual object and its (conventionalized) evocations of "immediacy" and bodily presence is representative of the role letters played in assembling the institutional church in this period of enormous transformation and expansion.

In particular, Peter's preference for a letter over a messenger marks the failures of face-to-face communication even as it focuses on how the presence of a speaker reveals the conventionality of "immediacy." In fact, the failure of face-to-face speech discloses the superiority of the epistolary supplement. At first glance, this may seem like a deconstructive or Lacanian substitution of a durative physical token of attenuated presence for the ephemeral and unobtainable real presence—in other words, a "fetish." In fact, the substitution of the letter for the presence of the sender transforms individual relationships into institutional roles; it reconfigures bodily presence into a conceptual vehicle for the lineaments of *association* that continuously enact the church as a body that transcends spatial and temporal location.[22]

What is striking about the way letters mediate this *incorporation* (considered as a process as much as an entity) is the degree to which they make embodied desire the motive force of the church's increasingly textualized institutionalization. This feature, too, is emblematized by Peter's letter to Bernard, not least with its optative (if counterfactual) statement marker *utinam*: "There does remain in me constantly, even as I hope [*utinam*] it does in you, the love which began together between us on account of Christ."[23] From their classical, patristic, and monastic origins, the intertwining threads of mediation, desire, and time emerge in high medieval epistolarity in a mode that is processed by the protocols of the *ars dictaminis*. This fact gives a different inflection to C. Stephen Jaeger's thesis about the idealization of physical presence during the period of transition to textualized bureaucratic administration during the long twelfth century.[24] This idealization depends precisely on that physical presence being already figured by epistolarity. The letter's reflective discourse about its own mediality combines its attention to bodily presence and absence with attention to the temporality of the letter's transmission and reception. Peter's letter to Bernard is a paradigmatic example of the dictaminal letter as the distillation of clerical society because it suggests how the representation of desired and desirous bodies organizes how letters enact the institutional routines that coordinate identities, relations, and systems in the clerical church. In the next section, I will turn to consider more broadly some of the ways in which we might apply this paradigm to think about medieval epistolarity more generally.

Letter, Institution, and Clerical Authority

The tension between the letter's monumentality and status as a situated act of communication from a specific sender to a specific recipient pervaded all kinds of medieval literary writing. Most conventional understandings of modern communications technology are predicated on a distinction between media and storage. And yet, as the example of Peter's letter 65 makes especially clear, letters can function both as transmission media and as storage media, and moreover these functions can not only fail to contradict each other but can be mutually reinforcing. Like modern technological mass media, letters "can be stored indefinitely," copied, reproduced, and reused for a variety of purposes at different times and places.[25] As tokens of exchange and objects of commercial consumption, letters were even subject to commodification like modern media, if at a much lower volume.[26] Letters persistently acknowledge the role played by the expectations and desires of specific readers in shaping the form and content of their letters. The sender also appeals to the personal history and mutual affiliation shared with the receiver, so that the letter itself perpetuates the connection as its material token and enactment—carried, exchanged, read out loud, copied, and collected.[27] The letter is both artifact and event: event *as* artifact, artifact *as* event.

This double nature manifests in several ways. As I have explained above, one of these is in the conventional contrast between the letter's self-characterization as spontaneous face-to-face discourse and its studied composition as prose. Another is in the expressions of longing for the correspondent's presence and sorrow at the absence, by reflections on distance and separation. These reveal complex and sometimes contradictory understandings of how letters mediate the presence and desire of writers and readers. The re-presentifying of the bodies of charismatic figures in an idealized way, made possible by the specific mediality of the letter—immaterial and yet touchable, transitory and yet available to be read and shared over and over again—was a central feature and perhaps motivating factor of that "golden age of epistolarity" identified with the twelfth century.

While it is difficult to overstate the importance of the letter to twelfth-century social, institutional, and religious practice, it bears acknowledging that this epistolary culture did not come out of nowhere. The greater part of the New Testament is made up of letters addressed to both individuals and communities. Likewise, a vast amount of patristic writing from the early apostolic fathers to Gregory the Great and Bede consisted of letters, and Christian epistolography was an outgrowth and species of a more widespread practice of letter-writing in the Greco-Roman world. This practice encompassed a great number of purposes: private, legal, administrative, diplomatic, didactic, and religious. Nor was this limited to European Christian culture. To pick only one other example, the rabbinical *responsa* offers a parallel legacy of ancient epistolography adapted to the use of a geographically dispersed religious community. Sita Steckel, among others, has expanded in detail on the continued and growing association of letter-writing with clerical culture through "networks of learning" in Western Europe from the ninth century.[28]

Nevertheless, the Investiture Controversy and reform movements beginning in the eleventh century gave letters a very specific form of prominence, because they served as the principal medium for propaganda for partisans on both sides.[29] Letters also grew in importance when their function expanded as the Roman Church transformed into a supranational bureaucracy.[30] The letter in the Middle Ages had already come to form the model not just for official and personal communication at a distance, but for deeds, charters, bulls, and other kinds of official legal documents. As such, letters were communication across time as well as space; the edict or charter served as a kind of letter to whom it may concern in the future.

As the importance of letters increased, procedures for making letters became increasingly codified and elaborate, and expertise in those procedures and codes became a mark of belonging to a distinct and self-regarding group. Writing letters was a central part of the education and work of clergy, both monastic and secular, in the Middle Ages.[31] From the eleventh through the fifteenth century, to learn to write prose was to learn to write letters. The work of institutional communication and network building was carried out by clerics occupying various institutional roles but sharing the *ars dictaminis* as a common protocol for communicating ideas and expressing and resolving conflicts.

The formality of the letter provides a unifying framework, a field for playing with various modes of address and types of discourse while anchoring them in the epistolary situation of the central and later Middle Ages.[32] This epistolary situation is a community fragmented in time and space but united by shared procedures and professional values. Thinking about the elaborate conventions of medieval epistolary rhetoric as mediating protocols brings into view the way the letter's sense of *immediacy* is attained through repeated formulas, genres, and rhetorical norms.[33] Of course Peter's claim that Bernard's love is more precious than any gem belongs to a standard repertoire of affective language that could signal a great many things. Nevertheless, to decode procedural and strategic meanings (e.g., "how a Benedictine abbot addresses a famous Cistercian he does not much like when challenging him to commit a position to writing") does not efface the literal and most historically proximate meaning. That literal meaning of this letter is a reflection on the value of a letter for monastic friendship in the context of the author's overwhelming reverence for the holiness of his recipient.

Above I have cited C. Stephen Jaeger's influential work, which has examined the cultural transformations that accompanied the shift in the church to a footing of administrative textuality.[34] It will help to clarify my own argument if I situate it briefly in relation to his influential narrative of these transformations. Jaeger begins this narrative in a "before time" when clerical authority was enacted through personal presence and an "after time" when texts became themselves dispositive of clerical authority. In the eleventh century, cathedral schools burgeoning in the imperial cities of the Rhine circulated "the accepted, normative, legitimate discourse" of *cultus virtutum*, the cultivation of virtue.[35] This *cultus* was learning manners and habits from a charismatic master whose body, rather than texts, was the object of imitation: "A charismatic culture makes the body and the physical presence into the mediator of cultural values.... Physical presence is the anchor of charismatic culture."[36] Jaeger's grand thesis is that the twelfth century witnessed the replacement of this charismatic culture centred on the cathedral schools of the eleventh century with a textual fabrication centred on the study and imitation of texts. The mediality of the dictaminal letters suggests a slightly more complicated situation—the charismatic body was already produced by textuality, and the authority of texts continued to issue from their connection to authorial bodies.

Jaeger describes the transformation of clerical culture from the eleventh to twelfth centuries in terms closely resembling how Gumbrecht describes the transition from a presence culture to a meaning culture, especially in the way it imagines meaning as something that transforms from the plenitude of presence ("the real") to the attenuated presence of verbal signification and mediation ("the symbolic").[37] According to Jaeger, "The eleventh century was oriented to personal presence; the twelfth tended more and more toward texts. It is a development closely related to the transition from an oral to a written culture. But the transition of media has received far more attention and intelligent commentary than the more embracing category, the transition from real to symbolic, from physical to textual presence, in the intellectual life of the two periods."[38] Jaeger's formulation of this shift as a "transition of media" tacitly acknowledges that the oral communication of personal presence is itself a kind of mediation. Oral communication, like the letter, produces the personal presence of the speaker under a set of protocols and conventions whose dependence on that speaker's personal presence is fixed within a wider range of practices and habits. Jaeger sees in the difference between bodily and textual presence a difference between real and symbolic, and sees in twelfth-century humanistic culture, such as John of Salisbury's celebrated portrait of Bernard of Chartres, an attitude of nostalgia toward the living, bodily presence of the master's charismatic body.[39]

Yet the eleventh century texts on which Jaeger bases his thesis are already retrospective, and have already textualized the physical presence in a way that marks the absence of the charismatic body and its representation in text. The twelfth-century text (itself an idealization based on periodizing assumptions) mediates the body, and in doing so remediates a creation already mediated and mediating—the idealized master's imaginary body, itself the instructive medium of virtue, grace, and good conduct. Jaeger's description of this charisma as "a kind of body-magic" that "makes the teacher's presence into a seal and the students into wax receiving his print" underscores the mediated nature of a supposedly immediate physical presence with a profound understanding of how medieval people looked for the mutual validation of seal, messenger, and letter.[40]

What emerges with the centrality of the dictaminal letter, then, is a valorization of the letter not as replacement, but as *remediation* of charismatic presence.[41] This remediation speaks not to its own insufficiency for translating that charisma, but on the contrary to a supersufficiency linking back to the letter's status as both transmission and storage. This allows not only mediation of the sender, but of the organization of the church that produces charisma as a function of the clerical office as much as the pure manners and sweet discourse described by the texts that Jaeger explores. It is the procedures of the *ars dictaminis* that bring together office and habitus. What were originally discretionary techniques for the orator become complex verbal protocols determined precisely by the institutional role of sender and recipient; the nested hierarchies produced by the arrangement of these protocols mediate the social structure imagined by the medieval clergy, and to use the compositional formulae of *ars dictaminis* is to realize that imaginary structure in institutional practice.[42]

A helpful framing for this is provided by critical discourse analysis (CDA), which teaches that face-to-face interactions and communications mediated by technology are equally formatted by "preconstructed elements" and "institutional routines" entailed by relations of class, status, and power.[43] The dictaminal letter is a particularly explicit instance of how discourse is configured by institutional routines and preconstructed elements. The routines include the protocols that inscribe status and social distance and proximity among the people, mostly men, of the medieval church's branching parallel hierarchies.[44] The preconstructed discursive elements belong to, and derive from, an art of rhetoric originating in ancient forensic discourse, but already thoroughly textualized in the eleventh century by centuries of educational practice.[45] Individual utterances and messages are produced by more or less explicit sets of conventions and protocols that reproduce relations of power.[46]

At the same time, CDA posits reciprocity between discourse and practice. Institutions and social structures are not just represented but regenerated by the elements and routines of discursive practices like the *ars dictaminis*.[47] In generating and structuring the discourse of the medieval letter, the *ars dictaminis* constitutes an authority that is immanent in textual self-representation. Letters point beyond themselves to an authorizing presence, but the authority is located in the text itself. If this authority is identified with an embodied voice, it must also be remembered that "the sound of the body often becomes an imitation of this part of itself that is produced and reproduced by the media: i.e., the copy of its own artifact."[48] The cultural fantasy of the master's charismatic body described by Jaeger depends already on the mediation of writing—"orality insinuates itself, like on the threads of which it is composed, into the network—an endless tapestry—of a scriptural economy."[49] Letters belong to an economy, an ordered but dynamic system of exchange, which is scriptural. And while "orality" or face-to-face interaction offers a fantasy of self-authorizing discourse, the "'scriptural' is that which separates itself from the magical world of voices and tradition" and in doing so, generates "legitimate practice," society as a text.[50]

This, then, is the story of the twelfth-century "golden age" of medieval epistolarity. As letters express longing for the co-presence of sender and recipient, they simulate the fantasy of immediacy, unachievable because its achievement would render the letters in which they exist unnecessary. Thus, the epistolary discourse of desire draws attention to the letter's mediation of word and presence across time, invoking spatial presence by displacing the temporal present. Reflections on the mediality of the letter like the one found in Peter the Venerable's Letter 65, reveal a nostalgia for the charismatic body of the eleventh-century master: "I composed this even while your absence—begrudgingly—was still concealing the look of your body from me against my wishes, since reputation, faster than the body, was already carrying the presence of your blessed soul to the eyes of my mind in what way it could."[51] Yet Peter's expressed desire for a letter reveals how bodily charisma has already become a textual phenomenon, just as the elaboration of dictaminal rhetoric calls attention to textuality in a way that ends up intensifying bodily reference. De Certeau talks about writing as displacing the originary voice of authority into the past, and in the course of doing so, transforming time into space. In this way, we can perhaps understand the reinscription of the voice into writing, the remediation of the body in text, as depending on the inscription of temporality into the text, which is a crucial feature of epistolarity as such.[52] In particular, Peter's letter helps us think through the way that absence is conceived more in temporal than spatial terms. In the next section, I will return to Peter's letter and address this question of temporality.

Absence, Temporality, and Desire

It is beyond the scope of this discussion but nonetheless helpful to note that scenes of people writing and reading letters to one another can be found throughout the literature of the central and later Middle Ages, in both official languages and unofficial dialects. These scenes articulate a persistent recognition of the absence felt as suffering and longing between the senders and recipients, as well their fetishistic desire to recover and maintain mutual presence through the letters themselves. In Marie de France's *Milun*, a young noblewoman kisses her lover's letter a "hundred times."[53] Several centuries later, Chaucer's Troilus bathes the seal of his letter to Criseyde in his tears, and later kisses Criseyde's response repeatedly.[54] These scenes are helpful context for the present argument because they suggest how the medieval imaginary makes the letter metonymical for the sender's body. In such fictions, the letter's materiality, including such appurtenances as the wax seal, mediates the physical presence of sender and receiver through a contiguity between physical bodies that replaces space with time as the distancing factor. In this section I will describe the similar play at work in the official letters that are the subject of my analysis.

As I have described above, the medieval art of letter writing, the *ars dictaminis*, includes specific protocols for formatting the text before its material transmission. But the entire set of practices that make up medieval letter writing involve a set of material practices as well as a set of textual protocols; it is therefore crucial that the overall picture of medieval epistolarity be understood to include such material practices De Ghellink here describes: "There are two stages to be crossed between the dictation by the author and the text as it is transmitted to us: first, the passage from the ear to the hand of the tachygrapher [the scribe working in shorthand, probably on a wax tablet] ... then, the second stage, from the eye to the hands of the scribe, who reconstituted the tachygraphy into ordinary writing, and, finally, the passage from the eye or the ear to the hands of the calligraphers, who definitively transcribed the copy, and thus the risks of textual corruptions were multiplied."[55] This description of letters as a communications medium registers how medieval fictions represent the exchange of letters as embedded in a matrix of bodies in motion and contact: multiple steps of material transmission, from voice to tablet to parchment, and then (often) to a secretary or cleric in the service of the recipient who will read the letter aloud and sometimes even translate it into a vernacular.[56]

The complexity of producing and exchanging letters raises a number of questions about what belongs to the message and what makes up the static obscuring it. The reference to eyes, hands, and ears points to the ways in which the letter, as a medium, overtly registers the mutual impositions it makes between itself and the bodies that handle it—scribes, messengers, and readers-out-loud. To compensate for the attenuation of the sender's presence, gestures of subscription—signatures and seals— imprint an indexical sign of the sender's bodily presence, as if to say that this seemingly mediated communication act is in fact immediate.

As I have suggested above, the letters that served as the ligaments of the institutional church were also a cultivated form of literary expression, especially in the long twelfth century that is my primary focus. Letter collections were assembled on account both of their author's significance and of their virtuosity with the epistolary medium. Some authors combined both, and indeed I have selected Peter the Venerable and Bernard of Clairvaux as my examples in part for the way that they exhibit this combination.[57] Through the letter genre's own discourse of presence, absence, and embodied desire, the letters found in such collections seemingly strive for immediate communication. As a necessary consequence of this striving, literary letters become thematically concerned with that distinction between communication as the act of sending a message and the medium as the method or material channel by which the message is sent. One cannot exist without the other, and so an "immediate" communication requires the co-presence of physical bodies in space and time, the body itself the irreducible material channel of communication.

Peter the Venerable's Letter 65, with its request to Bernard of Clairvaux for a letter, is a specimen from an exchange between two important churchmen and celebrated letter-writers that is precisely concerned with the combined literary and documentary task of representing and authorizing the mediality of their epistolary correspondence.[58] They were not friends, but ideological and institutional rivals whose many letters debated the purpose and conduct of monasticism at a time of institutional growth and tumult.[59] Nevertheless, as fellow monks and brothers in Christ, these letters drip with *caritas*, and in the passage cited above, Peter expresses the pain he feels at Bernard's absence in elaborately emotional language.

Conventionally, such emotional intensity was expressed not by simplicity but rhetorical amplification, and drew upon customary tropes expressing the feeling of missing their correspondent that have roots in classical, biblical, and patristic epistolography. I will cite again the passage in which Peter expresses his longing for Bernard. In order to clarify my reading of this passage, I will also mark out with their Latin words all the places in this sentence where Peter calls attention to time: "I composed this even while [*dum*] your absence—begrudgingly—was still [*adhuc*] concealing the look of your body from me against my wishes, since reputation was already [*iam*] carrying the presence [*faciem*] of your blessed soul to the eyes of my mind faster [*velocior*] than the body in that which it was able."[60] Adverbs of time—*dum, adhuc, iam*—call attention to the crucial role that time plays in the medium of letters.

This specific and in some ways unremarkable letter allows us to conceive how absence was conceived more in temporal than spatial terms, which indicates that letters conceive of their mediating work—of making absent correspondents present to each other—in temporal rather than spatial terms. The comparative *velocior* (faster) invokes speed and thus combines space and time, and the transference of focus from material to spiritual presence annihilates the materiality of distance, an operation intensified in the next sentence: "But when what had long been denied I have finally achieved, and the phantoms of dreams have vanished with the arrival of truth, my soul has stuck to you, nor has it been able to be further parted from your love."[61] The temporality of this sentence is markedly strange in idiom and grammar and defies easy translation. Attention to time is repeatedly marked by more temporal adverbs—*ubi* (when), *diu* (for a long time), *tandem* (at length)—and through verbal forms that invoke time through the idea of succession (*assecutus sum* and *succedente*—"I followed after" and "following"), but the sequence of tenses is peculiar. In the first clause, the pluperfect *fuerat* (had been) gives way to the perfect *sum assecutus* (I followed after) and *euanuerunt*—all of this is governed by the initial *ubi*. After *adhesit* (stuck), we are in the main clause, which continues in the perfect, but a perfect that drifts into an aorist aspect, which emphasizes completion of an action at some point in the past, rather than specifying a particular point in time. Past and present are collapsed as the grammar itself figures the sender's desire to overcome the distance between himself and his recipient through time. It is worth noting that the opening *ubi* can denote both where and when, but it quickly resolves its meaning as temporal in the context of the sentence that follows. This emphasis on time rather than space intensifies as the letter proceeds to where we began: "Thus, your love claimed me entirely for itself in turn, thus your character [*mores*] and virtues seized me, so that nothing was left to me of mine which was not yours, nothing not mine to you of yours was allowed to be. The love begun together for the sake of Christ remains in me constantly since that time, even as I hope it remains so in you—that love which alone, because it knows not how to perish, rightly has maintained its character as much in me as it keeps to you."[62] Here it will be useful to think analytically about the challenges to linguistic temporality posed by the letter itself. According to François Recanati, the "epistolary present" depends on an imaginary idealizing metaphor in which the time of sending and receiving are the same.[63] This metaphor depends, we might say, on the variety of immediacy identified by Bolter and Grusin, which is to say not the actual immediacy of technical transparency, as in a televised presence, but a conventionalized immediacy governed by beliefs and practices linking the epistolary situation to face-to-face interaction.[64]

This imaginary space furnishes the conditions for a textualized co-presence that permeates the understanding of epistolarity found in medieval letters. This co-presence, the metaphorical idealization, is a constant of epistolarity from the classical through the medieval period. We see this in Heloïse's quotation of Seneca in a letter to Abelard, occurring in one of the most celebrated letter collections in not only the twelfth century but in the European literary corpus:

> Letters from absent friends are welcome indeed, as Seneca himself shows us by his own example when he writes these words in one of his letters to his friend Lucilius: "Thank you for writing to me often, the one way in which you can make your presence felt, for I never have a letter from you without the immediate feeling that we are together. If pictures of absent friends give us pleasure, renewing our memories and relieving the pain of separation even if they cheat us with empty comfort, how much more welcome are letters, which come to us in the very handwriting of an absent friend?"[65]

Heloïse's citation of this ancient letter speaks to the indeterminate temporality of a letter, which undermines its presence and potentially makes its comfort "empty," even if Seneca says a letter is worth more than a picture. Temporality is ascribed not to the temporality of composition or reception but to the discourse of the text itself. This allows the epistolary text to convey the author's charismatic presence by virtue of its textuality, rather than simply recording an echo.

The elaborate discourse of medieval letters frequently draws attention to the role played by time. If mediation entails the overcoming of distance, then the medieval letter imagines that distance as being temporal rather than spatial. This aligns with Michel de Certeau's observation that writing displaces the originary voice into the past. If the originary voice of authority is imagined as present to the writer in the past—that time when the sender was recipient, the letter's desire expresses distance from future as well as past togetherness; the discourse of separation becomes one of longing and hope, and this mixture of nostalgia and longing (hopeful or desperate) belongs simultaneously to the medieval languages of religion, friendship, and erotic love. Since this longing extends to the future as to the past, the temporality of Peter's Letter 65 to Bernard rests finally on a note of apocalyptic unity. After a slightly fulsome description of Bernard as the *praelatior electus*, the chosen warrior of the church, Peter returns to a request for letters that specifically address the status of the pope: "In order that my complaints be put to sleep, commit the status of the Lord Pope and yours to be returned to me not only through my messengers but by your letters. I would also wish, as I have wished always, that one love might unite us, one Christ take us, and one place keep us, with you sped from your tedious court and me from dangerous care, never to be changed."[66] For a second time in the letter, Peter uses the wistful statement marker *utinam* ("would that it were so!") to express a desirable, but counterfactual event. This letter, then, uses the very conditions of its mediality to express the idea of connection but the fact of spatial and temporal separation that underscores institutional and political division.

Given that Peter and Bernard were not personal friends but institutional rivals, the desire for unity might strike modern readers as insincere to the degree that it is merely conventional. Indeed, if one contrasts the relative hardships they face—Peter's *cura periculosa* (dangerous concern) sounds rather worse than a *curia laboriosa* (hectic court)—then it may even be read as mildly aggressive. I would argue in response that it behooves modern readers of these letters not to foreclose too quickly on alternative readings. As media, letters can mediate, Peter hopes; they can communicate Bernard's whole and unadulterated intention. This letter thus represents epistolary mediation along the lines of the future communion of saints, and the work of mediation is imagined as working toward that future—a future that Peter even identifies with Bernard's charismatic body as a holy warrior. Yet gesturing toward an eschatological future unity also gestures toward present differences that arise from controversies and partisan affiliations within the broader church.

Peter's request for a letter over a messenger, while asking for Bernard's charismatic presence in his textualized voice, is also requesting that Bernard commit what he knows and what he wants as Cistercian abbot, friend of the pope, and reformer, to a written record of his knowledge, his wishes, and his affiliations. Thus, we see in Peter's letter 65 a reflection on its own mediality that pays strategic attention to its material and discursive aspects and to its capacity to both overcome and reinforce spatial and temporal distance. In this way it manages to be both a letter from one monk to another and an act of intra-institutional diplomacy between rivalrous factions, revealing the richness and complexity that a heavily conventionalized form can give to a medium of political communication and literary expression. Reading the letter in this way can not only lend new insight into the contradictions that drove the production of twelfth-century letters and letter collections, but also into medieval notions of mediality and their modern descendants.

CHAPTER 6

The *Gloss* on Genesis and Authority in the Cathedral Schools

Alice Hutton Sharp

The intellectual life of twelfth-century European schools was built around many different forms of authority: the authority of scripture, the writing of Late Antique and medieval *auctores*, the teaching authority of the "modern masters," and new texts that organized inherited, authoritative teaching in new ways. The biblical commentaries known as the *Ordinary Gloss* stand at the intersection of these interlinked forms, and they reflect the authority of the scriptural text and its inspired authors as well as that of the *auctores* whose works were excerpted to form the commentary.[1] This chapter will examine the origins of these biblical commentaries, to place them in the context of the performative, virtue-based model of education seen in medieval schools before the development of the universities.

The twelfth-century Bible was not a single volume, but a collection of books, each of which had its own tradition of commentaries. In the first decades of the twelfth century, commentaries on the most frequently taught books of the Bible, formatted as glosses copied in the margins of the page, spread around Europe thanks to their use in the influential cathedral schools of northern France. Their growing popularity and influence inspired the compilation of further glossed books of the Bible, chiefly under the influence of Parisian booksellers.[2] By the thirteenth century, almost every book of the Bible was provided with a *Gloss*, and they had become dominant influences on the interpretation of scripture, seen more and more as a single, magisterial entity: the *Ordinary Gloss*. As this chapter will demonstrate, the commentaries that would make up the *Gloss* did not originate as attempts to enshrine and codify authoritative interpretations of the biblical text, but were pieced together by students and scribes of the northern French cathedral schools because they aspired to the performed and embodied authority of their teachers.

This chapter's argument is built on a close study of the two oldest manuscripts of the *Gloss* on Genesis, supported by contemporary depictions of the masters of the French cathedral schools. It begins with a look at the context and history of the *Gloss*, as well as twentieth-century research on its authorship. From there, the argument discusses the challenges scribes faced when copying manuscripts of the *Gloss* and the techniques they developed to make their work easier. It then moves to the specific and unusual bibliographic characteristics of the two earliest manuscripts of Genesis—Paris, Bibliothèque nationale de France, latin 36 and Paris, Bibliothèque nationale de France, latin 14398—to show that the formatting and physical characteristics of these manuscripts' pages reflect a communal authorship of the text made possible by development in scribal techniques.[3] In particular, it shows that the Creation and Fall narratives were copied as texts distinct from the rest of Genesis in the two earliest manuscripts of the *Gloss*, and argues that the commentary on this section of Genesis was compiled as a distinct project. There was no single author of these texts, and this fact is important for understanding the transition between the older educational systems and intellectual traditions out of which the glosses arose and the newer systems and traditions that they helped to initiate.

The *Gloss* is a selection of biblical commentaries in which the interpretations from patristic and early medieval authorities, excerpted by a medieval compiler, are copied as "glosses"—i.e., between the lines and in the margins of the biblical text. The text is defined by its arrangement on the page, and as such its history is inseparable from the material evidence for how it was formatted, copied, and experienced by readers. For a commentary to be of use, it must be clear to the reader what passages in the principal text are under discussion. Both ancient and medieval commentaries were frequently written as what are called "continuous" commentaries, in which the commentary proceeds through the content of the main text without interruption, except for brief excerpts from the main text (called *lemmata*), which cued the reader to the topic under discussion. In gloss-format commentaries, however, the reader was guided by the format of the page, which contributed to the meaning of the text.

Although the *Gloss* is defined principally by its format, histories of that format have avoided questioning accepted attributions for the medieval authority behind the *Gloss*, accepting the common view that it took its influence from the teaching authority of its compiler.[4] For at least some books of the biblical *Gloss*, manuscript evidence breaks down the idea that there was any one twelfth-century authority whose thought was reproduced by the compiled text.

Here I will argue further that twelfth-century glosses on the Bible were not *authoritative* texts at all, but *aspirational*. Visually, the great blocks of text that make up the *Gloss* seem like a coherent and interwoven whole, though the text itself largely consisted of allegorical interpretations and questionable etymology. The schoolmasters to whom they have been attributed did not record their lessons to spread their teaching far and wide. The *Gloss* makes visible the twelfth-century study of the "sacred page," which included both sacred scripture and its received interpretation. If we place these pages in the lecture hall, it will reveal how the texts of the *Gloss* represent the aspirations of the students who hoped to acquire the same authority as the teachers before whom they sat.

In my analysis of the evidence to this effect I will focus on the earliest manuscripts of the *Gloss* on Genesis, which was one of the earliest books of the Bible to be glossed. The interpretation of Genesis has a peculiar history in the Christian tradition because the first chapters, which recount the creation of the world and the fall of humanity, were much more frequently discussed and hotly debated than the subsequent text. The unbalanced focus of the exegetical tradition has exaggerated some of the challenges of *Gloss* production in the manuscripts of the *Gloss*, contained a number of vexing theological challenges, and was thoroughly glossed. The course of its development shows that books of the *Gloss* were, at times, not the products not one single author, but of an intellectual community that made contributions through largely anonymous members, like scribes.[5] In order to look at the community that shaped the *Gloss* on Genesis, this chapter will first look at the figures at its head, whose names contributed to the popularity of the *Gloss* and whose teaching authority was sought out by ambitious and devoted students.

Authority and the School of Laon

The commentaries that made up the *Ordinary Gloss* were neither the first nor the only gloss-format commentaries on the Bible.[6] However, they were unusual for both their popularity and recognition, which grew rapidly over the course of the twelfth century. Their texts were also more stable from manuscript to manuscript than similar commentaries, although the textual history of the *Gloss* is revealing itself as more complex than previously recognized.[7] These characteristics, alongside the use of the *Gloss* by pre-scholastic and scholastic theologians, first inspired interest in identifying an author whose fame would offer the commentary authority. Identifying the author of the texts, however, long posed a problem for historians, particularly those working with the assumption that such influential commentaries must have been compiled by a figure of equal stature. Only the *Gloss* on Lamentations refers to its compiler, one Gilbert "the Universal" (d. 1134) who was briefly bishop of London. Evidence, therefore, is sparse.[8]

For many years, the biblical *Gloss* was credited to the Carolingian Walahfrid Strabo (to whom the *Gloss* is attributed in the *Patrologia Latina*), although Anselm of Laon was occasionally assigned authorship of the interlinear glosses. Fifteenth-century publishers of the *Gloss*, as Smalley notes, attributed the text to a collection of authorities.[9] Untangling medieval attributions to disprove these ahistorical claims was a matter of painstaking textual research linking medieval references to exegetical activity—usually taken from texts written after a scholar's death—to sources listed in later biblical commentaries.[10] In the first half of the twentieth century the *Gloss* was definitively linked to the cathedral School of Laon in northern France, under the leadership of Anselm and his brother Ralph. Anselm and Ralph were determined to have produced the preliminary forms of some of the *Glosses*, while a substantial number were credited to Gilbert, who was either their colleague or student before being raised to the episcopacy.[11] However, as will be shown, for some books of the *Gloss* the matter of authorship has been shown to be yet more complex than initially thought.

Anselm of Laon was already known to those seeking an author for the *Gloss* because of his school's role in the development of twelfth-century "sentence collections"—thematic collections of authoritative opinion, used as sources for classroom disputations. If Anselm's school produced both the *Gloss* and the earliest sentence collections (as it did), he can be identified as the teacher behind the two genres that gave medieval scholasticism its characteristic shape and essential texts.[12] Despite his influence, Anselm's life and teaching is known almost entirely from what others wrote about him. He is perhaps best known from his unflattering portrayal in Peter Abelard's autobiography: "If any one came to him impelled by doubt on any subject, he went away more doubtful still. He was wonderful, indeed, in the eyes of these who only listened to him, but those who asked him questions perforce held him as nought. He had a miraculous flow of words, but they were contemptible in meaning and quite void of reason. When he kindled a fire, he filled his house with smoke and illumined it not at all."[13]

Abelard's is one of the few detailed accounts of Anselm's teaching, so it is unfortunate that it comes to us from one of the most unreliable narrators of the Middle Ages.[14] In contrast, Anselm's supporters wrote with greater praise but less detail. Guibert of Nogent said that "[Anselm's] knowledge of the liberal arts made him a beacon for all of France and, indeed, the whole Latin world."[15] John of Salisbury praised the "lustre" Anselm and his brother Ralph brought to Laon with their teaching, and numerous elegies report his erudition.[16] Abelard's only companion in his disdain for the master of Laon was Rupert of Deutz, who was outraged to hear a rumour that Anselm taught that God willed evil. Taking the task of correction upon himself, Rupert travelled to Laon in 1117 to challenge Anselm to a debate. Portraying himself as a Christ-like figure, Rupert rode into Laon on a donkey. (This was practical as well as symbolic: the city sits on a high plateau.) Learning, on his arrival, that Anselm had just died, Rupert took it almost personally.[17]

Rupert's story—like Abelard's—is marked by a comical self-importance. However, Anselm did respond to his allegations, and this provides the only text in which he described his teaching. In a letter to Heribrand of Saint-Laurent, Rupert's abbot, Anselm said his task and teacher was teaching students to resolve the apparent disagreements found when comparing the writing of different *auctores*.[18] This line, which was part of an argument defending his orthodoxy, is the only surviving explanation of Anselm's teaching program, his approach to received authorities, and the educational system that underpinned his school and the texts it inspired.

But despite the established fact of Anselm's reputation, it is hard to find anything in the texts that came from Anselm's school that can be explicitly attributed to him. The contents of the school texts appear derivative, as they are rarely more than excerpts from the well-known patristic *auctores*. Recent research has questioned what role Anselm had in their composition,[19] and the question remains: What was the source of the authority of the *Gloss*, and what is its relationship to Anselm's teaching? The remainder of this chapter will address this question by looking at the medium and format of the *Gloss*. By looking at the symbiotic relationship between the text of the *Gloss* and developments in its format, this chapter will argue that the *Gloss* was developed in stages determined by input from a community of readers. It is only by understanding this anonymous, communal authorship that we can correctly gauge how the *Gloss* functioned as a source of authority. First, however, it is necessary to summarize some of the research on the authorship of the text in the years since Smalley's initial series of articles.

The further back in its history one goes—and thus, the closer to Anselm and his school one gets—the thinner becomes the evidence for a single, magisterial *Gloss* for most books of the Bible. Textual criticism of many books has revealed the survival of multiple versions, with varying degrees of difference. For some books, an early version of a commentary was eclipsed by a later; with others (like the *Glosses* on Ecclesiastes and Revelation), multiple versions circulated simultaneously, both in frequent use. The early *Gloss* on Genesis, the focus of this chapter, is found in two quite different versions, and there is textual evidence for at least one more, yet earlier, text.[20]

Questions have also been raised about how close the earliest versions of the *Gloss* are to the work of those to whom the text is attributed. The *Gloss* on John is an important example. Although this *Gloss* is usually attributed to Anselm, he did not write the commentary in its glossed form. Rather, Anselm's text was a continuous commentary that was later copied in the margins.[21] In a similar way, the early manuscripts of Genesis break down the idea that there was a single authority behind the production of the text. The evidence of the manuscripts does not point to the single *Gloss* author for whom so many historians have searched. Instead, as will be argued in this chapter, the manuscripts reveal the importance of scholarly communities and anonymous actors like scribes and students in the production, development, and dispersal of pre-scholastic texts.

These communities come into focus when we look at the material challenges of copying the *Gloss*. The unique history of the *Gloss* on

Genesis, as well as the rich history of theological inquiry that compilers attempted to distil in its pages, makes it an exceptional source for these anonymous communities. As manuscript production methods developed to make copying the text easier and more efficient, they also made possible new forms of the text itself. By reading the early *Gloss* through its medium, we can see it as a text that reflects the work and needs of the community, rather than of a single schoolmaster. We also gain new insights into the role of a teacher's authority in the intellectual culture of the cathedral schools. In the next section, I will discuss some of the techniques used in producing a glossed manuscript and how they developed over the first decades of the twelfth century; from there, I will move to the specific ways in which these techniques are seen in the two earliest manuscripts of the *Gloss* on Genesis and what they show about the manner in which it was compiled.

The Making of a Gloss Manuscript

The *Gloss* on Genesis exemplifies a number of the formatting challenges faced by scribes of the glossed Bible in the early twelfth century, because the commentary tradition on accounts of the creation of the world and the fall of humanity, found in chapters 1–3, was much more extensive than commentary on the remaining forty-seven chapters. With consideration for the cost of parchment, scribes struggled to copy such texts without leaving unused, wasted space.

When beginning a new manuscript, a scribe faced a blank gathering of parchment (usually four sheets folded in half, for eight folios). He first used an awl to prick holes at the top and bottom of each folio; lines were drawn between these holes to mark the outer border of the writing space and to divide it into three columns with two narrow gutters. These lines were drawn with a dry point, scoring the parchment and marking both sides of the folio simultaneously—on one side by a trench, the other by a ridge. The innermost column, by the fold, was usually narrower than the outer two. The central column was reserved for the biblical text while the *Gloss* was copied to its left and right, and the relative width of the columns stayed consistent throughout the manuscript.[22]

Next, the central column was ruled, again with a dry point. The biblical text for the whole gathering (or even manuscript) was copied first, in the central column. On its completion, the scribe returned to the beginning of the gathering and ruled the two outer columns. For this, he used lines closer together than those used for the main text, so that the text would be smaller, and he ruled only where glosses were to be added. Scribes avoided copying glosses in the upper and lower margins of the page, but for heavily glossed passages like the first three chapters of Genesis it was unavoidable. At times, one gloss column would be split into two in order to allow two glosses to begin beside the same line of the main text.[23]

This method was relatively simple, but it had its problems. Chiefly, how could one use parchment efficiently when the density of the glosses varies wildly between different biblical passages—especially without separating the gloss from the relevant text so much that understanding was impeded? Biblical passages of little interest (those infamous "begats," for example) were surrounded by empty columns, which offended aesthetics and wasted parchment. On the other hand, commentary on passages that carried great doctrinal or spiritual meaning for their audience was limited by the space available on the page (and, at times, the pages immediately adjacent). If glosses could not be copied in some proximity to the text they discussed, the organizational principle of the *Gloss* broke down.

Scribes responded to this inefficiency by changing the relative width of the columns from page to page, depending on how much space was needed for the glosses in the outer columns. On pages with many glosses, the central column was narrowed, increasing the amount of space available for commentary. Where there were fewer glosses, they made the central column wider.[24] Manuscripts of the *Gloss* on Genesis could not be copied with unchanging column widths, because there was too much marginal text in the commentary on the Creation and Fall narratives to fit in such restricted columns. In order for the commentary to be compiled into the text we know, scribes had to change how they copied manuscripts and vary the widths of the columns.

The result of these changes was that scribes no longer copied the biblical text and glosses in two stages, as two separate but concurrent texts. Instead, the individual page became the unit on which the text was built. The page had already added meaning to the *Gloss* by providing a boundary that tied subject and commentary to one another. It offered a visual constraint for the reader and a literal constraint on glossing. However, as the manuscript was no longer copied text by text, but rather page by page, the scripture and its glosses began to function as a single unified text, with each page existing as a unit of the scribe's labour and the reader's attention.[25] Margins were kept to certain parameters, according to fashion (with larger margins meaning greater expense), but within the writing frame the arrangement of each page was new and irregular, in order to successfully bring the two texts together.

Once a scribe had achieved a format that answered the many demands of a *Gloss*, with the glosses arranged in such a way that one could easily navigate from biblical text to glosses without wasting undue space, it could not necessarily be copied into a new manuscript. As a result of the variability of parchment and the writing of individual scribes, every page was a new canvas that had to be arranged according to the text, the size of the page, and the scribe's individual hand. The changing width of columns added yet another variable.[26] While the text of the *Gloss* was relatively stable within the different versions, the placement of different elements varied according to the material constraints of each individual manuscript. Changes in the size of the parchment, the distance of the ruled lines, and the scribe's individual hand made the formatting of each glossed page a new project. With changing columns, scribes had acquired flexibility; what was needed, as the popularity of these manuscripts increased, was simplicity. The *Gloss* on Genesis, however, was developed while scribal techniques were in these early stages, and the ways in which the manuscripts reflect the limitations of layout methods available also shows the steps through which members of the community contributed to the text itself.

The Manuscripts of the Gloss on Genesis

As was noted previously, numerous versions of a *Gloss* on one book of the Bible often circulated simultaneously. Genesis was no exception: two versions survive, although the earlier version was clearly eclipsed by the latter, which probably developed in Paris alongside many other late additions to the biblical *Gloss*.[27] The earlier version of the commentary, however, appears to be connected to the school of Laon and should reflect the teaching practices of its cathedral school and the authority of Master Anselm.[28] The early version is known in only two manuscripts, each of which is bibliographically distinctive for the way in which its formatting changes at the end of the Creation account—a change, it will be shown, that reflects the history of the *Gloss* text and its dependence on manuscript production techniques. This, in turn, demonstrates the importance of scribal innovation in the development of new texts in the twelfth-century schools and brings new light to bear on how texts could develop, not through the work of a single author, but as part of an intellectual community.

The complete text of the early *Gloss* on Genesis is found in Bibliothèque nationale de France, latin 14398, digitized and available online.[29] This manuscript was likely copied in Laon and dates to before 1140. The text is also found in the (also digitized) manuscript Bibliothèque nationale de France, latin 64.[30] This manuscript is of unknown provenance and is incomplete: gatherings are missing, and the glossing disappears in later chapters.[31] However, as will be argued, the cobbled-together aspect of this manuscript reflects the history of the text more clearly than, and elucidates some of the unusual features of, latin 14398.

In the *Gloss* found in these two manuscripts, the commentary on the first three chapters is simultaneously dense and expansive. Many biblical passages were glossed multiple times, and those glosses are long. In fact, there is so much commentary that latin 14398 breaks away from the traditional three-column gloss format to include six pages that held only the *Gloss*, copied in two columns, interrupting the biblical text and the three-column format.[32] Latin 14398 was copied page-by-page, with variable column width; it had to be copied page-by-page, or the scribe would not have known where to place the all-gloss folios that interrupt the biblical text. The width of the columns varies throughout the first three chapters of Genesis. They had to, or the unusually substantial gloss text would not have fit.

Latin 64 contains the same text, but copied in a very different format— one rarely seen in a manuscript of the *Gloss*.[33] For the commentary on the first chapters of Genesis, latin 64 is copied, not as a gloss, but as an "interwoven" commentary.[34] Each verse or passage of the scriptural text is followed immediately by commentary upon that passage, written in the same text column but with a smaller script. The interlinear glosses remain between the lines of the scriptural text, just as they are in the three-column format.[35] This ends at Genesis 3:19. At this point, on a new folio, the manuscript returns to a three-column gloss format, with static column widths and the biblical text copied first.[36] (Hence the missing glosses in later parts of the manuscript—the columns of biblical text—were copied, but commentary was unfinished.)

This change is sudden, but it is not accidental. In fact, the move from an interwoven commentary format to a three-column gloss occurs across an intact gathering of parchment. Looking closely at the first three-column folios shows that someone drew rulings with ink to divide the page into three columns, changing the two-column dry-point borders that were drawn first. In short, the scribe appears to have prepared the entire gathering for the interwoven gloss format. The change in formatting is not because of a change in materials, but because of some change in the text.

The idea that the scribe of latin 64 chose the unusual interwoven format specifically for copying the first three chapters of Genesis with its *Gloss* is supported by returning to latin 14398, which, on the surface, appears more cohesive than its mysterious counterpart. However, it too displays a change in scribal technique at the end of the third chapter of Genesis, albeit a subtler one. This is principally visible in the hand and decoration. For the first three chapters of Genesis, the decoration scheme includes a variety of letter forms and colours in the initials.[37] The gatherings are also irregular—the first is of only two folios (one sheet), followed by two gatherings of ten. None of these gatherings is numbered or marked. However, from the beginning of Genesis 4, the hand of the scribe copying the biblical text changes subtly.[38] The decoration becomes regular, with constant red initials and highlighting. In addition, from the beginning of Genesis 4 the gatherings are numbered—and numbered beginning with the number one. (It is important to remember here that the formatting change in latin 64 takes place at Genesis 3:20—but in latin 14398, the new quires begin with Genesis 4. However, in latin 14398 the text and formatting are simpler, and more like their counterparts in latin 64, from Genesis 3:20 to 4:1, and I suspect the lack of a sudden break reflects a scribe's attempt to make the transition less obvious than it is in latin 64.)

The placement of this change in format or technique at approximately the same point in the sole surviving manuscripts of the text suggests that the external appearance reflects a phenomenon internal to the *Gloss* on Genesis. In fact, when looking at the glosses themselves, from Genesis 3:20—the point at which latin 64 changes format—the number of glosses is rapidly reduced. The glosses are also shorter, on average, than the many extended glosses found in the first three chapters of Genesis. The glosses for the first three chapters of Genesis are often composed of multiple sources woven together. After Genesis 3:20, each individual gloss is taken from a single source. (This explains, in part, their relative brevity.) Finally, for the Creation and Fall narratives, the two manuscripts of the primitive *Gloss* on Genesis present exactly the same text. The glosses are even presented in exactly the same order—a phenomenon almost unheard of in later manuscripts of the *Gloss* on Genesis. From Genesis 3:20, however, the texts of the two manuscripts begin to diverge. The order of glosses changes, and some glosses appear in one manuscript that are not found in the other.[39]

Having observed these unusual characteristics in the manuscripts and acquired a sense of the challenges of gloss production, one can make reasonable inferences about the history of the *Gloss* on Genesis and how it was composed. The text seems to have begun with a three-column gloss-format commentary on the whole of Genesis, which included both marginal and interlinear glosses. This ur-commentary does not survive, but it was likely copied with the simplest, two-stage method of copying a glossed manuscript.[40] At some point in the early twelfth century, the commentary on the Creation narrative was expanded by adding passages from another distinct commentary, which was not originally a gloss. Those who undertook this project of expansion then faced a problem of formatting: chiefly, how do you accurately estimate the amount of space needed for the marginal commentary when you are in the process of expanding that very commentary?

One practical solution to this problem is indeed what we see in latin 64: the use of an interwoven commentary for the section of the *Gloss* that is being expanded.[41] With such a format, there would be no need to estimate the amount of column space needed, as one simply added new glosses after the old ones, all under the heading of the passage discussed.[42] However, at Genesis 3:20—presumably the end of the continuous commentary, although it could just be where the person expanding the text decided to stop—the interwoven format was no longer necessary, and the scribes returned to the three-column format. Any additions after this point are from later projects of expansion. The format of latin 14398, as suggested above, reflects attempts to make the patchwork *Gloss* on Genesis appear more cohesive—and perhaps to disguise the history of the text and its multiple contributors. This was not entirely successful: the all-gloss folios seen in latin 14398 are likely holdovers from the interwoven format.

The *Gloss* on Genesis found in these two manuscripts shows how the material constraints of medieval manuscript production—specifically, the management and arrangement of text in a limited space—could direct the development of a text by encouraging scribes to develop innovative copying techniques for producing manuscripts efficiently and effectively. It also shows how problematic the question of authorship can be for the school texts of the early twelfth century. The *Gloss* on Genesis is a collection of excerpts from Latin authorities, but it has no single compiler: it is an interweaving of multiple medieval source commentaries that was made possible by new methods for copying glossed manuscripts. It is a product of the community.[43]

Authorship and the Gloss on Genesis

When we use the formatting of the page to challenge the traditional notion of authorship and individual agency in intellectual history, we may return to a question with which began: How were these supposedly authoritative texts used in schools, and what do they say about medieval authorship? If the *Gloss* was chiefly a project of a community, what was the role of those who were claimed to be its authors? If one is looking for innovation, Abelard's insults seem almost correct. The excerpts found in the *Gloss* muster the received tradition, with emphasis on including as many passages as possible. Almost everything could have been found in another book, albeit with a different format. Even the three-column gloss format, however, was not particularly innovative, as it appears in some Carolingian manuscripts, as well as in commentaries on classical texts.[44] But these critiques, in which we read the schools of the Middle Ages through the narratives of modern intellectual history, are not a useful way of thinking about how a school text contributed to the medieval concept of authority.

What *was* new to the glossed Bible was the flexibility that scribes brought to the production of the gloss text. As the text grew in popularity, scribes further developed their variable-width column formats by changing how they ruled the page horizontally, as well as vertically. Rather than ruling the central column for the larger biblical text and the gloss columns only where necessary, they ruled the entire page at the small size used for the gloss text. To copy the scriptural text at a larger size, they simply wrote on every other line. This allowed them to change the height, as well as the width, of columns, or to change the width of only part of a column. With this method, one gloss might span two columns, while two glosses copied below it were vertically divided by the dry-point gutter.[45] The complex piecing together of texts that can be seen in the most advanced manuscripts of the *Gloss* was made possible by this innovation of writing on alternate lines—an innovation that, it has been suggested, was first seen in interwoven commentaries like latin 64.[46]

The scribal skills that mastered a challenging medium contributed to the popularity of the glossed Bible by making it expandable. However, the scribes did not create the market for this kind of manuscript. They were responding to a current demand for a book that could represent a master's teaching. We see this in Abelard's account of his time in Laon: when he astounds his fellow students with his lecture on Ezekiel, he is asked to produce glosses that record what he has already said in the classroom.[47] Anselm's comments on his teaching imply that his students were not simply memorizing these excerpts, as he says he taught students to reconcile disagreement in received authorities. In a similar way, it has been argued that the sentence collections that originated in Anselm's school were principally case books offering collections of potentially contradictory statements, in order to give students practice in disputing and reconciling their differences.[48] The books of the *Gloss* are similar to sentence collections in their inclusion of many interpretations, occasionally contradictory. Like the sentence collections, the books of the biblical *Gloss* were probably first used to teach students how to read the scriptural text in the light of traditional interpretations, resolving contradictions in the scriptural text itself, or disagreements between patristic authorities. However, Abelard's account and the textual history of the gloss suggest that this was due to demands from the students, not a project of the masters. Students may have studied the pages of the *Gloss*, but the master's teaching was found in the classroom.

What were students doing with this education? Few would become schoolmasters themselves. Most would use their time in the schools as a bridge to positions in the growing church and state bureaucracies of the twelfth century. In the century previous to Anselm's, it has been argued, the principal lessons of the cathedral schools were lessons in manners and bearing, which prepared students to take positions of authority.[49] The same seems to be true in the twelfth century. Abelard's disgust with Anselm's lectures may thus offer an account of new ideas of education running up against an earlier model that focused on manners and personality.[50] Even in the later twelfth century, when Peter Lombard was teaching, the masters not only lectured to their students, but also preached.[51] Masters taught both academic matters and morals.

Given this context, it is notable that one of our few accounts of Anselm outside the classroom focuses on his almost perfect behaviour in a time of unrest and unease. In Guibert of Nogent's account of the communal uprising of Laon, which took place shortly before Abelard's arrival, Anselm is discussed as the only elector who was not swayed by a prospective bishop's bribery. When the bishop (having successfully purchased his position) was assassinated for his disruption of the city's growing self-rule, Anselm is said to have taken pity on his corpse for the sake of his ecclesiastical station and to have ensured that he had a Christian burial.[52] (Gilbert the Universal, to whom Genesis is frequently attributed, did not leave such a sterling record. The monks of London remembered him principally for his avarice as bishop.)[53]

Looking to the *Gloss* as an aid in teaching mores or bearing brings us to the limit of what the surviving evidence can tell us about the intellectual history of the period, as the discipline is traditionally understood.

However, it also opens a new way of looking at the twelfth-century concept of authority. The *Gloss* is made up of excerpts from the "authorities," the accepted sources of Christian doctrine. But the authority of the early *Gloss* is not a received heritage from the ancients, adhered to for fears of heterodoxy. Nor is it a magisterial document from on high. The authority seen in the *Gloss* was the aspirational authority of students who saw a beloved teacher speaking with erudition and clarity, and asked for their notes to be copied into a new and technically demanding form. The authority of the *Gloss* was a lived authority, enacted in both bearing and education of the one who acquired it—who, by studying the sacred page, came to emulate the learning of both ancient authorities and their beloved modern masters.

PREFACE

1   Friedrich Kittler, *Discourse Networks 1800/1900,* trans. Michael Metteer and Chris Cullens (Stanford, CA: Stanford University Press, 1990).
2   Sigfried Zielinski, *Deep Time of the Media* (Cambridge, MA: MIT Press, 2006).

INTRODUCTION

1   John Unsworth, "Medievalists as Early Adopters of Information Technology," *Digital Medievalist* 7 (2011), https://journal.digitalmedievalist.org/articles/10.16995/dm.34; S. Hockey, "History of Humanities Computing," in *A Companion to Digital Humanities,* ed. Susan Schreibman, Ray Siemens, and John Unsworth (London: Blackwell, 2004), 4, cited in David J. Birnbaum, Sheila Bonde, and Mike Kestemont, "The Digital Middle Ages: An Introduction," *Speculum* 92, no. S1 (2017): S2.
2   John Guillory, "The Genesis of the Media Concept," *Critical Inquiry* 36 (2010): 321–62. On the exclusion, definition, and limitation at play, see especially Sylvia Wynter, "Unsettling the Coloniality of Being/Power/Truth/Freedom: Towards the Human, after Man, Its Overrepresentation—An Argument," *CR: The New Centennial Review* 3, no. 3 (2003): 257–337; and Michel Foucault, *The Order of Things: An Archaeology of the Human Sciences* (London: Routledge, 2002). For a comparison of these thinkers, see Denise Ferreira da Silva, "Before Man: Sylvia Wynter's Rewriting of the Modern Episteme," in *Sylvia*

Wynter: On Being Human as Praxis, ed. Katherine McKitterick, 90–105 (Durham, NC: Duke University Press, 2015).

3 For a survey of the history of Latin script in Europe, see Bernhard Bischoff, *Latin Paleography: Antiquity and the Middle Ages*, trans. Dáibhí Ó Cróinín and David Ganz (Cambridge: Cambridge University Press, 1990).

4 Sven Trakulhun and Ralph Weber, "Modernities: Editors' Introduction," in *Delimiting Modernities: Conceptual Challenges and Regional Responses*, ed. Trakulhun and Weber (Lanham, MD: Lexington Books, 2015), x–xi. Kathleen Davis, *Periodization and Sovereignty: How Ideas of Feudalism and Secularization Govern the Politics of Time* (Philadelphia: University of Pennsylvania Press, 2008); David Matthews, *Medievalism: A Critical History* (Cambridge: Boydell & Brewer, 2015).

6 Ted Underwood, *Why Literary Periods Mattered: Historical Contrast and the Prestige of English Studies* (Stanford, CA: Stanford University Press, 2013). See also Helge Jordheim, "Against Periodization: Koselleck's Theory of Multiple Temporalities," *History and Theory* 51, no. 2 (2012): 151–71; and chapter 2 in this volume.

7 Austin Grossman, *YOU* (New York: Mulholland, 2013).

8 On medievalism and computer programming, see S. Turkle, *Second Self: Computers and the Human Spirit* (New York: MIT Press, 1985), 79; Daniel Pargman, "Word and Code, Code as World," *Digital Arts and Culture*, 2003 Online Proceedings, https://www.researchgate.net/publication/228881105_Word_and_code_code_as_world; Matt Barton and Shane Stacks, *Dungeons and Desktops: The History of Computer Role-Playing Games*, 2nd ed. (Boca Raton, FL: CRC, 2019), 21–40; D. M. Ewalt, *Of Dice and Men: The Story of Dungeons & Dragons and the People Who Play It* (New York: Scribner, 2013), 182; M. T. Saler, *As If: Modern Enchantment and the Literary Prehistory of Virtual Reality* (Oxford: Oxford University Press, 2012); B. King and J. Boreland, *Dungeons and Dreamers: A Story of How Computer Games Created a Global Community* (Pittsburgh: ETC, 2014); Stephen Yeager, "Protocol, or 'The Chivalry of the Object,'" *Critical Inquiry* 45, no. 3 (2019): 747–61.

9 Carol L. Robinson, "Electronic Tolkien: Characterization in Film and Video Games," in *Medieval Afterlives in Contemporary Culture*, ed. Gail Ashton (London: Bloomsbury, 2015), 126.

10 Still available at the time of this writing: https://www.amc.com/shows/halt-and-catch-fire/exclusives/colossal-cave-adventure.

11 On the "manuscript matrix," see Stephen Nichols, "Introduction: Philology in a Manuscript Culture," *Speculum* 65 (1990): 1–10; M. D. Rust, *Imaginary Worlds in Medieval Books: Exploring the Manuscript Matrix* (New York: Palgrave Macmillan, 2007). On the development of technical "communities of practice" from online fanworks, see Casey Fiesler, Shannon Morrison, R. Benjamin Shapiro, and Amy S. Bruckman, "Growing Their Own: Legitimate Peripheral Participation for Computational Learning in an Online Fandom Community," *Proceedings of the 20th ACM Conference on Computer Supported Cooperative Work and Social Computing* (2017): 1375–86, doi: 10.1145/2998181.2998210. Classic studies of fandom and "geek culture" respectively are Henry Jenkins, *Convergence Culture: Where Old and New Media Collide* (New York: New York University Press, 2006); J. A. McArthur, "Digital Subculture: A Geek Meaning of Style," *Journal of Communication Inquiry* 33 (2009): 58–70.

12 Andrew Taylor, "Getting Technology and Not Getting Theory," *Florilegium* 32 (2015): 131–2. In Gibson's novel and its many imitations, most obviously Cline's *Ready Player One* (2011), cyberspace is depicted as a feudal landscape of corporate fiefdoms with hackers in the role of magic-wielding knights errant. On these novels' "cyberpunk" subgenre see, for example, Veronica Hollinger, "Cybernetic Deconstructions: Cyberpunk and Postmodernism," *Mosaic* 23, no. 2 (1990): 29–44.

13 Wendy Hui Kyong Chun, *Control and Freedom: Power and Paranoia in the Age of Fiber Optics* (Cambridge, MA: MIT Press, 2006), 171–245. On transmedia world-building, see Kavita Finn, *Fan Phenomena: Game of Thrones* (Chicago: Intellect Books, 2017); Colin B. Harvey, *Fantastic Transmedia: Narrative, Play and Memory across Science Fiction and Fantasy Storyworlds* (New York: Palgrave Macmillan, 2015); Mark J. P. Wolf, *Building Imaginary Worlds: The Theory and History of Subcreation* (New York: Routledge, 2012).

14 Surveyed by Daniel T. Kline, "Participatory Medievalism, Role-Playing, and Digital Gaming," in *The Cambridge Companion to Medievalism,* ed. Louise D'Arcens, 75–88 (Cambridge: Cambridge University Press, 2016). On the "magic circle," see Johan Huizinga, *Homo Ludens: A Study of the*

Play Element in Culture (Boston: Beacon, 1955). Huizinga developed this concept through his study of late-medieval culture, published, for example, in his important volume *The Autumn of the Middle Ages*, trans. Rodney J. Payton and Ulrich Mammitzsch (Chicago: University of Chicago Press, 1997). On the interconnection between these texts, see Laura Kendrick, "Games Medievalists Play: How to Make Earnest of a Game and Still Enjoy It," *New Literary History* 40, no. 1 (2009): 43–61.

15 The fullest exploration of this analogy may be found in Daniel T. Kline, ed., *Digital Gaming Re-imagines the Middle Ages* (New York: Routledge, 2014). For broader studies of games and historiography generally, see Matthew Kapell and Andrew B. R. Elliott, eds., *Playing with the Past: Digital Games and the Simulation of History* (London: Bloomsbury, 2013).

16 There are many studies of how modern notions of race derive from readings of medieval evidence. See, for example, Cord Whitaker, *Black Metaphors: How Modern Racism Emerged from Medieval Race-Thinking* (Philadelphia: University of Pennsylvania Press, 2019); and Whitaker, "Race-ing the Dragon: The Middle Ages, Race and Trippin' into the Future," *postmedieval* 6, no. 3 (2015): 3–11; Matthew X. Vernon, *The Black Middle Ages: Race and the Construction of the Middle Ages* (New York: Palgrave Macmillan, 2018); Geraldine Heng, *The Invention of Race in the European Middle Ages* (Cambridge: Cambridge University Press, 2018); Maria Elena Martinez-Lopez, *Genealogical Fictions: Limpieza de Sangre, Religion, and Gender in Colonial Mexico* (Stanford, CA: Stanford University Press, 2008); and the many works cited by Jonathan Hsy and Julie Orlemanski, "Race and Medieval Studies: A Partial Bibliography," *postmedieval* 8, no. 4 (2017): 500–31. On the ongoing problem of white supremacy in the field of medieval studies as currently practised, see Dorothy Kim, "Introduction to the Literature Compass Special Cluster: Critical Race and the Middle Ages," *Literature Compass* 16, no. 9–10 (2019): e1249; the rest of this special issue; and Donna Beth Ellard, *Anglo-Saxon(ist) Pasts postSaxon Futures* (New York: Punctum Books, 2019).

17 Amanda Phillips, *Gamer Trouble: Feminist Confrontations in Digital Culture* (New York: New York University Press, 2020); Shira Chess,

Ready Player Two: Woman Gamers and Designed Identity (Minneapolis: University of Minnesota Press, 2017); Kishonna Gray, *Race, Gender, and Deviance in Xbox Live: Theoretical Perspectives from the Virtual Margins* (New York: Routledge, 2014).

18 On #Gamergate and its implications see, for example, Kishonna L. Gray and David Leonard, "Introduction," in *Woke Gaming: Digital Challenges to Oppression and Social Injustice*, ed. Gray and Leonard, 9–14 (Seattle: University of Washington Press, 2018); Torill Elvira Mortensen, "Anger, Fear, and Games: The Long Event of #GamerGate," *Games and Culture* 13, no. 8 (2018): 787–806; Adrienne Massanari, "#Gamergate and The Fappening: How Reddit's Algorithm, Governance, and Culture Support Toxic Technoculture," *new media & society* 19, no. 3 (2017): 329–46; Shira Chess and Adrienne Shaw, "Conspiracy of Fishes, or, How We Learned to Stop Worrying about #Gamergate and Embrace Hegemonic Masculinity," *Journal of Broadcasting & Electronic Media* 59, no. 1 (2015): 208–20.

19 Ruha Benjamin, *Race after Technology: Abolitionist Tools for the New Jim Code* (Cambridge: Polity, 2019); Safaiya Umoja Noble, *Algorithms of Oppression: How Search Engines Reinforce Racism* (New York: New York University Press, 2018); Clemens Apprich, Wendy Hui Kyong Chun, Florian Cramer, and Hito Steryl, *Pattern Discrimination* (Minneapolis: University of Minnesota Press, 2018); Charlton McIlwain, "Racial Formation, Inequality and the Political Economy of Web Traffic," *Information, Communication & Society* 20, no. 7 (2017): 1073–89; Shaka McGlotten, "Black Data," in *No Tea, No Shade: New Writings in Black Queer Studies*, ed. E. Patrick Johnson, 262–86 (Durham, NC: Duke University Press, 2016); Lisa Nakamura, *Digitizing Race: Visual Cultures of the Internet* (Minneapolis: University of Minnesota Press, 2007). On the origins of digital organizational forms in medieval bureaucratic forms see Yeager, "Protocol."

20 See Thora Brylowe, *Romantic Art in Practice: Cultural Work and the Sister Arts, 1760–1820* (Cambridge: Cambridge University Press, 2018).

21 David Matthews, *Medievalism: A Critical History* (Cambridge: Boydell & Brewer, 2015), 51–2; John D. Niles, *The Idea of Anglo-Saxon England 1066–1901* (London: Wiley-Blackwell, 2015), 302–77; Fred Robinson,

"Medieval, The *Middle Ages*," in *The Tomb of Beowulf and Other Essays on Old English* (Oxford: Blackwell, 1992), 308.

22 Michael Snodin and Cynthia Roman, *Horace Walpole's Strawberry Hill* (New Haven, CT: Yale University Press, 2009).

23 On nineteenth-century neogothicism and medievalism, see, for example, "The Ghosts of the Nineteenth Century and the Future of Medieval Studies," ed. Cord Whitaker and Matthew Gabriele, special issue, *postmedieval* 10, no. 2 (2019); John Ganim, *Medievalism and Orientalism* (New York: Palgrave, 2008), esp. 83–108; Kathleen Biddick, *The Shock of Medievalism* (Durham, NC: Duke University Press, 1998). On the related contradictions in academic medieval studies in nineteenth-century North America, see Mary Dockray-Miller, *Public Medievalists, Racism, and Suffrage in the American Women's College* (New York: Palgrave, 2017).

24 On these figures and their impact see, for example, Timothy H. Evans, "Folklore as Utopia: English Medievalists and the Ideology of Revivalism," *Western Folklore* 47, no. 4 (1988): 245–68.

25 John Ganim, "Medievalism and Architecture," in *The Cambridge Companion to Medievalism*, ed. Louise d'Arcens, 29–44 (Cambridge: Cambridge University Press, 2016).

26 Franklin Toker, *Pittsburgh: A New Portrait* (Pittsburgh: University of Pittsburgh Press, 2009), 324.

27 Andi Harriman and Marloes Bontje, *Some Wear Leather, Some Wear Lace: The Worldwide Compendium of Postpunk and Goth in the 1980s* (Chicago: Intellect Books, 2014); Paul Hodkinson, *Goth: Identity, Style and Subculture* (Oxford: Berg Publishers, 2002).

28 In manuscript paleography, for example, *gothic* remains the preferred technical term for late-medieval book hands, despite the reservations of critics—expressed, for example, by Albert Derolez, *The Paleography of Gothic Manuscript Books from the Twelfth to the Early Sixteenth Century* (Cambridge: Cambridge University Press, 2003), 10–11.

29 Lisa Gitelman, *Paper Knowledge: Towards a Media History of Documents* (Durham, NC: Duke University Press, 2014); Bonnie Mak, *Why the Page Matters* (Toronto: University of Toronto Press, 2011); David Edgerton, *The Shock of the New: Technology and Global History since 1900* (Oxford: Oxford University Press, 2011); Wolfgang Ernst, *Digital Memory and*

the Archive (Minneapolis: University of Minnesota Press, 2013); Jussi
Parikka, *What Is Media Archaeology* (Boston: MIT Press, 2012); Sigfried
Zielinski, *Deep Time of Media: Towards an Archaeology of Seeing and
Hearing by Technical Means,* trans. Gloria Custance (Boston: MIT Press,
2008). For a response to Edgerton specifically, see Kathleen Kennedy's
chapter in this volume.

30 On this potential see, for example, Carolyn Dinshaw, *Getting Medieval:
Sexualities and Communities, Premodern and Postmodern* (Durham, NC:
Duke University Press, 1999).

31 Bruno Latour, *We Have Never Been Modern,* trans. Catherine Porter
(Cambridge, MA: Harvard University Press, 1993), 69.

32 On "darkness" in particular, see Whitaker, *Black Metaphors.* On medievalism and the "dark ages" more generally see, for example, Matthews,
Medievalism; Ganim, *Medievalism*; Lisa Lampert, "Race, Periodicity, and
the (Neo-) Middle Ages," *Modern Language Quarterly* 65, no. 3 (2004):
391–421.

33 On the allusion to this phrase in the title of her book, see the coda of
Dinshaw, *Getting Medieval.*

34 Kline, "Participatory Medievalism," 77–8. On the connections between
nostalgia for the medieval period, fantasy world-building, and twenty-
first-century racism see, for example, Ebony Elizabeth Thomas, *The Dark
Fantastic: Race and the Imagination from Harry Potter to the Hunger
Games* (New York: New York University Press, 2019); Mark C. Jerng,
Racial Worldmaking: The Power of Popular Fiction (New York: Fordham
University Press, 2018); Andrew B. R. Elliott, *Medievalism, Politics and
Mass Media: Appropriating the Middle Ages in the Twenty-First Century*
(Oxford: D. S. Brewer, 2017); Helen Young, *Race and Popular Fantasy
Literature: Habits of Whiteness* (New York: Routledge, 2016).

35 Daniel T. Kline, "Introduction: Medieval Children's Literature:
Problems, Possibilities, Parameters," in *Medieval Literature for Children,*
ed. Kline, 1–11 (New York: Psychology, 2003); Clare Bradford, *The
Middle Ages in Children's Literature* (New York: Palgrave Macmillan,
2015). On Disney and Tolkien respectively as imitators of medieval writing, see Tison Pugh and Susan Aronstein, eds., *The Disney Middle Ages:
A Fairy-Tale and Fantasy Past* (New York: Palgrave Macmillan, 2012);

Thomas Shippey, *The Road to Middle Earth: How J. R. R. Tolkien Created a New Mythology* (Boston: Houghton Mifflin, 2003).

36 On popular medievalism and labour, see Kevin Moberly and Brent Moberly, "There Is No Word for Work in the Dragon Tongue," *Year's Work in Medievalism* 28 (2013): 1–9.

37 On medievalism in D&D and its antecedent war games, see Jon Peterson, *Playing at the World* (San Diego, CA: Unreason, 2012), 81–202; Kline, "Participatory Medievalism," 78–83. On tabletop RPGs generally, see Sarah Lynne Bowman, *The Function of Role-Playing Games: How Participants Create Community, Solve Problems, and Explore Identity* (Jefferson, NC: McFarland, 2010); Jennifer Grouling Cover, *The Creation of Narrative in Tabletop Role-Playing Games* (Jefferson, NC: McFarland, 2010).

38 Daniel T. Kline, "Metamedievalism, Gaming, and Teaching Medieval Literature in the Digital Age," in *Teaching Literature at a Distance: Open, Online and Blended Learning,* ed. Takis Kayalis and Anastasia Natsina (London: Bloomsbury, 2010), 149–51; Carolyn Dinshaw, *How Soon Is Now? Medieval Texts, Amateur Readers and the Queerness of Time* (Durham, NC: Duke University Press, 2012). One standard touchstone for analyzing such medievalisms is Umberto Eco, "Dreaming the Middle Ages," in *Travels in Hyperreality,* trans. William Weaver (New York: Harvest, 1986), 61–72.

39 Michael Witwer, *Empire of Imagination: Gary Gygax and the Birth of Dungeons & Dragons* (New York: Bloomsbury, 2015).

40 Michael J. Tresca, *The Evolution of Fantasy Role-Playing Games* (Jefferson, NC: McFarland, 2011), 67.

41 For examples of such eruptions, see Helen Young, ed., *Fantasy and Science Fiction Medievalisms: From Isaac Asimov to A Game of Thrones* (Amherst, NY: Cambria, 2015).

42 On this culture, see the studies in the "Affective Affordances" section of this volume.

43 See, for example, Daniel T. Kline's study of the game series *Age of Empires:* "Virtually Medieval: The Age of Kings Interprets the Middle Ages," in *Mass Market Medieval: Essays on the Middle Ages in Popular*

Culture, ed. David W. Marshall, 154–70 (Jefferson, NC: McFarland, 2007).

44 On medieval studies, and postcolonial studies in particular, see, for example, Bruce Holsinger, "Medieval Studies, Postcolonial Studies, and the Genealogies of Critique," *Speculum* 77 (2002): 1195–1227; Patricia Clare Ingham and Michelle Warren, "Introduction," in *Postcolonial Moves: Medieval through Modern,* ed. Ingham and Warren, 1–15 (New York: Palgrave Macmillan, 2003); Andrew Cole, "What Hegel's Master/Slave Dialectic Really Means," *Journal of Medieval and Early-Modern Studies* 34 (2004): 577–610; Kathleen Davis, *Periodization and Sovereignty: How Ideas of Feudalism and Secularization Govern the Politics of Time* (Philadelphia: University of Pennsylvania Press, 2008); Heng, *Invention of Race.*

45 See, for example, Wolfgang Ernst, *Signale aus der Vergangenheit: Eine kleine Geschichtskritik* (Munich: Fink, 2013), 12; cited in Markus Stock and Anne-Marie Rasmussen, "Introduction: Medieval Media," *Seminar* 52, no. 2 (2016): 100.

46 Friedrich Kittler, *Discourse Networks, 1800/1900,* trans. Michael Meteer with Chris Cullens (Stanford, CA: Stanford University Press, 1990).

47 Guillory, "Genesis." See also chapter 1 in this volume.

48 Robinson, *"Medieval."*

49 Guillory, "Genesis," 321–2.

50 Guillory, "Genesis," 325.

51 On remediation and its importance to the development of new media forms, see also Jay David Bolter and Richard Grusin, *Remediation: Understanding New Media* (Cambridge, MA: MIT Press, 2000).

52 Guillory, "Genesis," 324. For recent considerations of the term *print culture* in medieval studies and media studies respectively, see Michael Johnston and Michael Van Dussen, "Introduction," *The Medieval Manuscript Book,* ed. Johnston and Van Dussen (Cambridge: Cambridge University Press, 2015), 10–12; Gitelman, *Paper Knowledge,* 7–8.

53 Guillory, "Genesis," 323.

54 Guillory, "Genesis," 323 (emphasis in the original).

55 Guillory, "Genesis," 324n6.

56 Guillory, "Genesis," 323–4.

57 It is noteworthy that Bacon's rejection of Islamic influence on Christian intellectual traditions persists in the academy: see María Rosa Menocal, *The Arabic Role in Medieval Literary History* (Philadelphia: University of Pennsylvania Press, 1987); Suzanne Conklin Akbari and Karla Mallette, "Introduction: The Persistence of Philology: Language and Connectivity in the Mediterranean," in *A Sea of Languages: Rethinking the Arabic Role in Medieval Literary History*, ed. Akbari and Mallette, 3–22 (Toronto: University of Toronto Press, 2013).

58 This (highly truncated) account of the medieval reception of Aristotle's *Poetics* is based on Karla Mallette, "Beyond Mimesis: Aristotle's Poetics in the Medieval Mediterranean," *PMLA* 124 (2009): 583–91.

59 For an introduction to the aesthetic theories and practices of Islamic cultures, see Shahab Ahmed, *What Is Islam?: The Importance of Being Islamic* (Princeton, NJ: Princeton University Press, 2016).

60 Our emphasis. For Latin text, see Latin Library, http://www.thelatinlibrary.com/bacon/bacon.liber1.shtml. Taken from Francis Bacon, *Novum Organum*, ed. Thomas Fowler (Oxford, 1878).

61 Guillory, "Genesis," 324, citing Francis Bacon, *The New Organon*, ed. Lisa Jardine and Michael Silverthorne (Cambridge: Cambridge University Press, 2000), 86–7.

62 Guillory, "Genesis," 324.

63 Wynters, "Unsettling"; Da Silva, "Before Man."

64 Guillory, "Genesis," 388.

65 We are thinking here of Marshall McLuhan, *The Gutenberg Galaxy: The Making of Typographic Man* (Toronto: University of Toronto Press, 1962, repr. 2011); and McLuhan, *Understanding Media: The Extensions of Man*, rev. ed. (Cambridge, MA: MIT Press, 1996); Walter Ong, *Orality and Literacy*, 30th Anniversary Edition (London: Routledge, 2002); and even Harold Innis, who in *Empire and Communications* (Toronto: University of Toronto Press, 2007) makes the distinction between vellum and paper.

66 John Durham Peters, *The Marvelous Clouds: Toward a Philosophy of Elemental Media* (Chicago: University of Chicago Press, 2016).

67 Peters, *Marvelous Clouds*, 316. See also chapter 3 in this volume.

68 Key expressions of the ideology of print in relation to both "orality" and later media appear in McLuhan, *Gutenberg Galaxy*; Walter Ong, "The Literate Orality of Popular Culture," in *Rhetoric, Romance, and Technology, Studies in the Interaction of Expression and Culture*, ed. Walter Ong, 284–303 (Ithaca, NY: Cornell University Press, 1971).

69 Hoyt Duggan, "Some Un-Revolutionary Aspects of Computer Editing," in *The Literary Text in the Digital Age*, ed. Ruth Finneran (Ann Arbor, MI: University of Michigan Press, 1996), 79.

70 For example in Hockey, "History of Humanities"; Jerome McGann, *Radiant Textuality: Literature after the World Wide Web* (New York: Palgrave, 2001); Willard McCarty, *Humanities Computing* (New York: Palgrave Macmillan, 2005); L. Shillingsburg, *From Gutenberg to Google: Electronic Representations of Literary Texts* (Cambridge: Cambridge University Press, 2006); Martin Foys, *Virtually Anglo-Saxon: Old Media, New Media, and Early Medieval Studies in the Late Age of Print* (Gainesville: University Press of Florida, 2007); Alan Liu, *Transcendental Data: Toward a Cultural History and Aesthetics of the New Encoded Discourse. Local Transcendence: Essays on Postmodern Historicism and the Database* (Chicago: University of Chicago Press, 2008); H. W. Gabler, "Theorizing the Digital Scholarly Edition," *Literature Compass* 7 (2010): 43–56; Susan Schreibman, "Digital Scholarly Editing," in *Literary Studies in the Digital Age: An Evolving Anthology*, ed. Kenneth M. Price and Ray Siemens (2013), https://dlsanthology.mla.hcommons.org/digital-scholarly-editing/.

71 Alan Liu, "Where Is Cultural Criticism in the Digital Humanities," in *Debates in the Digital Humanities*, ed. Matthew K. Gold (Minneapolis: University of Minnesota Press, 2012), 494.

72 Cliff Siskin and William Warner, *This Is Enlightenment* (Chicago: University of Chicago Press, 2010).

73 Patricia Jane Roylance, "Winthrop's Journal in Manuscript and Print: The Temporalities of Early-Nineteenth-Century Transmedial Reproduction." *PMLA* 133, no. 1 (2018): 88–106.

74 Roylance, "Winthrop's Journal," 92.

75 Adrian Johns, *The Nature of the Book* (Chicago: University of Chicago Press, 2000).

76 Patrick Jagoda, *Network Aesthetics* (Chicago: University of Chicago Press, 2016).

77 Jay David Bolter and Richard Grusin, *Remediation: Understanding New Media* (Cambridge, MA: MIT Press, 1999).

CHAPTER I

1 Richard Holden, "Digital," *Aspects of English: Word Stories* (Oxford: Oxford University Press, 2014), http://public.oed.com/aspects-of-english/word-stories/digital/. Unless otherwise noted, translations from Latin and English are my own.

2 Holden, "Digital."

3 Recent examples include Martin K. Foys, *Virtually Anglo-Saxon: Old Media, New Media, and Early Medieval Studies in the Late Age of Print* (Gainesville: University Press of Florida, 2007); Elaine Treharne, "The Architextual Editing of Early English," *Poetica* 71 (2008): 1–13; Martin K. Foys, "Media," in *A Handbook of Anglo-Saxon Studies*, ed. Jacqueline Stodnick and Renée R. Trilling, 133–48 (Malden, MA: Wiley-Blackwell, 2012); Elaine Treharne, "Fleshing Out the Text: The Transcendent Manuscript in the Digital Age," *postmedieval* 4 (2013): 465–78; Thomas A. Bredehoft, *The Visible Text: Textual Production and Reproduction from* Beowulf *to* Maus (Oxford: Oxford University Press, 2014); Kathleen E. Kennedy, *Medieval Hackers* (Brooklyn: punctum books, 2014); Fiona Somerset, "Introduction," in *Truth and Tales: Cultural Mobility and Medieval Media*, ed. Fiona Somerset and Nicholas Watson, 1–16 (Columbus, OH: Ohio State University Press, 2015); and Martin K. Foys, "Medieval Manuscripts: Media Archaeology and the Digital Incunable," in *The Medieval Manuscript Book: Cultural Approaches*, ed. Michael Johnston and Michael Van Dussen, 119–39 (Cambridge: Cambridge University Press, 2015). See also Brandon W. Hawk, *Preaching Apocrypha in Anglo-Saxon England*, Toronto Anglo-Saxon Series 30 (Toronto: University of Toronto Press, 2018), esp. 20–4 and 201–7.

4 Kennedy, *Medieval Hackers*, esp. lexical overview of the term *hacker* at 9–11. For another notable, recent, historical examination of a lexical

keyword related to media studies and our digital age, see Paul Duguid's study of information in the eighteenth century, "The Ageing of Information: From Particular to Particulate," *Journal of the History of Ideas* 76 (2015): 347–68.

5 Raymond Williams, *Keywords: A Vocabulary of Culture and Society*, rev. ed. (Oxford: Oxford University Press, 1983).

6 *Oxford English Dictionary Online* (hereafter OED), http://www.oed.com, s.v. *digital*, n. and adj., quotation from sense B. adj. 1., but found throughout; for example, within the same entry, see the definition for "digital computer."

7 For specific instances of defining these key terms both in relation and in contrast to each other, see, for example, Andrew Mall, "analog, digital," in *Keywords of Media Theory*, ed. W. J. T. Mitchell, Eduardo de Almeida, and Rebecca Reynolds (Chicago: University of Chicago Press, 2003), http://csmt.uchicago.edu/glossary2004/analogdigital.htm; and Jake Buckley, "Analog versus Digital," in *The Johns Hopkins Guide to Digital Media*, ed. Lori Emerson, Marie-Laure Ryan, and Benjamin J. Robertson, 7–11 (Baltimore, MD: Johns Hopkins University Press, 2014).

8 A. M. Turing, "Computing Machinery and Intelligence," *Mind* 59 (1950): 436.

9 See Ryan Singel and Kevin Poulsen, "Your Own Personal Internet," *Wired*, 29 June 2006, https://www.wired.com/2006/06/your-own-person/.

10 John Guillory, "Genesis of the Media Concept," *Critical Inquiry* 36 (2010): 321–62. See also the introduction to this volume.

11 Guillory, "Genesis," 321.

12 Guillory, "Genesis," 326.

13 It may be noted that this examination, focused on medieval texts in Latin and English, by necessity omits many aspects of this concept contributed from other linguistic domains; these also remain parts of history yet to be written. There are, of course, many relevant sources in other languages like Anglo-Norman, or the Celtic languages used in medieval Britain, but I only gesture toward them, since they are beyond the scope of this study.

14 Foys, *Virtually Anglo-Saxon*, 28.

15 Foys, *Virtually Anglo-Saxon*, 29–31, quotation at 31, and reproduction of the engraving at 30, figure 2. See Jacob Leupold, *Theatrum arithmetic-geometricum* (Leipzig, 1727), table 1.

16 Foys, *Virtually Anglo-Saxon*, 34.

17 *OED*, s.v. *digit*, n. and adj., and s.v. *digital*, n. and adj.; and *Middle English Dictionary* (hereafter *MED*) (Ann Arbor: University of Michigan Press, 2001–14), http://quod.lib.umich.edu/m/med/, s.v. *digit*, n., and s.v. *digital*, adj. & n. See also *Dictionary of Medieval Latin from British Sources* (hereafter *DMLBS*), ed. R. E. Latham, D. R. Howlett, and R. K. Ashdowne (Oxford: Oxford University Press, 1975–2013), s.v. *digitus*, esp. 3 (math.) digit; and *Thesaurus linguae Latinae* (hereafter *TLL*) (Leipzig: Teubner, 1900–), s.v. *digitus.*

18 On mathematics in the classical world, see esp. S. Cuomo, *Ancient Mathematics* (New York: Routledge, 2015).

19 *Isidori Hispalensis Episcopi Etymologiarum sive Originum Libri XX*, ed. W. M. Lindsay, 2 vols. (Oxford: Clarendon, 1911), n.p.; translations adapted from *The Etymologies of Isidore of Seville*, trans. Stephen A. Barney, W. J. Lewis, and J. A. Beach (Cambridge: Cambridge University Press, 2006).

20 See *Texts and Transmission: A Survey of the Latin Classics*, ed. L. D. Reynolds (Oxford: Oxford University Press, 1983), 194–6, with further bibliography there.

21 1.29.3–4: "Sunt autem etymologiae nominum aut ex causa datae ... aut ex origine ... aut ex contrariis.... Quaedam etiam facta sunt ex nominum derivatione ... quaedam etiam ex vocibus ... quaedam ex Graeca etymologia orta et declinata sunt in Latinum."

22 "Digiti nuncupati, vel quia decem sunt, vel quia decenter iuncti existunt. Nam habent in se et numerum perfectum et ordinem decentissimum." Lindsay, *Isidori Hispalensis*, 11.1.70; and *Etymologies*, trans. Barney, Lewis, and Beach, 235.

23 See T. G. Tucker, *A Concise Etymological Dictionary of Latin* (Halle: Max Niemeyer, 1931), s.v. *decem, dextra,* and *digitus*; Michiel de Vaan, *Etymological Dictionary of Latin and the Other Italic Languages* (Leiden: Brill, 2008), s.v. *decem, dextra,* and *digitus.*

24 *Bedae Venerabilis opera, pars VI: Opera didascalica 2*, ed. Ch. W. Jones, CCSL 123B (Turnhout: Brepols, 1977); and *Bede: The Reckoning of Time*, trans. Faith Wallis, Translated Texts for Historians 29 (Liverpool: Liverpool University Press, 1999).

25 See *Reckoning of Time*, trans. Wallis, 85–97; cf. George Hardin Brown and Frederick M. Biggs, "De temporum ratione," in *Bede: Part 1, Fascicles 1–4* (Amsterdam: Amsterdam University Press, 2017), 84–116, esp. 92–6.

26 See commentary in *Reckoning of Time*, trans. Wallis; and Francisca del Mar Plaza Picón and José Antonio González Marrero, "*De computo uel loquela digitorum*: Bede y el computo digital," *Faventia* 28 (2006): 115–23.

27 "Cum ergo dicis unum, minimum in laeua digitum inflectens, in medium palmae artum infiges." Jones, *Bedae Venerabilis opera*, 269, lines 25–6; and *Reckoning of Time*, trans. Wallis, 10.

28 "Decies autem centena millia cum dicis, ambas sibi manus, insertis inuicem digitis implicabis." Jones, *Bedae Venerabilis opera*, 271, lines 69–71; and *Reckoning of Time*, trans. Wallis, 11.

29 On (re)mediation, see Jay David Bolter and Richard Grusin, *Remediation: Understanding New Media* (Cambridge, MA: MIT Press, 1999); Guillory's complication of this concept in "Genesis"; and most recently, Richard Grusin, "Radical Mediation," *Critical Inquiry* 42 (2015): 124–48.

30 See Karol Berger, "The Guidonian Hand," in *The Medieval Craft of Memory: An Anthology of Texts and Pictures*, ed. Mary Carruthers and Jan M. Ziolkowski, 71–82 (Philadelphia: University of Pennsylvania Press, 2002).

31 "Visions of the Cistercian Abbey at Ham," in *Revelations of Peter of Cornwall*, ed. and trans. Robert Easting and Richard Sharpe, British Writers of the Middle Ages and Early Modern Period 5 (Toronto: Pontifical Institute for Mediaeval Studies, 2013), 226–7.

32 See Scott G. Bruce, *Silence and Sign Language in Medieval Monasticism: The Cluniac Tradition, c.900–1200* (Cambridge: Cambridge University Press, 2007), esp. appendix A: "The Cluniac Sign Lexicon," 177–82; and *The Anglo-Saxon Monastic Sign Language: Monasteriales Indicia*, ed.

Debby Banham (Norfolk: Anglo-Saxon Books, 1991). On monastic sign language and media, see Martin K. Foys, "A Sensual Philology for Anglo-Saxon England," *postmedieval* 5 (2014): 456–72.

33 See *Gesture in Medieval Drama and Art*, ed. Clifford Davidson (Kalamazoo, MI: Medieval Institute Publications, 2001); J. A. Burrow, *Gestures and Looks in Medieval Narrative*, Cambridge Studies in Medieval Literature 48 (Cambridge: Cambridge University Press, 2002); and C. R. Dodwell, *Anglo-Saxon Gestures and the Roman Stage* (Cambridge: Cambridge University Press, 2000).

34 *OED*, s.v. *manuscript*, adj. and n. There were premodern uses of the terms *manuscriptio* (manuscript) and *manuscriptus* (handwritten), as well as *manus* and *scriptus* together, to indicate handwritten media, which therefore set a sort of precedent for the early modern uses; see *DMLBS*, s.v. *manuscriptus*; and *TLL*, s.v. *manuscriptio*.

35 *OED*, s.v. *manual*, adj. and n.; *DMLBS*, s.v. *manual* and related terms; and *TLL*, s.v. *manualis* and related terms.

36 "manus fortium dominabitur quae autem remissa est tributis serviet." *Biblia sacra iuxta Vulgatam versionem*, ed. Robert Weber, 5th ed. (Stuttgart: Deutsche Bibelgesellschaft, 2007); translation from *The Holy Bible: Douay Version Translated from the Latin Vulgate* (London: Catholic Truth Society, 1956).

37 See *DMLBS*, s.v. *digitus* and related terms.

38 *Byrhtferth's Enchiridion*, ed. and trans. Peter S. Baker and Michael Lapidge, EETS s.s. 15 (Oxford: Oxford University Press, 1995).

39 On specific correspondences, see entries for "Beda" and "Byrhtferth" in *Fontes Anglo-Saxonici: World Wide Register*, http://fontes.english.ox.ac.uk/; and Brown and Biggs, "De temporum ratione."

40 See Patrizia Lendinara, "Abbo of Fleury," *Sources of Anglo-Saxon Literary Culture*, vol. 1, *Abbo of Fleury, Abbo of Saint-German-des-Prés, and Acta Sanctorum*, ed. Frederick M. Biggs, Thomas D. Hill, Paul E. Szarmach, and E. Gordon Whatley, with the assistance of Deborah A. Oosterhouse, 1–15 (Kalamazoo, MI: Medieval Institute Publications, 2001).

41　For the latter, see *Byrhtferth's Enchiridion*, ed. and trans. Baker and Lapidge, 140, lines 76 and 78–9; trans. at 141.

42　"In tricentario numero digitus digito iungitur.... In trecentario ungues indicis et pollicis blando coniunges amplexu; in sexagenario pollicem curuatum indice circumflexo diligenter a fronte precinges." *Byrhtferth's Enchiridion*, ed. and trans. Baker and Lapidge, 222, lines 312–13 and 317–19; trans. at 223.

43　"Istius centenarii perfectio in ipsa digitorum computatione ostenditur, quia de leua manu transit in dexteram, circulum exprimendo in modum corone, 'illam inmarcescibilem coronam' ostendendo." *Byrhtferth's Enchiridion*, ed. and trans. Baker and Lapidge, 222, lines 322–5; trans. at 223.

44　*Byrhtferth's Enchiridion*, ed. and trans. Baker and Lapidge, 228, quotation at lines 408–9; trans. at 229.

45　*Byrhtferth's Enchiridion*, ed. and trans. Baker and Lapidge, 186 and 188, figs. 26 and 27.

46　*Bullettino di bibliografia e di storia delle scienze matematiche et fisiche xv*, ed. Enrico Narducci (1882), 137–40, with an image of the constructed table at 139.

47　*Bullettino di bibliografia e di storia delle scienze matematiche et fisiche xv*, 137, lines 26–37.

48　"Unde si quid in digitis et articulis abaci numeralibus ex multiplication creuerit, id utrum recte processerit, divisione eiusdem summe probatur." *Adelard of Bath, Conversations with His Nephew:* On the Same and the Different, Questions on Natural Science, *and* On Birds, ed. and trans. Charles Burnett, Cambridge Medieval Classics 9 (Cambridge: Cambridge University Press, 1998), 20, trans. at 21.

49　"sicut idem est multiplicare compositum cum composito, et multiplicare vtramque partem compositi cum vtraque parte compositi, vt sic fiat quadruplex multiplicatio, scilicet articuli cum articulo et digiti cum articulo, deinde articuli cum digito, et quarto digiti cum digito." *Robert of Chester's Latin Translation of the Algebra of Al-Khowarizmi*, ed. and trans. Louis Charles Karpinski (Ann Arbor, MI: University of Michigan, 1915), 136, trans. at 137.

50 Since no full critical edition exists, I quote from the early printed version in *Barthomeus anglicus de Proprietatibus rerum* (Nuremberg: Anton Koberger, 1492). I have consulted the digital facsimile in the collection of the Corning Museum of Glass, https://www.cmog.org/library/de-proprietatibus-rerum-bartholomeusanglicus. I have also compared this to the text printed in Basel, 1470, which contains the same readings. I have standardized spelling, expanded abbreviations, and modernized punctuation.

51 *Petri Philomeni de Dacia in algorismum vulgarem Johannis de Sacrobosco commentarius*, ed. Maximillian Curtze (Copenhagen: Hauniæ, 1897), 1, lines 11–12.

52 *On the Properties of Things: John Trevisa's Translation of Bartholomaeus Anglicus De Proprietatibus Rerum: A Critical Text*, ed. M. C. Seymour and Gabriel M. Liegey, 3 vols. (Oxford: Oxford University Press, 1975–88), 2:1360.

53 *The Earliest Arithmetics in English*, ed. Robert Steele, EETS e.s. 118 (London: Early English Text Society, 1922; repr. 1988), 3–32 and 33–51.

54 *Earliest Arithmetics in English*, 33, lines 23–4.

55 *Earliest Arithmetics in English*, 50, line 9.

56 *Earliest Arithmetics in English*, 72–80.

57 See, for example, articles in "The Vernacularization of Science, Medicine, and Technology in Late Medieval Europe," special issue, *Early Science and Medicine* 3 (1998); and William Crossgrove, "The Vernacularization of Science, Medicine, and Technology in Late Medieval Europe: Broadening Our Perspectives," *Early Science and Medicine* 5 (2000): 47–63.

58 See *Catalogue of Additions to the Manuscripts in the British Museum in the Years 1882–1887* (London: Trustees of the British Museum, 1889), e.g., no. 2622.

59 See William Henry Black, *A Descriptive, Analytical, and Critical Catalogue of the Manuscripts Bequeathed unto the University of Oxford by Elias Ashmole, Esq., M.D., F.R.S., Windsor Herald, Also Some Additional MSS. Contributed by Kingsley, Lhuyd, Borlase, and Others* (Oxford: Oxford University Press, 1845), no. 396.

60 See, for example, articles in *Conceptualizing Multilingualism in England, c.800–c.1250*, ed. Elizabeth M. Tyler (Turnhout: Brepols, 2011); and

Multilingualism in Medieval Britain (c. 1066–1520): Sources and Analysis, ed. Judith A. Jefferson and Ad Putter (Turnhout: Brepols, 2012).

61 For example, there is no entry for *digital* in Frédéric Godefroy, *Dictionnaire de l'ancienne langue française et de tous ses dialectes du IXe au XVe siècle*, 10 vols. (Paris: Vieweg, 1881–1902); Adolf Tobler and Erhard Lommatzsch, *Altfranzösisches Wörterbuch*, 11 vols. to date (Berlin: Weidmann, 1925–); or the *Anglo-Norman Dictionary*, http://www.anglo-norman.net/.

62 *DMLBS*, s.v. *digitaliter*. On date and contexts, see Williell R. Thomson, *The Latin Writings of John Wyclyf: An Annotated Catalog*, Subsidia Mediaevalia 14 (Toronto: Pontifical Institute of Mediaeval Studies, 1983), 227–9 (nos. 378–80).

63 "sed vere dicit quod non est per se, ex specie vel genere, propheta, vel falsus propheta, sicut dicit autem Johannes non est propheta, cum hoc quod nunc digitaliter ostendit Messiam, ad quem sunt prophetiae." *Fasciculi Zizaniorum Magistri Johannis Wyclif Cum Tritico, Ascribed to Thomas Netter of Walden*, ed. Walter Waddington Shirley, Rolls Series 5 (London: Longmans, 1858), 462. My thanks to Fiona Somerset for helping me to translate this passage and discussing Wyclif's meaning.

64 On the Continent, a near-contemporary use of *digitaliter* appears in *De ornatu spiritualium nuptiarum* by Willem Jordaens (ca. 1322–1372), a Latin translation of *Die geestelike brulocht* by the Flemish mystic Jan van Ruusbroec (1293–1381); see *Ioannis Rusbrochii, De ornatu spiritualium nuptiarum, Wilhelmo Iordani interprete*, ed. Kees Schepers, CCSM 207 (Turnhout: Brepols, 2004), 207, line 47: "Primo in hoc aduerbio demon-strandi Ecce uisum nostrum digitaliter excitat et preceptum quodam-modo dat uidendi." This is the only instance of the term in the Brepols *Library of Latin Texts* (Turnhout: Brepols, 2014), series A, http://clt.brepolis.net/llta/, and series B, http://clt.brepolis.net/lltb/; no instance of the term appears in the Patrologia Latina Database (1996–2015), http://pld.chadwyck.com; nor in TLL.

65 *OED*, s.v. -*al*, suffix1. See also Mark Kaunisto, *Variation and Change in the Lexicon: A Corpus-Based Analysis of Adjectives in English Ending in -ic and -ical*, Language and Computers: Studies in Practical Linguistics 63 (Amsterdam: Rodopi, 2007), esp. 8–12; and R. M. W. Dixon, *Making*

New Words: Morphological Derivation in English (Oxford: Oxford University Press, 2014), 250–3.

66 *OED*, s.v. *digitally*, adv.

67 Oliver Yorke, "The Sock and the Buskin. No. III: Miss Fanny Kemble's 'Francis the First,' and Mr. Sheridan Knowles's 'Hunchback,'" *Fraser's Magazine for Town and Country* 5 (1832): 432.

68 John W. Mauchly, "Digital and Analog Computing Machines," *The Moore School Lectures (1946)*, ed. Martin Campbell-Kelly and Michael R. Williams (Cambridge, MA: MIT Press, 1985), 25–42.

69 *DMLBS*, s.v. *manual, manualis*, and related terms; and *TLL*, s.v. *manualis* and related terms.

70 *OED*, s.v. *manual*, adj. and n.; and *MED*, s.v. *manual*, adj. Cf. *OED*, s.v. *manually*, adv.; and *MED*, s.v. *manualli*, adv.

71 "Manus dicta, quod sit totius corporis munus. Ipsa enim cibum ori ministrat; ipsa operatur omnia atque dispensat; per eam accipimus et damus. Abusive autem manus etiam ars vel artifex, unde et manupretium dicimus." Lindsay, *Isidori Hispalensis*, 11.1.66; *Etymologies*, trans. Barney et al., 235.

72 *DMLBS*, s.v. *dexter*; *TLL*, s.v. *dexter*; and *OED*, s.v. *dexterous*, adj.

73 *Fr. Rogeri Bacon: Opera quaedam hactenus inedita*, ed. J. S. Brewer (London: Longman, Green and Roberts, 1859), 1:309.

74 *"My Compleinte" and Other Poems*, ed. Roger Ellis (Exeter: University of Exeter Press, 2001), 74, lines 364–6.

75 Quoted from London, Wellcome Library, MS 564, fol. 146b. See quotations in *MED*, s.v. *manuel*.

76 On analogue computers, see Paul E. Ceruzzi, *A History of Modern Computing*, 2nd ed. (Cambridge, MA: MIT Press, 2003); James S. Small, *The Analogue Alternative: The Electronic Analogue Computer in Britain and the USA, 1930–1975* (New York: Routledge, 2001; repr. 2013); Eric G. Swedin and David L. Ferro, *Computers: The Life Story of a Technology* (Baltimore, MD: Johns Hopkins University Press, 2005); and, situating analogue computers among other types, George Dyson, *Turing's Cathedral: The Origins of the Digital Universe* (New York: Penguin Books, 2012), 5–6, 69–70, 280–1.

77 See Turing, "Computing Machinery and Intelligence"; and L. F. Menabrea, "Sketch of the Analytical Engine Invented by Charles Babbage," trans. with notes by Ada Augusta, Countess of Lovelace, *Scientific Memoirs, Selected from the Transactions of Foreign Academies of Science and Learned Societies, and Foreign Journals,* ed. Richard Taylor (London, 1843), 3:666–707.

78 See, for example, Larry Hardesty, "Analog Computing Returns," *MIT News,* 20 June 2016, http://news.mit.edu/2016/analog-computing-organs-organisms-0620; and N. Guo, Y. Huang, T. Mai, S. Patil, C. Cao, M. Seok, S. Sethumadhavan, and Y. Tsividis, "Energy-Efficient Hybrid Analog/Digital Approximate Computation in Continuous Time," *IEEE Journal of Solid-State Circuits* 51 (2016): 1514–24.

79 For editions, see John Reidy, "A Treatise on the Astrolabe with Explanatory and Textual Notes," in *The Riverside Chaucer,* gen. ed. Larry D. Benson, 3rd ed. (Boston: Houghton Mifflin, 1987), 622–83, 1092–1102, and 1193–7; and *A Variorum Edition of the Works of Geoffrey Chaucer,* vol. 6, *Prose Treatises, Part One: A Treatise on the Astrolabe,* ed. Sigmund Eisner (Norman, OK: University of Oklahoma Press, 2002). For summaries of scholarship, with further references, see esp. Eisner, *Treatise on the Astrolabe,* 3–100; Jenna Mead, "Geoffrey Chaucer's *Treatise on the Astrolabe,*" *Literature Compass* 3 (2006): 973–91; Edgar Laird, "Chaucer and Friends: The Audience for the Treatise on the Astrolabe," *Chaucer Review* 41 (2007): 439–44; and Simon Horobin, "The Scribe of Bodleian Library MS Bodley 619 and the Circulation of Chaucer's *Treatise on the Astrolabe,*" *Studies in the Age of Chaucer* 31 (2009): 109–24.

80 *OED,* s.v. *computation,* n.; and *MED,* s.v. *computacioun,* n.

CHAPTER 2

1 Marshall McLuhan, *The Gutenberg Galaxy: The Making of Typographic Man* (Toronto: University of Toronto Press, 2011). A cogent critique of McLuhan and his forebears remains Leroy Vail and Landeg White, *Power and the Praise Poem: South African Voices in History* (Charlottesville, VA: University Press of Virginia, 1991), 1–39.

2 These terms have a long afterlife (of both use and rejection), but both appear already in *Gutenberg Galaxy*, for instance, on pages 150 and 167 respectively.

3 Raymond Williams, "Ideology," in *Keywords: A Vocabulary of Culture and Society* (New York: Croom Helm, 1976), 126–30; Louis Althusser, *For Marx*, trans. Ben Brewster (New York: Verso, 2006), 233–4.

4 Elizabeth Eisenstein, *The Printing Press as an Agent of Change*, 2 vols. (Cambridge: Cambridge University Press, 1979).

5 Michael Johnston and Michael Van Dussen, "Introduction," in *The Medieval Manuscript Book*, ed. Johnston and Van Dussen (Cambridge: Cambridge University Press, 2015), 9–10.

6 *Thesaurus Linguae Graecae*, ed. Maria C. Pantelia, University of California Irvine, http://www.tlg.uci.edu, accessed 7 November 2019, s.v. πρωτό-χολλον, τό. See also Alexander Galloway, *Protocol: How Control Exists after Decentralization* (Cambridge, MA: MIT Press, 2004), 7; E. G. Turner, *Greek Papyri: An Introduction* (Oxford: Clarendon, 1968), 4–5; H. I. Bell, "The Greek Papyrus Protocol," *Journal of Hellenic Studies* 37 (1917): 56–8; E. M. Thompson, *An Introduction to Greek and Latin Paleography* (Cambridge: Cambridge University Press, 1906), 24–5.

7 Novels (*Novellae*) 44 Cap. 2: *Corpus juris civilis*, ed. Paul Krueger and Theodor Mommsen, 3 vols. (Berlin: Apud Weidmannos, 1888).

8 The history of protocol summarized here is laid out more fully in Stephen M. Yeager, "Protocol: The Chivalry of the Object," *Critical Inquiry* 45, no. 3 (2019): 747–61.

9 For a fuller exploration of this definition of *literacy*, as applied to the "transitional literacy" of early medieval England, see also Stephen M. Yeager, *From Lawmen to Plowmen: Anglo-Saxon Legal Tradition and the School of Langland* (Toronto: University of Toronto Press, 2014), 27–59.

10 *Dictionary of Medieval Latin from British Sources*, s.v. *revolutio*, n. The classical definition of the term is "a revolving, revolution (late Lat. for *conversio*)": Lewis and Short, *A Latin Dictionary*. Both of these dictionaries were accessed through Logeion 2, built by Philip Posner, Ethan Della Rocca, and Josh Day, https://logeion.uchicago.edu/.

11 *OED*, s.v. *Revolution*, n., II; *Industrial Revolution*, n.

12 Bruno Latour, *We Were Never Modern*, trans. Catherine Porter (Cambridge, MA: Harvard University Press, 1993).

13 Kathleen Davis, *Periodization and Sovereignty: How Ideas of Feudalism and Secularization Govern the Politics of Time* (Philadelphia: University of Pennsylvania Press, 2008), 5.

14 Michael Clanchy, *From Memory to Written Record*, 3rd ed. (Oxford: Wiley Blackwell, 2012), 23–45. For a contrary view of this periodization and its value, see Elaine Treharne, *Living through Conquest* (Oxford: Oxford University Press, 2012).

15 E.g., Andrew B. R. Elliott, *Medievalism, Politics, and Mass Media: Appropriating the Middle Ages in the Twenty-First Century* (Oxford: D. S. Brewer, 2017); Bruce Holsinger, *The Premodern Condition* (Chicago: University of Chicago Press, 2005); Carolyn Dinshaw, *Getting Medieval: Sexualities and Communities, Premodern and Postmodern* (Durham, NC: Duke University Press, 1999); John Ganim, *Medievalism and Orientalism* (New York: Palgrave Macmillan, 2005); Fred Robinson, "*Medieval*, The *Middle Ages*," in *The Tomb of Beowulf and Other Essays on Old English*, 304–15 (Oxford: Wiley Blackwell, 1992).

16 Davis, *Periodization*, 30–1.

17 Davis, *Periodization*, 52–3.

18 Davis, *Periodization*, 55.

19 Henry Spelman, "Feuds and Tenure," in *Reliquiæ Spelmannianæ the posthumous works of Sir Henry Spelman, Kt., relating to the laws and antiquities of England: publish'd from the original manuscripts: with the life of the author* (Oxford, 1698), 5–6. For a recent consideration of a possible "feudal revolution" after William's reign, see Stephen Baxter, "Lordship and Labour," in *A Social History of England 900–1200*, ed. Julia Crick and Elisabeth Van Houts, 98–114 (Cambridge: Cambridge University Press, 2011).

20 Davis, *Periodization*, 56–9.

21 Witnessed, for example, in the opening lines of the law code Athelred I: "Ðis is seo gerædnys, ðe æþelred cyning & his witan geræddon, eallon folce to friþes bote, æt Wudestoce on Myrcena lande, æfter Engla lage (This is the decree [*gerædnys*] that King Athelred and his *witan* advised,

as a remedy of peace to all folk, at Woodstock in Mercian land, according to English law)." Felix Liebermann, *Die Gesetze der Anglesachsen*, 3 vols. (Halle: Max Niemeyer, 1903–16), 1:216.

22 Patrick Wormald notes that Robert Talbot glossed his copy of V Atr "an act of parlament as ytt were": BL Cotton MS Nero A.i f. 89r; Wulfstan MS ed. Loyn p. 40; Wormald, *The Making of English Law: King Alfred to the Twelfth Century* (London: Blackwell, 2001), 6. Nor is this the first occurrence of using the word *parliament* to refer to a convening of the *witan*: see also the fourteenth-century Anglo-Norman *Mirror of Justices*, ed. W. J. Whittaker (Selden Society 7, 1895), 8. On the historical question of the actual role of the *witan*, see H. R. Loyn, *The Governance of Anglo-Saxon England, 500–1087* (Stanford, CA: Stanford University Press, 1984), 100–6; Maddicott, *Origins of English Parliament* (Oxford: Oxford University Press, 2010), 25–31; Levi Roach, *Kingship and Consent in Anglo-Saxon England, 871–978* (Cambridge: Cambridge University Press, 2013).

23 Davis, *Periodization*, 9.

24 Davis, *Periodization*, 55–6.

25 This brief summary is drawn from Wendy Chun, *Control and Freedom: Power and Paranoia in the Age of Fiber Optics* (Cambridge, MA: MIT Press, 2006); Alexander Galloway, *Protocol: How Control Exists after Decentralization* (Cambridge, MA: MIT Press, 2004); Barry M. Leiner, Vinton G. Cerf, David D. Clark, Robert E. Kahn, Leonard Kleinrock, Daniel C. Lynch, Jon Postel, Larry G. Roberts, and Stephen Wolff, "Brief History of the Internet," 1997, http://www.internetsociety.org/internet/what-internet/history-internet/brief-history-internet; and from my own conversations with industry professionals.

26 Galloway, *Protocol*, 44–6, 131–7, citing Jonathan Postel, "Transmission Control Protocol," RFC 793, September 1981; "Internet Protocol," RFC 791, September 1981; Eric Hall, *Internet Core Protocols: The Definitive Guide* (Sebastopol, CA: O'Reilly Media, 2000).

27 Chun, *Control*.

28 Chun, *Control*, 37–76.

29 Attempts to separate the true views of Deleuze and Guattari from their vulgar appropriations include, for example, Richard Coyne, "The Net Effect: Design, the Rhizome, and Complex Philosophy," *Futures* 40 (2008): 552–61; Jason J. Wallin, "Rhizomania: Five Provocations on a Concept," *Complicity: An International Journal of Complexity and Education* 7 (2010): 83–9; Peter Lenco, "(Re-)Introducing Deleuze: New Readings of Deleuze in International Studies," *Millennium: Journal of International Studies* 43 (2014): 124–44.

30 Gilles Deleuze and Felix Guattari, *A Thousand Plateaus: Capitalism and Schizophrenia* (Minneapolis: University of Minnesota Press, 1987), 21.

31 Deleuze and Guattari, *Thousand Plateaus*, 21.

32 Galloway, *Protocol*, 8; Alexander Galloway, *Laruelle: Against the Digital* (Minneapolis: University of Minnesota Press, 2014), 96; Chun, *Control*, 23–4.

33 Stefan Wray, "Rhizomes, Nomads, and Resistant Internet Use," http://www.thing.net/~rdom/ecd/rhizomatic.html#THE%20 LITERATURE; Stuart Moulthrop, "Rhizome and Resistance: Hypertext and the Dreams of a New Culture," in *Hyper/Text/Theory*, ed. George P. Landow, 1–18 (Baltimore, MD: Johns Hopkins University Press, 1994); cited by Mark Gartler, "rhizome," Chicago School of Media Theory, https://lucian.uchicago.edu/blogs/mediatheory/keywords/rhizome/. See also Ian Buchanan, "Deleuze and the Internet," *Australian Humanities Review* 43 (2007): 1–21.

34 Galloway, *Protocol*, 8.

35 Galloway also articulates his views about the emancipatory potential of rhizomatic networks in "Networks," in *Critical Terms for Media Studies*, ed. W. J. T. Mitchell and Mark B. N. Hansen, 280–96 (Chicago: University of Chicago Press, 2010).

36 On such privileging of decentralized/rhizomatic over heirarchical/arborescent organization, see Vita Peacock, "The Negation of Hierarchy and Its Consequences," *Anthropological Theory* 15 (2015): 3–21.

37 See Dorothy Kim, "Introduction to the Literature Compass Special Cluster: Critical Race and the Middle Ages," *Literature Compass* 16, nos. 9–10 (2019): e1249, and the rest of this special issue.

38 Jacques Derrida, "Archive Fever: A Freudian Impression," trans. Eric Prenowitz, *Diacritics* 25, no. 2 (1995): 9–63.

39 Bernard Stiegler, *Technics and Time 1: The Fault of Epimetheus*, trans. Richard Beardsworth and George Collins, 21–179 (Stanford, CA: Stanford University Press, 1998).

CHAPTER 3

1 See, for example, Tom Simonite, "Moore's Law Is Dead. Now What?" *MIT Technology Review*, 13 May 2016, https://www.technologyreview.com/s/601441/moores-law-is-dead-now-what/.

2 This claim was one of Innis's basic interventions in *Empire and Communications* (Oxford: Clarendon, 1950), which he continued to support and expand on in later works such as *The Bias of Communication* (Toronto: University of Toronto Press, 1951).

3 Paul Levinson, "McLuhan and Media Ecology," *Proceedings of the Media Ecology Association* 1 (2000): 17.

4 Levinson, "McLuhan and Media Ecology," 17–18.

5 Levinson, "McLuhan and Media Ecology," 19.

6 Neil Postman, "The Humanism of Media Ecology," *Proceedings of the Media Ecology Association* 1 (2000): 10.

7 Postman, "Humanism of Media Ecology," 10.

8 Postman, "Humanism of Media Ecology," 10–11.

9 Michael Goddard, "Media Ecology," in *The Johns Hopkins Guide to Digital Media*, ed. Marie-Laure Ryan, Lori Emerson, and Benjamin J. Robertson (Baltimore, MD: Johns Hopkins University Press, 2014), 331.

10 Goddard, "Media Ecology," 332; and see also Félix Guattari, *Les trois écologies* (Paris: Éditions Galilée, 1989); Félix Guattari, *The Three Ecologies*, trans. Ian Pindar and Paul Sutton (London: Athlone, 2000).

11 The history of the adoption of the fork in Europe and its American colonies remains under-explored. Though short, one of the better treatments supported by historical evidence is Travis J. Lybbert, "The Economic Roots of the American 'Zig-zag': Knives, Forks, and British Mercantilism," *Economic Inquiry* 48 (2010): 810–15, which highlights the

colonial legal roots behind the social and technological practices explored by James Deetz, *In Small Things Forgotten: An Archaeology of Early American Life*, expanded and rev. ed. (New York: Anchor Books, 1996); and Henry Petroski, *The Evolution of Useful Things* (New York: Vintage Books, 1994).

12 Such a statement is also callously ableist. John Durham Peters, *Speaking into the Air: A History of the Idea of Communication* (Chicago: University of Chicago Press, 1999), 269.

13 Peters, *Speaking into the Air*, 269.

14 David Edgerton, *The Shock of the Old: Technology and Global History since 1900* (Oxford: Oxford University Press, 2007), xvii.

15 Norton tackles this prejudice head-on in "Subaltern Technologies and Early Modernity in the Atlantic World," *Colonial Latin America Review* 26 (2017): 18–38. For an excellent monograph exemplifying this newer branch of scholarship, see E. R. Truitt, *Medieval Robots: Mechanism, Magic, Nature and Art* (Philadelphia: University of Pennsylvania Press, 2015).

16 Norton, "Subaltern Technologies and Early Modernity," 27.

17 Edgerton, *Shock of the Old*, ix–xviii.

18 Edgerton, *Shock of the Old*, xiii.

19 Benchmark species are commonly used in the sciences, and an example describing some of the method involved in identifying benchmark species can be found in Mark O. Hill, "Local Frequency as a Key to Interpreting Species Occurrence Data When Recording Effort Is Not Known," *Methods in Ecology and Evolution* 3 (2012): 195–205. doi: 10.1111/j.2041-210X.2011.00146.x.

20 *Wife of Bath's Prologue*, lines 99–101: "a lord in his household, / He nath nat every vessel al of gold; / Somme been of tree." Quoted from *The Riverside Chaucer*, 3rd ed., ed. Larry D. Benson (New York: Oxford University Press, 1987). For archeological data on woodenware in England, see Geoff Egan, "Medieval Vessels of Other Materials: A Non-Ceramic View from London," *Medieval Ceramics* 21 (1997): 109–14; and more recently Robin Wood, "What Did Medieval People Eat From?" *Medieval Ceramics* 29 (2005): 19–20.

21 T. F. Reddaway and Lorna E. M. Walker, *The Early History of the Goldsmiths' Company 1327–1509 Including the Book of Ordinances 1478–83* (London: Edward Arnold, 1975), 246.

22 See, for example, those landed from a Venetian galley at London in 1480–81, in H. S. Cobb, ed. *The Overseas Trade of London: Exchequer Customs Accounts 1480–1* (London: London Record Society, 1990), 46.

23 See Kathleen E. Kennedy, "Gripping It by the Husk: The Medieval English Coconut," *Medieval Globe* 3 (2017): 19–21, on mazers.

24 "Ho so ys lengyst a lyve Take this cope with owtyn stryfe," *Testamenta Eboracensia or Wills Registered at York Illustrative of the History, Manners, Language, Statistics, Etc., of the Province of York from the Year MCCC Downwards. Part 1*, ed. James Raine (London: J. B. Nichols and Son, 1835), hereafter TE1, 209; and "Quod wele ware hym yat wyste in whome yat he myght tryste," "Mazer," The Metropolitan Museum of Art, New York, gift of Irwin Untermyer, 1968, 68.141.179.

25 For example, "vas precor et potum cristum benedicere totum" and "MISEREMINI.MEI.MISEREMINI.MEI SALTEM.VOS.AMICI MEI," British Museum, London, 1909,0624.1 and AF.3118.

26 *Calendar of Wills Proved and Enrolled in the Court of Husting, London, A.D. 1258–A.D. 1688, Preserved among the Archives of the Corporation of the City of London, at the Guildhall*, 2 Pts., ed. Reginal Sharpe (London: John C. Francis, 1889), 2:207 (God Morwe); 2:305 (Pardoncuppe).

27 *Calendar of Wills*, 1:557.

28 This sense is confirmed by the archaeological record, Egan, "Medieval Vessels of Other Materials," 112–13.

29 See, for example, the seventeenth-century mazer 68.141.179 in n16, and "Bute Mazer," National Museum of Scotland, Edinburgh, on loan from the Bute Collection at Mount Stuart, IL.2001.182.1.1. The last mazer donated to a Cambridge college was 1521–22 and Oxford 1529; Alfred Jones, *The Old Plate of the Cambridge Colleges* (Cambridge: Cambridge University Press, 1910), 113; and Harold Charles Moffatt, *Old Oxford Plate* (London: Archibald, Constable, 1906), 199.

30 René T. J. Cappers, "Exotic Imports of the Roman Empire: An Exploratory Study of Potential Vegetal Products from Asia," in *Food, Fuel and Fields: Progress in African Archaeobotany*, ed. Katharina Neumann,

Ann Butler, and Stefanie Kahlheber, 197–206 (Cologne: Brill, 2003); Marijke van der Veen, *Consumption, Trade and Innovation: Exploring the Botanical Remains from the Roman and Islamic Ports at Quseir al-Qadim, Egypt* (Frankfurt am Main: Africa Magna Verlag, 2011), 48. For a study showing very early cultivation of coconut palms in both India and the Philippines, see B. F. Gunn, L. Baudouin, and K. M. Olson, "Independent Origins of Cultivated Coconut (*Cocos nucifera* L.) in the Old World Tropics," *PLoS ONE* 6 (2011): e21143. http://dx.doi.org/10.1371/journal.pone.0021143.

31 For evidence in the Middle Ages, see van der Veen, *Consumption, Trade and Innovation*, 49; and van der Veen, "Trade and Diet at Roman and Medieval Quseir al-Qadim, Egypt: A Preliminary Report," in *Food, Fuel and Fields*, ed. Neumann, Butler, and Kahlheber, 208.

32 The etymology of *coconut* remains vexed, but there is no evidence of it before the sixteenth century, and its usage in English regularized only gradually in the seventeenth: *OED*, s.v. *coconut*, n. Wills and probate inventories continue to use the medieval English term *nut*, until at least the mid-seventeenth century. See a 1620 will in J. A. Atkinson, B. Flynn, V. Portass, K. Singlehurst, and J. J. Smith, eds., *Darlington Wills and Inventories 1600–1625* (Newcastle: Boydell, 1993), 172. This particular coconut cup may have been a covered sugar-bowl style, as it is listed together with three small boxes. See also an instance in 1611, John Parsons Earwaker, ed. *Lancashire and Cheshire Wills and Inventories 1572–1696 Now Preserved at Chester* (Manchester: Chetham Society, 1893), 178. As late as 1669, the probate inventory of Queen Henrietta Maria listed a "Nutt-cup garnished with silver" and an "Indian Nutt with a bottome and lower of fillagrime of silver," descriptions common for several hundred years at that point. In addition, the dowager queen had three "Indian Nut Shells" apparently used as boxes for "Balms"; see Erin Griffey, *On Display: Henrietta Maria and the Materials of Magnificence at the Stuart Court* (New Haven, CT: Yale University Press, 2015), 282 and 286.

33 Philippe Cordez, *Trésor, Mémoire, Merveilles: Les Objets des Églises au Moyen Âge* (Paris: EHESS, 2016), 147–9.

34 See Cordez, *Trésor, Mémoire, Merveilles*, 148; Rolf Fritz, *Die Gefäße aus Kokosnuß in Mitteleuropa 1250–1800* (Mainz: Ph. Von Zabern, 1983),

41–2. While I am not aware of any research that explicitly discusses reliquaries as media, both Patrick Geary's now-classic discussion of *furta sacra* and David Perry's more recent intervention about relics as cultural vectors, come close. Patrick Geary, *Furta Sacra: Thefts of Relics in the Central Middle Ages* (Princeton, NJ: Princeton University Press, 1978); and David Perry, *Sacred Plunder: Venice and the Aftermath of the Fourth Crusade* (University Park: Pennsylvania State University Press, 2015).

35 Kennedy, "Gripping It by the Husk," 7–10.

36 See Jones, *Old Plate of the Cambridge Colleges*, 113; and Moffatt, *Old Oxford Plate*, 199.

37 Reddaway and Walker, *Early History of the Goldsmiths' Company*, 257–8; and Lisa Jefferson, ed., *Wardens' Accounts and Court Minute Books of the Goldsmiths' Mistery of London, 1334–1446* (Woodbridge: Boydell, 2003), 480–1.

38 Kennedy, "Gripping It by the Husk," 13.

39 For example, see *The Logge Register of Prerogative Court of Canterbury Wills 1479–1486*, ed. Lesley Boatwright, Moira Habberjam, and Peter Hammond, 2 vols. (Gorsedene: Richard III Society, 2008), 2:410.

40 Fritz, *Die Gefäße aus Kokosnuß*, 55; Rabia Gregory, "Black as a Coconut and White as a Tusk: African Materials and European Displays of Christ before Columbus," *Journal of African Religions* 2 (2014): 396–7.

41 For an example of an ostrich vessel, see "Ornamental Vessel," Museum of Applied Arts, Budapest, 19038.

42 For examples of relief carving, see Fritz, *Die Gefäße aus Kokosnuß*, plate 110. For native American caryatids, see Fritz, *Die Gefäße aus Kokosnuß*, plate 85, 116: these are both hybrid figures and bear characteristics that might have been viewed as African, such as dark skin and a turban. However, the feather skirt and hat, and the bow were closely associated with native Americans in European iconography. See, for example, the frontispiece of Philippe Sylvestre Dufour, *Traitez nouveaux et curieux du café, du thé et du chocolate* (Lyon: Jean Girin and B. Rivere, 1685).

43 Formerly scholarship argued that Spanish colonizers maintained a distinct, separate European lifestyle in the Americas, but more recently scholars have documented pervasive, practical blending of cultures and traditions. See, for example, Enrique Rodríguez-Alegría, "Eating Like an

Indian: Negotiating Social Relations in the Spanish Colonies," *Current Anthropology* 46 (2005): 551–73; and Marcy Norton, *Sacred Gifts, Profane Pleasures: A History of Tobacco and Chocolate in the Atlantic World* (Ithaca, NY: Cornell University Press, 2008), for just two examples of the new consensus.

44 Daniel Zizumbo-Villarreal and Hermilo J. Quero, "Re-evaluation of Early Observations on Coconut in the New World," *Economic Botany* 52 (1998): 71.

45 Zizumbo-Villarreal and Quero, "Re-evaluation of Early Observations," 74. Carlos F. Duarte, *El Arte del Tomar el Chocolate: Historia del Coco Chocolatero en Venezuela* (Caracas: C. F. Duarte, 2005) claims that the Mexicas drank chocolate from coconut shell cups, but the passages he cites accord with known decoration used on gourd *jícaras* and so we cannot assume that coconuts were also referenced without additional evidence (51).

46 Matthew Fuller, *Media Ecologies: Materialist Energies in Art and Technoculture* (Cambridge, MA: MIT Press, 2005), 2 and 45.

47 Logan Kistler, Álvaro Montenegro, Bruce D. Smith, John A. Gifford, Richard E. Green, Lee A. Newsom, and Beth Shapiro, "Transoceanic Drift and the Domestication of African Bottle Gourds in the Americas," *Proceedings of the National Academy of Sciences of the United States of America* III (2014): 2937–41, https://www.ncbi.nlm.nih.gov/pmc/articles/PMC3939861/.

48 Daniel H. Janzen and Paul S. Martin, "Neotropical Anachronisms: The Fruits the Gomphotheres Ate," *Science* 215 (1982): 19–27.

49 Norton, *Sacred Gifts, Profane Pleasures*, 16, 28, 54–5.

50 For example, Christine Folch, "Stimulating Consumption: Yerba Mate Myths, Markets, and Meanings from Conquest to Present," *Comparative Studies in Society and History* 52 (2010): 6–36, uses the term *yerba*, while Adalberto López, "The Economics of Yerba Mate in Seventeenth-Century South America," *Agricultural History* 48 (1974): 493–509, employs the full *yerba mate*. In contrast, in Spanish, María Marschoff, "La Sociedad Virreinal en Buenos Aires: Un Análisis desde la Cultura Material y la Alimentación," *Revista des Indias* 74 (2014): 67–100, calls yerba maté "mate."

51 See, for example, the Argentine study that employs *jícara* generically, and also identifies yerba cups as "mate." Marschoff, "La Sociedad Virreinal en Buenos Aires," 83.

52 Folch, "Stimulating Consumption," 24–5.

53 On the gestures of yerba-drinking, López, "Economics of Yerba Mate," 497.

54 That this hospitality was especially gendered is also suggested by Ross W. Jamieson, "The Essence of Commodification: Caffeine Dependencies in the Early Modern World," *Journal of Social History* 35 (2001): 278. For the importance of yerba and its utensils to upper-class women in Spanish-American culture of South America, see Jorge F. Rivas Pérez, "Domestic Display in the Spanish Overseas Territories," ed. Richard Aste, *Behind Closed Doors: Art in the Spanish American Home 1492–1898* (Brooklyn: Brooklyn Museum, 2013), 91–3.

55 López, "Economics of Yerba Mate," 494–6, 498–9.

56 Vera Blinn Reber, "Commerce and Industry in Nineteenth Century [*sic*] Paraguay: The Example of *Yerba Mate*," *Americas* 42 (1985): 48–9; and Folch, "Stimulating Consumption," 14.

57 See Folch, "Stimulating Consumption," 17–22; and Reber, "Commerce and Industry," 50.

58 Marschoff, "La Sociedad Virreinal en Buenos Aires," 83. For examples of such zoomorphic tripod designs see "Cup," British Museum, London, donated by George Rose-Innes, Am1943,07.5; and "Cup," British Museum, London, Am1924,0507.1.

59 Folch, "Stimulating Consumption," 10.

60 Marschoff, "La Sociedad Virreinal en Buenos Aires," 83. For an example, see "Cup," British Museum, London, donated by George Rose-Innes, Am1943,07.14.a.

61 Folch, "Stimulating Consumption," 23–4; and Pérez, "Domestic Display in the Spanish Overseas Territories," 91–3, who notes examples of yerba sets that were part of marriage agreements.

62 See, for example, "Cup," British Museum, London, Am1924,0507.3.a, apparently owned by the Peruvian Marquis of Negreiros, Domingo Negreiros y Gondra, and carved with his name and the date, 1778; or the probably more recent "Mate Cup and Stand," Brooklyn Museum,

Brooklyn, bequest of Margarita H. Button, 2011.60.14a-b. For a Peruvian coconut yerba cup in context with Peruvian harnessed yerba *jícaras,* see Elena Phipps, Johanna Hecht, and Cristina Esteras Martin, *The Colonial Andes: Tapestries and Silverwork* (New York: Metropolitan Museum of Art, 2004), 349–50.

63 Amaro Villanueva, *El Arte de Cebar: El Lenguaje Del Mate*, intro. Sergio Delgado, chronology Guillermo Mondejar (Paraná: Ediciones UNL, 2018), 65 and 75.

64 Norton, *Sacred Gifts, Profane Pleasures*, 20–8.

65 Caracas even became a cacao production and shipping centre: Jamieson, "Essence of Commodification," 281. A range of documentary evidence shows chocolate, *jícaras,* and *cocos chocolateros* in Spanish Florida by the mid-seventeenth century, and chocolate was drunk in present-day Texas and California by the eighteenth century; Margaret A. Graham and Russel K. Skowronek, "Chocolate on the Borderlands of New Spain," *Journal of Historical Archaeology* 20 (2016): 650.

66 Jamieson, "Essence of Commodification," 280–1.

67 Duarte, *El Arte del Tomar el Chocolate*, 61–2.

68 Jamieson uses the term this way, discussing "porcelain *jícara*" in "Essence of Commodification," 285, and describes a "tall, flaring" shape not found in gourd *jícaras.* Marcy Norton, "Tasting Empire: Chocolate and the European Internalization of Mesoamerican Aesthetics," *American Historical Review* 111 (2006): 667n25 and 672, where Norton notes the original term for a painted chocolate gourd as *xicalli.* See also 686.

69 Graham and Skowronek, "Chocolate on the Borderlands of New Spain," 661.

70 Norton, "Tasting Empire," 682–3. For *jícaras* involved in a famous property dispute in 1641–2, see Beatriz Cabezon and Louis Evan Grivetti, "Symbols from Ancient Times: Paleography and the St. Augustine Chocolate Saga," in *Chocolate: History, Culture, and Heritage*, ed. Louis Evan Grivetti and Howard-Yana Shapiro (Hoboken, NJ: Wiley, 2009), 678–81. Notably, the *jícaras* described are not "harnessed" or "garnished" as the *cocos* are, but described as painted (*pintadas*) or perhaps gilded (*doradas*), though when the coconut harness was gilded a different term was used, *sobredorada.*

71 Graham and Skowronek, "Chocolate on the Borderlands of New Spain," 658; and Louis Evan Grivetti, Patricia Barriga, and Beatriz Cabezon, "Sailors, Soldiers and Padres: California Chocolate, 1542?–1840," in *Chocolate: History, Culture, and Heritage*, ed. Grivetti and Shapiro, 439–63.

72 For example, see the harnessed morro *jícara* from Guatemala and commentary in Cristina Esteras Martin, *La Platería en el Reino de Guatemala Siglos XVI–XIX* (Guatemala City: Fundación Albergue Hermano Pedro, 1994), 98–9. Guatemala was a hub of cacao farming in the seventeenth century. Norton, "Tasting Empire," 676n48. For a less ornate example showing use of a different type of gourd, see "Cup," British Museum, London, Am1924,0507.2. For an example in art, see Antonio de Pereda's 1652 work, "Still Life with an Ebony Chest," ΓЄ-377, Hermitage Museum, St. Petersburg. *Jícara* identified as Venezuelan were among the chocolateware being exported to Spain in 1641. Cabezon and Grivetti, "Symbols from Ancient Times," 680.

73 An early Coliman will even identifies a harnessed coconut cup as having a cover, hinting that more *cocos* were covered than extant examples suggest: Paulina Machuca, "De Porcelanas Chinas y Otros Menesteres. Cultura Material de Origen Asiático en Colima, Siglo XVI–XVII," *Relaciones* 33 (2012): 78.

74 As with harnessed gourds, *cocos* occasionally feature in visual art as well, such as Antonio Pérez de Aguilar's 1769 work, "Cupboard." Antonio Pérez de Aguilar, "Cupboard," Museo National de Arte, Mexico City.

75 Exceptions prove the rule, as a few examples of tankard-style or standing coconut cups of purely European design exist that were manufactured in Central and South America. See, for example, "Cup," British Museum, London, donated by Col. F. H. Ward, Am1924,0609.1.a.

76 Duarte, *El Arte del Tomar el Chocolate*, 62.

77 For another example of a Mexican *coco*, see "Coconut-Shell Cup (*Coco Chocolatero*)," Los Angeles County Museum of Art, Los Angeles, gift of Ronald A. Belkin, Long Beach, California, in memory of Charles B. Tate, M.2015.69.2. For examples from the Museo Franz Mayer collection, see *The Grandeur of Viceregal Mexico: Treasures from the Museo Franz*

Mayer, ed. Héctor Rivero and Bonnelli Miranda (Houston: University of Texas Press, 2002), 256–62.

78 For examples, see cups in n77.

79 For evidence of painted or paste inlay, see Martin, *La Platería en el Reino de Guatemala*, 99. For an example of an inlaid *coco*, see Gustavo Curiel, "Los Ajuares Domésticos Novohispano," in *Museo Franz Mayer: 20 Año de Arte y Cultura en México*, ed. Federico Rubli Kaiser (Mexico: Chapa, 2006), 342; and for discussion of this cup in English, see Rivero, *Grandeur of Viceregal Mexico*, 260–1.

80 For example, see the very similar lion handles on the following cups: "Coconut-Shell Cup (*Coco Chocolatero*)," Los Angeles County Historical Museum of Art, Los Angeles, gift of Ronald A. Belkin, Long Beach, California, in memory of Charles B. Tate, M.2015.69.3; "Cup," Brooklyn Museum, Brooklyn, 61.117.3, gift of Mr. and Mrs. Henry C. Stockman; Rivero, *Grandeur of Viceregal Mexico*, 257; Roberto López Bravo, "Iconografía y Uso del Chocolate en el Museo Regional Chiapas," *Gaceta de Museos* 50 (2011): 29; and the *morro* in Martin, *La Platería en el Reino de Guatemala*, 99.

81 Pascal Rihouet, "Veronese's Goblets: Glass Design and the Civilizing Process," *Journal of Design History* 26 (2013): 133–51. One can see Spanish examples of these gestures as adopted by peasants in two early seventeenth-century paintings by Diego Velázquez: *The Waterseller of Seville*, Apsley House, London; and *The Lunch*, Hermitage Museum, St. Petersburg.

82 Barnet Pavao-Zuckerman and Diana DiPaolo Lauren, "Presentation Is Everything: Foodways, Tablewares, and Colonial Identity at Presidio Los Adaes," *International Journal of Archaeology* 16 (2012): 221–3. Pavao-Zuckerman and Lauren do not discuss *cocos* specifically, but identify tableware as a vital status-marker in border communities where diet was similar across classes. The association of coconut cups with the Spanish leave me skeptical of Alfredo Taullard's claim that coconut cups were employed in Peru for chicha, Alfredo Taullard, *Platería Sudamericana* (Buenos Aires: Peuser, 1941), 33. In 1941, Taullard was not expected to support this claim, but more recent research highlights the persistent low

class (and indigenous) associations of chicha: Esteban Mira Caballos, "Vinos y élites en la América de la Conquista," *Iberoamericana* 15 (2015): 20. While more research is certainly called for, if coconut cups were adopted for chicha-drinking in Peru, it may have been a deliberately mestizing adoption or post-date independence.

83 Peter Villella, *Indigenous Elites and Creole Identity in Colonial Mexico, 1500–1800* (Cambridge: Cambridge University Press, 2016), 307.

84 Pérez, "Domestic Display in the Spanish Overseas Territories," 91–4.

85 Duarte, *El Arte del Tomar el Chocolate*, 103.

CHAPTER 4

1 I investigate the versions of this verse and its *mouvance* across Europe in more detail in "Unde Versus," a chapter in the book I am writing about late medieval theories of consent.

2 Liber Extra with the *Glossa Ordinaria* of Bernard of Parma, gloss on 1.29.1 "pari pena," in the Editio Romana, 1582, col. 327, available online at http://digital.library.ucla.edu/canonlaw/.

3 London, British Library, MS Royal 10 e iv, fol. 59r, col. i, see http://www.bl.uk/manuscripts/Viewer.aspx?ref=royal_ms_10_e_iv_fs001r.

4 https://imagines.manuscriptorium.com/loris/AIPDIG-NKCR__XI_E_3_____49DL3VD-cs/ID0013v/full/full/0/default.jpg.

5 N. Kathleen Hayles, "How We Read: Close, Hyper, Machine," *ADE Bulletin* 150 (2011): 62–79, reviews research on how reading is affected by technology and different modes of reading. However, our understanding of associative reading would profit from considering older technologies as well as newer ones. See also Jerome McGann, *Radiant Textuality: Literary Studies after the World Wide Web* (New York: Palgrave, 2001).

6 On memes see, for example, Limor Shifman, *Memes in Digital Culture* (Cambridge, MA: MIT Press, 2014).

7 See C. W. Marx, "The Middle English Verse 'Lamentation of Mary to Saint Bernard' and the 'Quis dabit,'" in *Studies in the Vernon Manuscript*, ed. Derek Pearsall, 137–57 (Cambridge: Brewer, 1990).

8 Gen. 1:22, 1:28, 8:17, 9:1, 9:7.

9 *The Book of Margery Kempe*, ed. Lynn Staley, TEAMS Middle English
   Texts Series (Kalamazoo, MI: Medieval Institute Publications, 1996),
   http://d.lib.rochester.edu/teams/text/staley-book-of-margery-kempe-
   book-i-part-ii, chap. 51, line 2843. See also Naoë Kukita Yoshikawa,
   "The Making of The Book of Margery Kempe: The Issue of Discretio
   Spirituum Reconsidered," *English Studies* 92 no. 2 (2011): 119–37,
   doi: 10.1080/0013838X.2011.553919.

10 Geoffrey Chaucer, "General Prologue," in *The Riverside Chaucer*, 3rd ed.,
   gen. ed. Larry D. Benson et al. (Boston: Houghton Mifflin, 1987), frag. 1,
   line 646.

11 James M. Dean, ed., *Mum and the Sothsegger*, in *Richard the
   Redeless and Mum and the Sothsegger*, TEAMS Middle English
   Text Series (Kalamazoo, MI: Medieval Institute Publications,
   2000), lines 743–9, http://d.lib.rochester.edu/teams/publication/
   dean-richard-the-redeless-and-mum-and-the-sothsegger.

12 Thank you to Stephen Yeager for discussion of this point.

13 For a comprehensive guide to the sources of legal and penitential quotation in *Piers Plowman*, see John A. Alford, *Piers Plowman: A Guide to the
   Quotations* (Binghamton, NY: MRTS, 1992). This intensively researched
   volume is in itself a guide to the sources of quotation in the tradition
   more broadly.

14 On the development of legal tags as a means of argument, see Peter
   Stein, *Regulae Iuris: From Juristic Rules to Legal Maxims* (Cambridge:
   Cambridge University Press, 1966). On legal language in narrative
   poetry, the foundational study is R. Howard Bloch, *Medieval French
   Literature and Law* (Berkeley: University of California Press, 1977);
   most recently see Candace Barrington and Sebastian Sobecki, eds., *The
   Cambridge Companion to Literature and Law* (Cambridge: Cambridge
   University Press, 2019). For an introduction to medieval legal procedures,
   see Anthony Musson, *Medieval Law in Context: The Growth of Legal
   Consciousness from Magna Carta to the Peasants' Revolt* (Manchester:
   Manchester University Press, 2001); James A. Brundage, *The Medieval
   Origins of the Legal Profession: Canonists, Civilians, and Courts* (Chicago:
   University of Chicago Press, 2008).

15 Rachel Koopmans, *Wonderful to Relate: Miracle Stories and Miracle Collecting in High Medieval England* (Philadelphia: University of Pennsylvania Press, 2011).

16 For a preliminary survey, see Fiona Somerset, "Lollards and Religious Writings," in Barrington and Sobecki, eds., *Cambridge Companion to Literature and Law*, 167–77. Previous attention to Wycliffite attitudes to canon law can be found in Anne Hudson, *The Premature Reformation; Wycliffite Texts and Lollard History* (Oxford: Oxford University Press, 1988); Christina Von Nolcken, *The Middle English Translation of the Rosarium Theologie: A Selection*, Middle English Texts, 10 (Heidelberg: Carl Winter, 1979); Ian Christopher Levy, "Texts for a Poor Church: John Wyclif and the Decretals," *Essays in Medieval Studies* 20, no. 1 (2003): 94–107.

17 Brundage, *Medieval Origins*.

18 For an introductory study, see James A. Brundage, *Medieval Canon Law* (Harlow: Pearson, 1995). For a comprehensive introductory bibliography, see Edward Peters and Melodie H. Eichbauer, "Canon Law," in *Oxford Bibliographies Online*, doi: 10.1093/OBO/9780195396584-0033.

19 For a brief introduction to Gratian's *Decretum*, see Katherine Christensen, "Introduction," in *Gratian: The Treatise on Laws*, trans. Augustine Thompson O. P. and James Gordley, ix–xxvii (Washington, DC: Catholic University of America Press, 1993).

20 For a detailed investigation of the stages of the text's composition, see Anders Winroth, *The Making of Gratian's Decretum* (Cambridge: Cambridge University Press, 2000).

21 On canon law commentators, see Kenneth Pennington and Charles Donahue, "Bio-Bibliographical Guide to Medieval and Early Modern Jurists," Ames Foundation, http://amesfoundation.law.harvard.edu/BioBibCanonists/HomePage_biobib2.php. For a more detailed survey history of canon law, see Wilfried Hartmann and Kenneth Pennington, eds., *The History of Medieval Canon Law in the Classical Period, 1140–1234* (Washington, DC: Catholic University of America Press, 2008).

22 A description is available in the British Library online catalogue: http://searcharchives.bl.uk/IAMS_VU2:IAMS040-002106542 , accessed 9 November 2019.

23 On these pledges and the history of the loan chests at Oxford, see
   Jennifer Adams, "John Wyclif's Loan and the Production of Oxford's
   Academic Community," with thanks to the author for the opportunity to
   read this essay in draft.

24 Kathryn Kerby-Fulton, "Afterword," *The Medieval Manuscript Book:
   Cultural Approaches*, ed. Michael Johnston and Michael Van Dussen
   (Cambridge: Cambridge University Press, 2015), 248.

25 See J. I. Catto, "Wyclif and Wycliffism at Oxford, 1356–1450," in *The
   History of the University of Oxford*, ed. J. I. Catto and Ralph Evans
   (Oxford: Oxford University Press, 1992), 2:175–261; Anne Hudson,
   "'Who Is My Neighbour?' Some Problems of Definition on the Borders
   of Orthodoxy and Heresy," in *Wycliffite Controversies*, ed. Mishtooni
   C. A. Bose and J. Patrick Hornbeck, 79–96 (Turnhout: Brepols, 2012).

26 On the distinction between *latria* and *dulia*, and its use by Wycliffite
   writers, see Anne Hudson, ed., *Two Wycliffite Texts*, EETS 301 (1993),
   120, note to lines 1051–61. For a brief bibliography of Wycliffite and
   anti-Wycliffite writings on images, see Anne Hudson, ed., *Selections from
   English Wycliffite Writings* (Cambridge: Cambridge University Press,
   1978), headnote to "Images and Pilgrimages," 179–81.

27 The biblical prefaces and a number of tracts in favour of biblical
   translation appear in Mary Dove, ed., *The Earliest Advocates of the
   English Bible: The Texts of the Medieval Debate* (Exeter: University
   of Exeter Press, 2010). The Bible summary in Oxford, Trinity College
   MS 93 contains a summary of the whole Bible; see Fiona Somerset,
   Feeling Like Saints: Lollard Writings after Wyclif (Ithaca, NY: Cornell
   University Press, 2014), 166–202. The text now known as the *Thirty-
   Seven Conclusions* was published as the *Remonstrance against Romish
   Corruptions*, ed. J. Forshall (London, 1851).

28 A convenient translation is *Gratian: The Treatise on Laws*, trans.
   Thompson and Gordley, but note Anders Winroth's reservations, *Making
   of Gratian's Decretum*, 9n20.

29 "Littera gesta docet, quid credas allegoria, / Moralis quid agas, quo
   tendas anagogia." This distich is attributed to Augustine of Dacia, and
   very widely quoted. Sixteen examples appear in the In Principio database,
   for example.

30 Lucie Doležalova has published several articles on biblical mnemonics: see especially "Latin Mnemonic Verses Combining the Ten Commandments with the Ten Plagues of Egypt Transmitted in Late Medieval Bohemia," in *The Ten Commandments in Medieval and Early Modern Culture*, ed. Youri Desplenter, Jürgen Pieters, and Walter Melion, 152–72 (Leiden: Brill, 2017).

31 "Hoc vetus hoc nouum sic soluere non valet omnium / Cum promptum sit iura iuribus concordare."

32 On the influence of grammar school teaching and its fundamental texts on medieval literary culture more broadly, see Christopher Cannon, *From Literacy to Literature: England, 1300–1400* (Oxford: Oxford University Press, 2016).

33 John Wyclif, *Tractatus de Officio Regis*, ed. Alfred W. Pollard and Charles Sayle, Wyclif's Latin Works vol. 8 (London, 1887), esp. 83–97.

34 See, for example, Karla Taylor, "Proverbs and the Authentication of Convention in Troilus and Criseyde," in *Chaucer's 'Troilus': Essays in Criticism*, ed. Stephen A. Barney, 277–96 (Hamden, CT: Archon, 1980); Christopher Cannon, "Proverbs and the Wisdom of Literature: The Proverbs of Alfred and Chaucer's Tale of Melibee," *Textual Practice* 24 (2010): 407–34; Emily Steiner, *Reading Piers Plowman* (Cambridge: Cambridge University Press, 2013), 101–3, 209–10; Alexandra Gillespie, "Unknowe, unkow, Vncovthe, uncouth: From Chaucer and Gower to Spenser and Milton," in *From Medieval into Renaissance: Essays for Helen Cooper*, ed. Andrew King and Matthew Woodcock, 15–34 (Woodbridge: D. S. Brewer, 2016).

35 Fourteen examples (not including the ones discussed here) appear in the In Principio database, for example.

36 Perhaps the fullest exposition of this point of view may be found in *Book to a Mother*, which seeks to persuade its addressee (and all subsequent readers) that a holy life may best be pursued outside a convent; see Adrian James McCarthy, *Book to a Mother: An Edition with Commentary* (Salzburg, Austria: Institut für Anglistik und Amerikanistik, Universität Salzburg, 1981).

37 On this trend, see Nicole Rice, *Lay Piety and Religious Discipline in Middle English Literature* (Cambridge: Cambridge University Press, 2012).

38 *The Castle of Perseverance*, ed. David N. Klausner (Kalamazoo, MI: Medieval Institute Publications, 2010), line 2364a.

CHAPTER 5

1 Martin Camargo, *Ars Dictaminis, Ars Dictandi* (Turnhout: Brepols, 1991).
2 On protocols, see chapter 2 in this volume.
3 On the explosion of documentary culture in the twelfth century, see Robert L. Benson and Giles Constable, *Renaissance and Renewal in the Twelfth Century* (Toronto: University of Toronto Press, 1999); Giles Constable, *Letters and Letter-Collections* (Turnhout: Brepols, 1976); M. T. Clanchy, *From Memory to Written Record: England 1066–1307* (London: Wiley Blackwell, 1979).
4 *The Letters of Peter the Venerable*, ed. Giles Constable (Cambridge, MA: Harvard University Press, 1967).
5 Gillian R. Knight, *The Correspondence between Peter the Venerable and Bernard of Clairvaux: A Semantic and Structural Analysis* (New York: Routledge, 2017).
6 C. Stephen Jaeger, *The Envy of Angels: Cathedral Schools and Social Ideals in Medieval Europe, 950–1200* (Philadelphia: University of Pennsylvania Press, 1994).
7 "As research in the fields of medieval history, cultural studies and literary studies has shown, the performative acts of people co-present in shared spaces are foundational for aristocratic practices." Markus Stock, "Letter, Word, and Good Messengers: Towards an Archaeology of Remote Communication," *Interdisciplinary Science Reviews* 37, no. 4 (2012): 300.
8 "Mansit in me constanter ex illo tempore, et utinam sic in te maneat Christi causa coepta mutua caritas,... Cumque hanc omni auro cariorem, omni gemma clariorem in sinu meo reposuerim, in thesauris abscond-erim, miror, quod tanto tempore non qualia uellem indicia huius a te michi custoditae caritatis accaeperim. Ago quidem gratias, quod sepe per quoslibet salutationibus missis, non penitus te amici oblitum signasti. Sed queror, quod certiora per litteras indicia hactenus non dedisti. Certiora dixi, quia nescit carta impressum mutare sermonem, cum lo-quentium lingua addendo uel demendo iniuncta mutet sepius ueritatem."

All quotations from the letter are from the edition of Giles Constable (see note 4), 194–5. Translations of Peter's letter are my own.

9 See Stock, "Letter, Word, and Good Messengers," 299–313, on the persistent anxiety about messengers in medieval German literature.

10 Ann Marie Rasmussen and Markus Stock, "Medieval Media," *Seminar* 52, no. 2 (2016): 101.

11 Stock, "Letter, Word, and Good Messengers," 300–1; Horst Wenzel, "Boten und Briefe: Zum Verhältnis Körperlicher und Nichtkörperlicher Nachrichtenträger," in *Gespräche—Boten—Briefe: Körpegedächtnis und Schriftgedächtnis im Mittelalter*, ed. Horst Wenzel, Philologische Studien und Quellen 143 (Berlin: Erich Schmidt, 1997), 97–101. On the possibility of message failure as a condition of mediality, see John Guillory, "Genesis of the Media Concept," *Critical Inquiry* 36, no. 2 (2010): 321–62.

12 Constable, *Letters and Letter-Collections*, 18.

13 Constable, *Letters and Letter-Collections*, 18.

14 For a lucid exposition of the Peircean terminology used here with respect to media theory, see Elayne Oliphant, "sign," Chicago School of Media Theory, https://lucian.uchicago.edu/blogs/mediatheory/keywords/sign/; and Drew Huening. "symbol/index/icon," Chicago School of Media Theory, https://lucian.uchicago.edu/blogs/mediatheory/keywords/symbolindexicon/.

15 This is the topic of Jacques Derrida's *The Postcard: From Socrates to Freud and Beyond*, trans. Alan Bass (Chicago: University of Chicago Press, 1987).

16 Stock, "Letter, Word, and Good Messengers," 300, citing Wenzel, "Boten und Briefe," u.a.

17 This point is made elsewhere in Peter's letters: "Words that are conveyed to the hearts of others through foreign ears have a way of increasing, changing, or losing their true meaning, which is either misunderstood, or neglected, or distorted by the ignorance, carelessness, or assiduity of the messenger." Letter 69, Constable, *Letters and Letter-Collections*, 18.

18 Erving Goffman, "On Face-Work: An Analysis of Ritual Elements in Social Interaction," in *Interaction Ritual: Essays on Face-to-Face Behavior* (New York: Pantheon Books, 1982), 5–45; Bronisław Malinowski, "On

Phatic Communion," in *The Discourse Reader*, ed. Adam Jaworski and Nikolas Coupland (New York: Routledge, 2014), 296–8.

19 The concept of ratification used here is developed by Norman Fairclough, *Language and Power* (New York: Longman, 1989).

20 Hans Ulrich Gumbrecht, *Production of Presence: What Meaning Cannot Convey* (Stanford, CA: Stanford University Press, 2004).

21 In the introduction to the English translation of Kittler's *Discourse Networks 1800/1900*, David E. Welberry speaks of re-analyzing society as interacting subsystems endowed with their particular technologies and protocols. David Wellbery, "Foreword," in *Discourse Networks 1800/1900* (Stanford, CA: Stanford University Press, 2007), xvii; Discursive practice is the name that Norman Fairclough and other scholars working in critical discourse analysis give to such protocols, and to the protocols that order their interaction. Norman Fairclough, *Media Discourse* (London: Bloomsbury Academic, 2011), 16–18.

22 Bruno Latour, *Reassembling the Social: An Introduction to Actor-Network-Theory*, Clarendon Lectures in Management Studies (Oxford: Oxford University Press, 2007), 27–32.

23 "utinam sic in te maneat Christi causa coepta mutua caritas." See note 4.

24 Jaeger, *Envy of Angels.*

25 Fairclough, *Media Discourse*, 38.

26 The letters of Peter of Blois were a medieval "best-seller," surviving in over three hundred manuscripts, and this later Peter both wrote his letters and revised them for collection. In doing so he was following the example of celebrated letter-writers of previous generations including Peter the Venerable, Bernard of Clairvaux, John of Salisbury, and Peter of Celle; of these two pairs, their correspondence survives individually and as exchanges. John D. Cotts, *The Clerical Dilemma: Peter of Blois and Literate Culture in the Twelfth Century* (Washington, DC: Catholic University of America Press, 2009), esp. 50–5.

27 Jean Leclercq gave a vivid account of the "postal system" operating among monastic houses:

> A postal service which operated between abbeys, particularly at times when a death occurred, made it possible for the monks to carry on

correspondence with each other. On these occasions, announcements, called rolls (*rotuli*) would be sent to other religious houses. At the various stops on his journey, the roll-carrier (*rolliger*) would report the news vocally and also deliver business correspondence. The announcement was copied on a strip of parchment at the end of which a large space was left blank. Then the whole was rolled up and the "roll" entrusted to a special carrier who went off to display it at all the religious houses who were associated in the same compact of sharing in prayer, which were often quite numerous. The roll-carrier would start off with the letter announcing a death, enclosed in a wooden or metal cylinder hanging at his side. One after the other he would visit the appointed addresses. There, bells were rung to announce his visit, and the monks would gather in the cloister, the chapter or, more customarily, in the church. (Jean Leclercq, *The Love of Learning and the Desire for God: A Study of Monastic Culture* [New York: Fordham University Press, 2014], 179–80.)

28 Sita Steckel, *Kulturen des Lehrens im Früh- und Hochmittelalter: Autorität, Wissenskonzepte und Netzwerke von Gelehrten* (Wien, Köln, Weimar, 2010), https://doi.org/10.7788/boehlau.9783412213466.

29 Many of these letters are collected in Ernst Dümmler, *Libelli de lite imperatorvm et pontificvm saecvlis XI. et XII. conscripti*, Monumenta Germaniae Historica (Hannover: Brepols, 1956).

30 For a comprehensive overview of the role of letters and propaganda in the controversy, see Ian Stuart Robinson, *Authority and Resistance in the Investiture Contest: The Polemical Literature of the Late 11th Century* (Manchester: Manchester University Press, 1978).

31 Epistolary training for clerics was formalized in the Carolingian Empire, ran through the Ottonian Cathedral school reforms of the later 900s, and extended to the Low Countries and France during the 1000s. The centrality of letter-writing became intensified in the twelfth century when masters specialized in the *ars dictaminis* from England to Italy. See Steckel, *Kulturen des Lehrens im Früh- und Hochmittelalter*; and Ronald G. Witt, *The Two Latin Cultures and the Foundation of Renaissance*

Humanism in Medieval Italy (Cambridge: Cambridge University Press, 2012), 76, 113, 229; for a briefer overview focused more narrowly on English and French contexts, see John Van Engen, "Letters, Schools, and Written Culture in the Eleventh and Twelfth Centuries," in *Dialektik und Rhetorik im früheren und hohen Mittelalter: Rezeption, Überlieferung und gesellschaftliche Wirkung antiker Gelehrsamkeit vornehmlich im 9. und 12. Jahrhundert*, ed. Johannes Fried (Munich: Oldenbourg, 1997), 98–132.

32 William Doty formulated the phrase *epistolary situation* and its basic foundational definition: "Someone wishes to communicate in writing with someone else distant from them in space (primarily) or time." Doty, "The Classification of Epistolary Literature," *Catholic Biblical Quarterly* 31, no. 2 (1969): 183–99.

33 Jay David Bolter and Richard Grusin, *Remediation: Understanding New Media* (Cambridge, MA: MIT Press, 2000), 5–13, 30; Lisa Gitelman, *Always Already New: Media, History, and the Data of Culture* (Cambridge, MA: MIT Press, 2008), 7–9; Rasmussen and Stock review debates (especially in German-language scholarship) over the applicability of the media concept to studying medieval culture and finally argue carefully for its value. Rasmussen and Stock, "Medieval Media," 100–2.

34 A recent collection attests to the range and depth of Jaeger's influence on the study of medieval culture: Brigitte Miriam Bedos-Rezak and Martha Dana Rust, *Faces of Charisma* (Boston: Brill, 2018).

35 Jaeger, *Envy of Angels*, 316.

36 Jaeger, *Envy of Angels*, 7.

37 Gumbrecht, *Production of Presence*, esp. 78–110.

38 Jaeger, *Envy of Angels*, 190.

39 See John of Salisbury, *The Metalogicon: A Twelfth-Century Defense of the Verbal and Logical Arts of the Trivium*, trans. Daniel D. McGarry (Berkeley: University of California Press, 1955), 65–70.

40 Jaeger, *Envy of Angels*, 15.

41 Bolter and Grusin, *Remediation*, esp. 5–15. Swagato Chakravorty contextualizes Bolter and Grusin's concept of remediation within theories of mediation more broadly: "mediation," Chicago School of Media Theory, https://lucian.uchicago.edu/blogs/mediatheory/keywords/mediation/.

42 On the transition from ancient to medieval rhetoric, see James J. Murphy, *Rhetoric in the Middle Ages: A History of Rhetorical Theory from Saint Augustine to the Renaissance* (Berkeley: University of California Press, 1974); the picture of rhetoric given here differs from John Guillory's report of a rationalistic seventeenth-century definition of rhetoric as a set of techniques of "verbal seduction" designed to serve the "exploitation of fear and ignorance." Guillory, "Genesis," 325–6.

43 See M. M. Bakhtin, *Speech Genres and Other Late Essays*, ed. Michael Holquist and Caryl Emerson, trans. Vern McGee (Austin: University of Texas Press, 1986); Fairclough, *Media Discourse*, 14, 38.

44 Giles Constable, "The Structure of Medieval Society According to the *Dictatores* of the Twelfth Century," in *Law Church and Society: Essays in Honor of Stephan Kuttner*, ed. Kenneth Pennington and Robert Somerville (Philadelphia: University of Pennsylvania Press, 1977), 253–67.

45 See Steckel, *Kulturen des Lehrens im Früh- und Hochmittelalter*.

46 See Teun van Dijk, *Discourse as Social Interaction* (Los Angeles: SAGE, 2009), 6–7.

47 Fairclough, *Media Discourse*, esp. 63–7.

48 Michel de Certeau, *The Practice of Everyday Life*, trans. Steven Rendall (Berkeley: University of California Press, 2008), 132; this resembles the idea of *training*, "the regiment that bodies pass through" as replacing *praxis* in post-hermeneutical criticism. Wellbery, "Foreword," xv.

49 de Certeau, *Practice of Everyday Life*, 132.

50 de Certeau, *Practice of Everyday Life*, 134.

51 "Feci hoc, etiam dum adhuc absentia tua uultum corporis tui michi inuidens abscondebat, quia iam fama uelocior corpore beatae animae tuae faciem oculis mentis meae modo quo poterat inferebat."

52 For a recent collection exploring the role of temporality in late medieval and early modern Europe across a number of textual and visual media, see Christian Kiening and Martina Stercken, *Temporality and Mediality in Late Medieval and Early Modern Culture* (Turnhout: Brepols, 2018).

53 Marie de France, *Marie de France: Poetry*, ed. and trans. Dorothy Gilbert (New York: W. W. Norton, 2015), lines 229–30.

54 Geoffrey Chaucer, *Troilus and Criseyde*, in *The Riverside Chaucer*, 3rd ed., ed. Larry Benson et al. (Boston: Houghton Mifflin, 1987), book 2, lines 1089–90.

55 Giles Constable, "Medieval Letters and the Letter Collection of Peter the Venerable," in *The Letters of Peter the Venerable*, ed. Giles Constable (Cambridge, MA: Harvard University Press, 1967), 2:47.

56 If, as Guillory suggests, a medium is recognizable by its capacity for failure, the failure of this step sometimes had crucial consequences, as when the imperial chancellor Rainald of Dassel deliberately rendered the Latin *beneficium* in a letter from the pope in a way that might imply the emperor's feudal subjection.

57 Bruno Scott James, trans. and ed., *The Letters of St. Bernard of Clairvaux* (Sutton: Stroud, 1998).

58 See note 3.

59 Knight, *Correspondence Between Peter the Venerable and Bernard of Clairvaux*.

60 "Feci hoc, etiam dum adhuc absentia tua uultum corporis tui michi inuidens abscondebat, quia iam fama uelocior corpore beatae animae tuae faciem oculis mentis meae modo quo poterat inferebat."

61 "At ubi quod diu negatum fuerat tandem sum assecutus, et phantasmata somniorum ueritate succedente euanuerunt, adhesit anima mea tibi, nec ab amore tuo ultra divelli potuit."

62 "Ita caritas tua totum me sibi deinceps uendicauit, ita uirtutes tuae et mores rapuerunt, ut nichil michi de me quod tuum non esset relinquerent, nichil tibi de te non meum esse permitterent. Mansit in me constanter ex illo tempore, et utinam sic in te maneat Christi causa coepta mutua caritas, quae sola quia nunquam excidere nouit, morem suum quantum ad te pertinet in me optime conseruauit." On the centrality of *mores* to the idea of the charismatic master and the difficulty of translating a word that conflates morals, customs, and habits, see Jaeger, *Envy of Angels*, 9–10.

63 François Recanati, "Le présent épistolaire: une perspective cognitive," *L'Information grammaticale* 66, no. 1 (1995), 38, https://doi.org/10.3406/igram.1995.3046.

64 Bolter and Grusin, *Remediation*, 30.

65 "Quam iucunde uero sint absentium littere amicorum, ipse nos exemplo proprio Seneca docet, ad amicum Lucilium quodam loco scribens: 'Quod frequenter mihi scribis, gratias ago. Nam quo uno modo potes te mihi ostendis. Nunquam epistolam tuam accipio, quin protinus una simus. Si imagines nobis amicorum absentium iucunde sunt, que memoriam renouant et desiderium absentie falso atque inani solatio leuant, quanto iucundiores sunt littere que amici absentis ueras notas afferunt?'" David Luscombe, ed., *The Letter Collection of Peter Abelard and Heloise*, trans. Betty Radice (Oxford: Oxford University Press, 2013), 2.4, 125.

66 "Per quos ut querela mea sopiatur, esse tuum ac reditum et statum domini papae non solum legatis meis sed et litteris tuis committe. Vtinam et te a curia laboriosa, et me a cura periculos expeditum ut semper optaui, nunquam mutandus unus locus retineret, una caritas uniret, unus Christus susciperet."

CHAPTER 6

1 Lesley Smith, *The* Glossa Ordinaria: *The Making of a Medieval Bible Commentary* (Leiden: Brepols, 2009), 230–4.

2 Patricia Stirnemann has identified the earliest surviving manuscript of each book of the *Gloss*, dividing its history into two principal stages of production: that of Laon, and that of Paris. Patricia Stirnemann, "Où ont été fabriqués les livres de la glose ordinaire dans la première moitié du XIIe siècle," in *Le XIIe siècle: Méditations et renouveau en France dans la première moitié du XIIe siècle*, ed. Françoise Gasparri, Cahiers du léopard d'or 3, 257–301 (Paris: Léopard d'or, 1994). See also Christopher F. R. De Hamel, *Glossed Books of the Bible and the Origins of the Paris Booktrade* (Woodbridge: Brewer, 1984), 87; Smith, Glossa Ordinaria, 105.

3 On the page's functions of boundary and shaper of the text, see Bonnie Mak, *How the Page Matters* (Toronto: University of Toronto Press, 2011), especially the discussion 9–17.

4 The classic treatment of the *Gloss*'s format is found in De Hamel, *Glossed Books of the Bible*, 15–25. It has since been updated by Smith in Glossa Ordinaria, 94–114.

5 Gilbert the Universal (d. 1134) is usually said to have authored the *Gloss* on Genesis, but the attribution is problematic. See Alice Hutton Sharp, "'Gilbertus Universalis' Reevaluated and the Authorship of the *Gloss* on Genesis," *Recherches de Théologie et Philosophie Médiévales* 83, no. 2 (2016): 225–43.

6 For some Carolingian predecessors, see Margaret Gibson, "The Place of the *Glossa ordinaria* in Medieval Exegesis," 6, reprinted in Gibson, *"Artes" and Bible in the Medieval West* (Aldershot, UK: Ashgate Variorum, 1993), 5–27; M. C. Ferrari, "Before the *Glossa Ordinaria*: The Ezekiel Fragment in Irish Minuscule Zürich, Staatsarchiv W 3.19. XII, and Other Experiments towards a Bible Commentée in the Early Middle Ages," in *Biblical Studies in the Early Middle Ages: Proceedings of the Conference on Biblical Studies in the Early Middle Ages*, ed. Claudio Leonardi and Giovanni Orlandi (Florence: SISMEL/Edizioni del Galluzzo, 2005), 285.

7 Smith, Glossa Ordinaria, 73–4.

8 "venerabilis memorie magister Gislebertus, veteris et novi Testamenti glosator eximius, qui universalis merito est appellatus, huius ecclesie canonicus" (Master Gilbert of venerable memory, extraordinary glossa-tor of the old and new Testaments, who is rightly called "the Universal," canon of this church). *Obituaires de la Province du Sens*, vol. 3, *Diocèses d'Orléans, d'Auxerre, et de Nevers*, ed. Alexandre Vidier and Léon Mirot (Paris, 1909), 239; "in cunctis huius mundi sapientium litteris et studiis ludens, omnem quoque studuit et potuit divinam quodammodo revocare et renovare scripturum" (playing in all the letters and studies of the wise men of this world, he studied and could, in a way, revive and renew all sacred Scripture). Bernard of Clairvaux, *Epistola* 24, *S. Bernardi opera*, vol. 7: *Epistolae I Corpus epistolarum 1–180*, ed. Jean Leclercq (Rome: Editiones Cistercienses, 1974), 77.

9 Karlfried Froehlich, "Walahfrid Strabo and the *Glossa Ordinaria:* The Making of a Myth," in *Studia Patristica 28: Papers Presented at the Eleventh International Conference on Patristic Studies Held in Oxford 1991*, ed. E. A. Livingstone, 192–6 (Leuven: Peeters, 1993); Beryl Smalley, *The Study of the Bible in the Middle Ages*, 3rd ed. (Oxford: Blackwells, 1983), 56.

10 Beryl Smalley, "Gilbertus Universalis Bishop of London (1128–1134) and the Problem of the 'Glossa Ordinaria,'" *RTAM* 7 (1935): 235–62, and *RTAM* 8 (1936): 24–64. J. de Blick, working at the same time as Beryl Smalley, definitively removed Strabo from the history of the *Glossa* in "L'œuvre exégétique de Walafrid Strabon et la Glossa ordinaria," *RTAM* 16 (1949): 5–28.

11 Smalley, "Gilbertus." "Anselm was certainly responsible for the *Gloss* on St. Paul and the Psalter, probably for that on the Fourth Gospel. His brother Ralph compiled the *Gloss* on St. Mattthew; his pupil Gilbet the Universal compiled the *Gloss* on the Pentateuch and the Greater Prophets and Lamentations, sometime before he became bishop of London in 1128": Smalley, *Study of the Bible in the Middle Ages*, 60.

12 See Joseph de Ghellinck, "The Sentences of Anselm of Laon and Their Place in the Codification of Theology during the XIIth Century," *Irish Theological Quarterly* 6 (1911): 427–41; Franz Bliemetzrieder, "Autour de l'œuvre théologique d'Anselme de Laon," *RTAM* 1 (1929): 435–83; Bliemetzrieder, "Robert von Melun und die Schule Anselmus von Laon," *Zeitschrift für Kirchengeschichte* 53 (1934): 117–70; Bliemetzrieder, "L'œuvre d'Anselme de Laon et la littérature contemporaine, II: Hughes de Rouen," *RTAM* 6 (1934): 261–83, and *RTAM* 7 (1935): 28–51.

13 "Verborum usum habebat mirabilem, sed sensum contemtibilem et ratione vacuum. Cum ignem accenderet, domum suam fumo implebat, non luce illustrabat." Peter Abelard, *Historia calamitatum*, ed. J. Monfrin (Paris: Librairie Philosophique J. Vrin, 1959), 68. The translation here is mine, but see also J. T. Muckle, *The Story of Abelard's Adversities: A Translation with Notes of the Historia Calamitatum* (Toronto: Pontifical Institute of Mediaeval Studies, 1954), 20.

14 Michael Clanchy and Lesley Smith, "Abelard's Description of the School of Laon: What Might It Tell Us about Early Scholastic Teaching?" *Nottingham Medieval Studies* 54 (2010): 1–34.

15 Guibert of Nogent, *De vita sua* 3.4, ed. Georges Bourgin (Paris, 1903), 139. For an English translation, see *A Monk's Confession: The Memoirs of Guibert of Nogent*, trans. Paul J. Archambault (University Park: Pennsylvania State University Press, 1996), 130.

16 John of Salisbury, *Metalogicon* 1.5, ed. Clement Webb (Oxford: Clarendon, 1929), 18. For an English translation of this passage, see *The Metalogicon of John of Salisbury: A Twelfth-Century Defense of the Verbal and Logical Arts of the Trivium*, trans. Daniel D. McGarry (Berkeley: University of California Press, 1955), 22. To quote one example of an elegy: "Hic iacet Anselmus nunc in cinerem resolutus, Cuius doctrina climata cuncta Latina / Exponendo sacras scriptrus atque docendo / [In] Domini nomen preciosum fudit odorem" (Here lies Anselm, now reduced to ashes, whose teaching poured out an odour precious to the name of the Lord into all the Latin world by explicating and teaching the sacred scriptures): London, British Library Cotton Fragments I, f. 12v., published in Albert Derolez, "Le 'Liber Floridus' et l'énigme du manuscrit Cotton Fragments Volume I," *Mittellateinisches Jahrbuch* 17 (1982): 120–9.

17 Rupert's critique of Anselm's teachings on God's will—specifically on whether or not God could will evil—can be seen in Rupert of Deutz, *De uoluntate Dei, Patrologia Latina* 170:437c. On the debate that wasn't, see Cédric Giraud, *Per verba magistri: Anselme de Laon et son école au XIIe siècle* (Turnhout: Brepols, 2010), 163; John H. Van Engen, *Rupert of Deutz* (Berkeley: University of California Press, 1983), 211. Historians of the school of Laon can make this sound like a singular event, but as Van Engen's study shows, it was part of a larger tour Rupert was making of northern France.

18 "Sententie quidem omnium catholicorum diuerse, sed non aduerse, in unam concurrunt conuenientiam, in uerbis uero sonant quedam quasi contrarietates" (Indeed, the sentences of all the fathers are diverse, but they are not adverse, and they come together into one harmony, although in words certain of them sound as if they are contradictory). Odon Lottin, *Psychologie et morale aux XIIe et XIIIe siècles,* vol. 5 (Gembloux, Belgium: J. Duculot, 1959), 175–6. On the dating and other matters of this text, see Hubert Silvestre, "À propos de la lettre d'Anselme de Laon à Héribrand de Saint-Laurent," *RTAM* 28 (1961): 5–25.

19 Alexander Andrée, "The *Glossa ordinaria* on the Gospel of John: A Preliminary Survey of the Manuscripts with a Presentation of the Text and Its Sources," *Revue Bénédictine* 118 (2008): 109–34.

20 For books of the *Glossa* surviving in multiple versions, see *Gilbertus Universalis: Glossa ordinaria in Lamentationes Ieremie Prophete: Prothemata et Liber I. A Critical Edition with an Introduction and a Translation*, ed. Alexander Andrée (Stockholm: Almquist & Wiksell, 2005), 92–3; Guy Lobrichon, "Une nouveauté: Les gloses de la Bible," in *Le Moyen Âge et la Bible*, Bible de tous les temps, ed. Pierre Riche and Guy Lobrichon (Paris: Beauchesne, 1984), 4:158–72; Alexander Andrée, "Le *Pater* (Matth. 6,9–13 et Luc. 11,2–4) dans l'exégèse de l'école de Laon: la *Glossa ordinaria et autres commentaires*," in *Le Pater noster au XIIe siècle: Lectures et usages*, ed. Francesco Siri (Turnhout: Brepols, 2015), 46–8. The two recensions of the *Glossa* on Genesis were first discussed in Philippe Buc, *L'ambiguïté du livre: Prince, pouvoir, et peuple dans les commentaires de la Bible au Moyen Âge* (Paris: Beauchesne, 1994), 72–4. I laid out the argument for an earlier source text in Hutton Sharp, "Textual Format and the Development of the Early *Glossa* on Genesis," *Mediaeval Studies* 78 (2016): 125–65.

21 Andrée, "*Glossa ordinaria* on the Gospel of John," 304.

22 De Hamel, *Glossed Books of the Bible*, 4; Smith, Glossa Ordinaria, 94.

23 De Hamel, *Glossed Books of the Bible*, 15.

24 De Hamel, *Glossed Books of the Bible*, 16–17; Smith, Glossa Ordinaria, 116.

25 De Hamel, *Glossed Books of the Bible*, 17.

26 Smith, Glossa Ordinaria, 114; De Hamel, *Glossed Books of the Bible*, 17.

27 Buc, *L'ambiguïté du livre*, 72–4.

28 Stirnemann, "Où ont été fabriqués les livres de la glose," 259–60.

29 Available through Gallica: https://gallica.bnf.fr/ark:/12148/btv1b10036613p.

30 Also available through Gallica: https://gallica.bnf.fr/ark:/12148/btv1b10039219w.

31 A full description of this manuscript can be found in Alice Hutton Sharp, "*In Principio:* The Origins of the *Glossa ordinaria* on Genesis 1–3" (PhD diss., University of Toronto, 2015), 242–5. The manuscript is listed in Léopold Delisle, *Inventaire des Manuscrits Latins de Saint Victor Conservés à la Bibliothèque Impériale sous les Numéros 14232–15175* (Paris, 1869, repr. New York: Johnson Reprint, 1965), 12.

32 These are folios 12r–12v (https://gallica.bnf.fr/ark:/12148/
btv1b10036613p/f13.image), 14r–14v (https://gallica.bnf.fr/ark:/12148/
btv1b10036613p/f15.image), and 19v–20r (https://gallica.bnf.fr/ark:/
12148/btv1b10036613p/f21.image).

33 For a full description, see Hutton Sharp, "*In Principio*," 245–8. The
manuscript is also briefly described in Philippe Lauer, *Catalogue
Général des Manuscrits Latins*, vol. 1, nos. 1–1438 (Paris: Bibliothèque
Nationale, 1939), 28; and with great detail by Dominique Stutzmann, "La
Bibliothèque de l'abbaye cistercienne de Fontenay (Côte d'Or)" (thesis,
École nationale des Chartes, 2002), 2:213–15.

34 The interwoven commentary covers Genesis 1:1–3:19, beginning fol. 3r
(https://gallica.bnf.fr/ark:/12148/btv1b10039219w/f3.image) and ending
fol. 23r (https://gallica.bnf.fr/ark:/12148/btv1b10039219w/f23.image).

35 A Genesis 3:20–31:43 is copied, with glosses, beginning on fol. 23v
(https://gallica.bnf.fr/ark:/12148/btv1b10039219w/f24.image) and ending
fol. 97r.

36 Fol. 98r (https://gallica.bnf.fr/ark:/12148/btv1b10039219w/f101.image) to
fol. 109v contain Genesis 47:7–50:25, unglossed.

37 E.g., fol. 6r (https://gallica.bnf.fr/ark:/12148/btv1b10036613p/f7.image).
These first three chapters are found on fols. 1r–22v; the remainder of
Genesis is found on fols. 23r–133v.

38 https://gallica.bnf.fr/ark:/12148/btv1b10036613p/f24.image.

39 Further details of this textual argument can be found in Hutton Sharp,
"Textual Format," 142–61.

40 For proof of the existence of this ur-commentary, with a focus on Genesis
1–3, see Hutton Sharp, "Textual Format," 144–53.

41 Hutton Sharp, "Textual Format," 162.

42 This likely explains one unusual characteristic of this gloss, namely, that
patristic are usually cited in the same order in each gloss.

43 Similar arguments have been made by Alexander Andrée, who argued
that Anselm's *Gloss* on the Gospel of John was a continuous commentary transformed into a gloss by students, and by Cédric Giraud, who
has argued that sentence collections were the projects of a community.
Andrée, "*Glossa ordinaria* on the Gospel of John," 304; Cédric Giraud,
"Per verba magistri: la langue des maîtres théologiens au premie XIIe

siècle," in *Zwischen Babel und Pfingsten—Entre Babel et Pentecôte*, ed. Peter von Moos (Zurich: LIT Verlag, 2008), 357–73.

44 See note 7, above.

45 De Hamel, *Glossed Books of the Bible*, 24; Smith, Glossa Ordinaria, 105–6.

46 De Hamel claimed that the alternate-line format was first seen in manuscripts formatted for Peter Lombard, which would make it too late for this argument. However, since then a number of earlier examples have been found. See De Hamel, *Glossed Books of the Bible*, 25; Teresa Gross-Diaz, *The Psalms Commentary of Gilbert of Poitiers: From Lectio Divina to the Lecture Room* (Leiden: Brill, 1996), 30–40, n55; Margaret Gibson, *The Early Medieval Bible: Its Production, Decoration and Use* (Cambridge: Cambridge University Press, 1994), 99; Ferrari, "Before the *Glossa Ordinaria*," 302–3.

47 Abelard, *Historia Calamitatum*, 69; Muckle, *Story of Abelard's Adversities*, 21–2.

48 Giulio Silano, "Introduction," in *The Sentences, Book 1: The Mystery of the Trinity*, trans. Giulio Silano, xxiii–xxiv (Toronto: Pontifical Institute of Mediaeval Studies, 2007).

49 This is the central argument of C. Stephen Jaeger's *The Envy of Angels: Cathedral Schools and Social Ideals in Medieval Europe, 950–1200* (Philadelphia: University of Pennsylvania Press, 2000). Jaeger begins his study of the cathedral schools with a problem akin to that brought up at the beginning of this chapter: in the eleventh century, numerous teachers were praised by their students for their erudition and learning, but the teaching they passed on has not survived. Jaeger argues that their reputations were built on teaching, which leaves no textual trace, chiefly words and bearing. *Envy of Angels*, 76–80.

50 Jaeger himself makes this connection: *Envy of Angels*, 81.

51 Matthew Doyle, *Peter Lombard and His Students* (Toronto: Pontifical Institute of Mediaeval Studies, 2016), 123.

52 Guibert, *De Vita Sua*, 3.4 (for the election) and 3.10 (for burial), 139 and 174–6; English translation in *A Monk's Confession*, 130 and 162–3.

53 Beryl Smalley, "Gilbertus Universalis, Bishop of London (1128–34)," *RTAM* 7 (1935): 245.

PRIMARY SOURCES

Andrée, Alexander, ed. *Gilbertus Universalis: Glossa ordinaria in Lamentationes Ieremie Prophete: Prothemata et Liber I. A Critical Edition with an Introduction and a Translation*. Stockholm: Almquist & Wiksell, 2005.

Archambault, Paul J., trans. *A Monk's Confession: The Memoirs of Guibert of Nogent*. University Park: Pennsylvania State University Press, 1996.

Atkinson, J. A., B. Flynn, V. Portass, K. Singlehurst, and J. J. Smith, eds. *Darlington Wills and Inventories 1600–1625*. Newcastle: Boydell, 1993.

Bacon, Francis. *Novum Organum*. Edited by Thomas Fowler. Oxford: Clarendon Press, 1878.

—. *The New Organon*. Edited by Lisa Jardine and Michael Silverthorne. Cambridge: Cambridge University Press, 2000.

Baker, Peter S., and Michael Lapidge, ed. and trans. *Byrhtferth's Enchiridion*. EETS s.s. 15. Oxford: Oxford University Press, 1995.

Barney, Stephen A, W. J. Lewis, and J. A. Beach, trans. *The Etymologies of Isidore of Seville*. Cambridge: Cambridge University Press, 2006.

Barthomeus anglicus de Proprietatibus rerum. Nuremberg: Anton Koberger, 1492. In the Collection of the Corning Museum of Glass. https://www.cmog.org/library/de-proprietatibus-rerum-bartholomeus anglicus.

Benson, Larry D., gen. ed. *The Riverside Chaucer*, 3rd ed. New York: Houghton Mifflin, 1987.

Bernard of Clairvaux. *The Letters of St. Bernard of Clairvaux*. Edited and translated by Bruno Scott James. Stroud: Sutton, 1998.

—. *S. Bernardi opera*, vol. 7: *Epistolae* I *Corpus epistolarum 1–180*. Edited by
Jean Leclercq. Rome: Editiones Cistercienses, 1974.

Boatwright, Lesley, Moira Habberjam, and Peter Hammond, eds. *The
Logge Register of Prerogative Court of Canterbury Wills 1479–1486*. 2 vols.
Gorsedene: Richard III Society, 2008.

Brewer, J. S., ed. *Fr. Rogeri Bacon: Opera quaedam hactenus inedita, Vol. I*.
London: Longman, Green and Roberts, 1859.

Brown, George Hardin, and Frederick M. Biggs. "De temporum ratione,"
in *Bede: Part 1, Fascicles 1–4*, 84–116. Amsterdam: Amsterdam University
Press, 2017.

Burnett, Charles, ed. and trans. *Adelard of Bath, Conversations with his
Nephew:* On the Same and the Different, Questions on Natural Science,
and On Birds. Cambridge Medieval Classics 9. Cambridge: Cambridge
University Press, 1998.

Corpus juris civilis, edited by Paul Krueger and Theodor Mommsen, 3 vols.
Berlin: Apud Weidmannos, 1888.

Curiel, Gustavo. "Los Ajuares Domésticos Novohispano." In *Museo Franz
Mayer: 20 Año de Arte y Cultura en* México, edited by Federico Rubli
Kaiser, 81–108. Mexico: Chapa, 2006.

Curtze, Maximilian, ed. *Petri Philomeni de Dacia in algorismum vulgarem
Johannis de Sacrobosco commentarius*. Copenhagen: Hauniæ, 1897.

Dean, James M., ed. *Mum and the Sothsegger*. In *Richard the Redeless and
Mum and the Sothsegger*, edited by James M. Dean. TEAMS Middle English
Text Series. Kalamazoo, MI: Medieval Institute Publications, 2000.

de France, Marie. *Marie de France: Poetry (Norton Critical Editions)*. Edited
and translated by Dorothy Gilbert. New York: W. W. Norton, 2015.

Derolez, Albert. "Le 'Liber Floridus' et l'énigme du manuscrit Cotton
Fragments Volume I," *Mittellateinisches Jahrbuch* 17 (1982): 120–9.

Dove, Mary, ed. *The Earliest Advocates of the English Bible: The Texts of the
Medieval Debate*. Exeter: University of Exeter Press, 2010.

Dümmler, Ernst. *Libelli de lite imperatorvm et pontificvm saecvlis XI. et XII.
conscripti*. Hannover: Hahn, 1956.

Earwaker, John Parsons, ed. *Lancashire and Cheshire Wills and Inventories
1572–1696 Now Preserved at Chester*. Manchester: Chetham Society, 1893.

Easting, Robert, and Richard Sharpe, ed. and trans. *Revelations of Peter of Cornwall*. British Writers of the Middle Ages and Early Modern Period 5. Toronto: Pontifical Institute of Mediaeval Studies, 2013.

Eisner, Sigmund, ed. *A Variorum Edition of the Works of Geoffrey Chaucer, Volume VI: Prose Treatises, Part One: A Treatise on the Astrolabe*. Norman, OK: University of Oklahoma Press, 2002.

Ellis, Roger, ed. *"My Compleinte" and Other Poems*. Exeter: University of Exeter Press, 2001.

Fontes Anglo-Saxonici: World Wide Register. Oxford, 2002. http://fontes.english.ox.ac.uk/.

Forshall, J., ed. *Remonstrance against Romish Corruptions*. London: Longman, Brown, Green, and Longmans, 1851.

Fritz, Rolf. *Die Gefäße aus Kokosnuß in Mitteleuropa 1250–1800*. Mainz: Verlag Phillip von Zabern, 1983.

Grossman, Austin. *YOU*. New York: Mulholland, 2013.

Guibert of Nogent. *Histoire de sa vie*. Edited by Georges Bourgin. CTSEEH 40. Paris, 1903.

The Holy Bible: Douay Version Translated from the Latin Vulgate. London: Catholic Truth Society, 1956.

Hudson, Anne, ed. *Two Wycliffite Texts*. EETS o.s. 301. London: Early English Text Society, 1993.

— ed. *Selections from English Wycliffite Writings*. Cambridge: Cambridge University Press, 1978.

John of Salisbury. *The Metalogicon: A Twelfth-Century Defense of the Verbal and Logical Arts of the Trivium*. Translated by Daniel D. McGarry. Berkeley: University of California Press, 1955.

—. *Metalogicon*. Edited by Clement Webb. Oxford: Clarendon Press, 1929.

Jones, Alfred. *The Old Plate of the Cambridge Colleges*. Cambridge: Cambridge University Press, 1910.

Jones, Charles W., ed. *Bedae Venerabilis opera, pars VI: Opera didascalica 2*. CCSL 123B. Turnhout: Brepols, 1977.

Karpinski, Louis Charles, ed. and trans. *Robert of Chester's Latin Translation of the Algebra of Al-Khowarizmi*. Ann Arbor, MI: University of Michigan, 1915.

Klausner, David N., ed. *The Castle of Perseverance*. Kalamazoo, MI: Medieval Institute Publications, 2010.

Leupold, Jacob. *Theatrum arithmetic-geometricum*. Leipzig: Zufinden bey dem Autore und Joh. Friedr. Gleditschens seel. Sohn, 1727.

Library of Latin Texts. Turnhout: Brepols, 2014.

Liebermann, Felix, ed. *Die Gesetze der Anglesachsen*, 3 vols. Halle: Max Niemeyer, 1903–16.

Lindsay, W. M., ed. *Isidori Hispalensis Episcopi Etymologiarum sive Originum Libri XX*. 2 vols. Oxford: Clarendon Press, 1911.

Los Angeles. Wellcome Library, MS 564. https://wellcomelibrary.org/item/b19730925/.

Luscombe, David. *The Letter Collection of Peter Abelard and Heloise*. Translated by the Late Betty Radice. 1 edition. Oxford: Oxford University Press, 2013.

McCarthy, Adrian James. *Book to a Mother: An Edition with Commentary*. Salzburg, Austria: Institut für Anglistik und Amerikanistik, Universität Salzburg, 1981.

Menabrea, L. F. "Sketch of the Analytical Engine Invented by Charles Babbage." Trans. with notes by Ada Augusta, Countess of Lovelace. In *Scientific Memoirs, Selected from the Transactions of Foreign Academies of Science and Learned Societies, and Foreign Journals, Volume III*, ed. Richard Taylor, 666–707. London: R. and J. E. Taylor, 1843.

Middle English Compendium. University of Michigan. http://quod.lib.umich.edu/m/med/.

Muckle, J. T. *The Story of Abelard's Adversities: A Translation with Notes of the Historia Calamitatum*. Toronto: Pontifical Institute of Mediaeval Studies, 1954.

Paris. Bibliothèque nationale de France, Latin 64.

—. Bibliothèque nationale de France, Latin 14398.

Peter the Venerable. *The Letters of Peter the Venerable*. Edited by Giles Constable. Cambridge, MA: Harvard University Press, 1967.

Schepers, Kees, ed. *Ioannis Rusbrochii, De ornatu spiritualium nuptiarum, Wilhelmo Iordani interprete*. CCSM 207. Turnhout: Brepols, 2004.

Seymour, M. C., and Gabriel M. Liegey, eds. *On the Properties of Things: John Trevisa's Translation of Bartholomaeus Anglicus De Proprietatibus*

Rerum, A Critical Text. 3 vols. Oxford: Oxford University Press, 1975–1988.

Shirley, Walter Waddington, ed. *Fasciculi Zizaniorum Magistri Johannis Wyclif Cum Tritico, Ascribed to Thomas Netter of Walden*. Rolls Series 5. London: Longmans, 1858.

Spelman, Henry. "Feuds and Tenure." In *Reliquiæ Spelmannianæ the posthumous works of Sir Henry Spelman, Kt., relating to the laws and antiquities of England: publish'd from the original manuscripts: with the life of the author*. 1–46. Oxford, 1698.

Staley, Lynn, ed. *The Book of Margery Kempe*. TEAMS Middle English Texts Series. Kalamazoo, MI: Medieval Institute Publications, 1996.

Steele, Robert, ed. *The Earliest Arithmetics in English*. EETS e.s. 118. London: Early English Text Society, 1922; repr. 1988.

Tobler, Adolf, and Erhard Lommatzsch. *Altfranzosisches Worterbuch*. 11 vols. Berlin: Weidmann, 1925–.

Wallis, Faith, trans. *Bede: The Reckoning of Time*. Translated Texts for Historians 29. Liverpool: Liverpool University Press, 1999.

Weber, Robert, ed. *Biblia sacra iuxta Vulgatam versionem*. 5th ed. Stuttgart: Deutsche Bibelgesellschaft, 2007.

Whittaker, W. J., ed. *Mirror of Justices*. Selden Society 7, 1895.

Wilson, G. Willow. *Alif the Unseen*. New York: Corvus Books, 2012.

Wyclif, John. *Tractatus de Officio Regis*. Edited by Alfred W. Pollard and Charles Sayle. Wyclif's Latin Works, vol. 8. London: The Wyclif Society, 1887.

Yorke, Oliver. "The Sock and the Buskin. No. III: Miss Fanny Kemble's 'Francis the First,' and Mr. Sheridan Knowles's 'Hunchback'." *Fraser's Magazine for Town and Country* 5 (1832): 432–47.

SECONDARY SOURCES

Ahmed, Shahab. *What Is Islam? The Importance of Being Islamic*. Princeton, NJ: Princeton University Press, 2016.

Akbari, Suzanne Conklin, and Karla Mallette. "Introduction: The Persistence of Philology: Language and Connectivity in the Mediterranean." In *A Sea of Languages: Rethinking the Arabic Role in Medieval Literary History*, edited by Akbari and Mallette, 3–22. Toronto: University of Toronto Press, 2013.

Alford, John A. *Piers Plowman: A Guide to the Quotations*. Binghamton, NY: MRTS, 1992.

Althusser, Louis. *For Marx*. Translated by Ben Brewster. New York: Verso, 2006.

Andrée, Alexander. "Le *Pater* (Matth. 6,9–13 et Luc. 11,2–4) dans l'exégèse de l'école de Laon: la *Glossa ordinaria et autres commentaires*." In *Le Pater noster au XIIe siècle: Lectures et usages*, ed. Francesco Siri. Turnhout: Brepols, 2015.

—. "The *Glossa ordinaria* on the Gospel of John: A Preliminary Survey of the Manuscripts with a Presentation of the Text and Its Sources." *Revue Bénédictine* 118 (2008): 109–34.

Anglo-Norman Dictionary. http://www.anglo-norman.net/.

Apprich, Clemens, Wendy Hui Kyong Chun, Florian Cramer, and Hito Stereyl. *Pattern Discrimination*. Minneapolis: University of Minnesota Press, 2018.

Bakhtin, M. M. *Speech Genres and Other Late Essays*. Edited by Michael Holquist and Caryl Emerson. Translated by Vern McGee. Austin: University of Texas Press, 1986.

Banham, Debby, ed. *The Anglo-Saxon Monastic Sign Language: Monasteriales Indicia*. Norfolk: Anglo-Saxon Books, 1991.

Barrington, Candace, and Sebastian Sobecki, eds. *The Cambridge Companion to Literature and Law*. Cambridge: Cambridge University Press, 2019.

Barton, Matt, and Shane Stacks. *Dungeons and Desktops: The History of Computer Role-Playing Games*, 2nd ed. Boca Raton, FL: CRC Press, 2019.

Baxter, Stephen. "Lordship and Labour." In *A Social History of England 900–1200*, edited by Julia Crick and Elisabeth Van Houts, 98–114. Cambridge: Cambridge University Press, 2011.

Bell, H. I. "The Greek Papyrus Protocol." *Journal of Hellenic Studies* 37 (1917): 56–8.

Benjamin, Ruha. *Race after Technology: Abolitionist Tools for the New Jim Code*. Cambridge: Polity, 2019.

Benson, Robert L., and Giles Constable. *Renaissance and Renewal in the Twelfth Century*. Toronto: University of Toronto Press, 1999.

Berger, Karol. "The Guidonian Hand." In *The Medieval Craft of Memory: An Anthology of Texts and Pictures*, edited by Mary Carruthers and

Jan M. Ziolkowski, 71–82. Philadelphia: University of Pennsylvania Press, 2002.

Biddick, Kathleen. *The Shock of Medievalism.* Durham, NC: Duke University Press, 1998.

Birnbaum, David J., Sheila Bonde, and Mike Kestemont. "The Digital Middle Ages: An Introduction." *Speculum* 92, no. S1 (2017): S2.

Bischoff, Bernhard. *Latin Paleography: Antiquity and the Middle Ages.* Translated by Dáibhí Ó Cróinín and David Ganz. Cambridge: Cambridge University Press, 1990.

Black, William Henry. *A Descriptive, Analytical, and Critical Catalogue of the Manuscripts Bequeathed unto the University of Oxford by Elias Ashmole, Esq., M.D., F.R.S., Windsor Herald, Also Some Additional MSS. Contributed by Kingsley, Lhuyd, Borlase, and Others.* Oxford: Oxford University Press, 1845.

Bliemetzreider, Franz. "Robert von Melun und die Schule Anselmus von Laon." *Zeitschrift für Kirchengeschichte* 53 (1934): 117–70.

—. "L'œuvre d'Anselme de Laon et la littérature contemporaine, II: Hughes de Rouen." *RTAM* 6 (1934): 261–83, and *RTAM* 7 (1935): 28–51.

—. "Autour de l'œuvre théologique d'Anselme de Laon." *RTAM* 1 (1929): 435–83.

Bloch, R. Howard. *Medieval French Literature and Law.* Berkeley: University of California Press, 1977.

Bolter, Jay David, and Richard Grusin. *Remediation: Understanding New Media,* 1st ed. Cambridge, MA: MIT Press, 1999.

Bowman, Sarah Lynne. *The Function of Role-Playing Games: How Participants Create Community, Solve Problems, and Explore Identity.* Jefferson, NC: McFarland, 2010.

Bradford, Clare. *The Middle Ages in Children's Literature.* New York: Palgrave Macmillan, 2015.

Bravo, Roberto López. "Iconografía y Uso del Chocolate en el Museum Regional Chiapas." *Gaceta de Museos* 50 (2011): 26–9.

Bredehoft, Thomas A. *The Visible Text: Textual Production and Reproduction from Beowulf to Maus.* Oxford: Oxford University Press, 2014.

Bruce, Scott G. *Silence and Sign Language in Medieval Monasticism: The Cluniac Tradition, c.900–1200.* Cambridge: Cambridge University Press, 2007.

Brundage, James A. *The Medieval Origins of the Legal Profession: Canonists, Civilians, and Courts.* Chicago: University of Chicago Press, 2008.

—. *Medieval Canon Law.* Harlow: Pearson, 1995.

Brylowe, Thora. *Romantic Art in Practice: Cultural Work and the Sister Arts, 1760–1820.* Cambridge: Cambridge University Press, 2018.

Buc, Philippe. *L'ambiguïté du livre: Prince, pouvoir, et peuple dans les commentaires de la Bible au Moyen Age.* Paris: Beauchesne, 1994.

Buchanan, Ian. "Deleuze and the Internet." *Australian Humanities Review* 43 (2007): 1–21.

Buckley, Jake. "Analog versus Digital." In *The Johns Hopkins Guide to Digital Media*, edited by Lori Emerson, Marie-Laure Ryan, and Benjamin J. Robertson, 7–11. Baltimore, MD: Johns Hopkins University Press, 2014.

Burrow, J. A. *Gestures and Looks in Medieval Narrative.* Cambridge Studies in Medieval Literature 48. Cambridge: Cambridge University Press, 2002.

Caballos, Esteban Mira. "Vinos y élites en la América de la Conquista." *Iberoamericana* 15 (2015): 7–23.

Cabezon, Beatriz, and Louis Evan Grivetti. "Symbols from Ancient Times: Paleography and the St. Augustine Chocolate Saga." In *Chocolate: History, Culture, and Heritage*, edited by Louis Evan Grivetti and Howard-Yana Shapiro, 669–98. Hoboken: Wiley, 2009.

Camargo, Martin. *Ars Dictaminis, Ars Dictandi.* Turnhout: Brepols, 1991.

Cannon, Christopher. *From Literacy to Literature: England, 1300–1400.* Oxford: Oxford University Press, 2016.

—. "Proverbs and the Wisdom of Literature: The Proverbs of Alfred and Chaucer's Tale of Melibee." *Textual Practice* 24 (2010): 407–34.

Cappers, René T. J. "Exotic Imports of the Roman Empire: an Exploratory Study of Potential Vegetal Products from Asia." In *Food, Fuel and Fields: Progress in African Archaeobotany*, edited by Katharina Neumann, Ann Butler, and Stefanie Kahlheber, 197–206, Köln: Brill, 2003.

Catalogue of Additions to the Manuscripts in the British Museum in the Years 1882–1887. London: Trustees of the British Museum, 1889.

Catto, J. I. "Wyclif and Wycliffism at Oxford, 1356–1450." In *The History of the University of Oxford*, edited by J. I. Catto and Ralph Evans, 2:175–261. Oxford: Oxford University Press, 1992.

Certeau, Michel de. *The Practice of Everyday Life*. Translated by Steven Rendall. Berkeley, CA: University of California Press, 2008.

Ceruzzi, Paul E. *A History of Modern Computing*, 2nd ed. Cambridge, MA: MIT Press, 2003.

Chakravorty, Swagato. "Mediation." *The Chicago School of Media Theory* (blog). Accessed 24 July 2020. https://lucian.uchicago.edu/blogs/mediatheory/keywords/mediation/.

Chess, Shira. *Ready Player Two: Woman Gamers and Designed Identity*. Minneapolis: University of Minnesota Press, 2017.

Chess, Shira, and Adrienne Shaw. "Conspiracy of Fishes, or, How We Learned to Stop Worrying about #Gamergate and Embrace Hegemonic Masculinity." *Journal of Broadcasting & Electronic Media* 59, no. 1 (2015): 208–20.

Christensen, Katherine. "Introduction." In *Gratian: The Treatise on Laws*, translated by Augustine Thompson O. P. and James Gordley, ix–xxvii. Washington, DC: The Catholic University of America Press, 1993.

Chun, Wendy Hui Kyong. *Control and Freedom: Power and Paranoia in the Age of Fiber Optics*. Cambridge, MA: MIT Press, 2006.

Clanchy, Michael. *From Memory to Written Record*, 3rd ed. Oxford: Wiley Blackwell, 2012.

Clanchy, Michael, and Lesley Smith. "Abelard's Description of the School of Laon: What Might It Tell Us about Early Scholastic Teaching?" *Nottingham Medieval Studies* 54 (2010): 1–34.

Cobb, H. S., ed. *The Overseas Trade of London: Exchequer Customs Accounts 1480–1*. London: London Record Society, 1990.

Cole, Andrew. "What Hegel's Master/Slave Dialectic Really Means." *Journal of Medieval and Early-Modern Studies* 34 (2004): 577–610.

Constable, Giles. *Letters and Letter-Collections*. Turnhout: Brepols, 1976.

—. "Medieval Letters and the Letter Collection of Peter the Venerable." In *The Letters of Peter the Venerable*, edited by Giles Constable, II:1–45. Cambridge, MA: Harvard University Press, 1967.

—. "The Structure of Medieval Society According to the /Dictatores/ of the Twelfth Century." In *Law Church and Society: Essays in Honor of Stephan Kuttner*, edited by Kenneth Pennington and Robert Somerville, 253–67. Philadelphia: University of Pennsylvania Press, 1977.

Cordez, Philippe. *Trésor, Mémoire, Merveilles: Les Objets des Églises au Moyen Âge*. Paris: EHESS, 2016.

Cossgrove, William, ed. "The Vernacularization of Science, Medicine, and Technology in Late Medieval Europe." Special issue, *Early Science and Medicine* 3, no. 2 (1998).

—. "The Vernacularization of Science, Medicine, and Technology in Late Medieval Europe: Broadening Our Perspectives." *Early Science and Medicine* 5 (2000): 47–63.

Cotts, John D. *The Clerical Dilemma: Peter of Blois and Literate Culture in the Twelfth Century*. Washington, DC: Catholic University of America Press, 2009.

Cover, Jennifer Grouling. *The Creation of Narrative in Tabletop Role-playing Games*. Jefferson, NC: McFarland, 2010.

Coyne, Richard. "The Net Effect: Design, the Rhizome, and Complex Philosophy." *Futures* 40 (2008): 552–61.

Cuomo, S. *Ancient Mathematics*. New York: Routledge, 2015.

da Silva, Denise Ferreira. "Before Man: Sylvia Wynter's Rewriting of the Modern Episteme." In *Sylvia Wynter: On Being Human as Praxis*, edited by Katherine McKitterick, 90–105. Durham, NC: Duke University Press, 2015.

Davidson, Clifford, ed. *Gesture in Medieval Drama and Art*. Kalamazoo, MI: Medieval Institute Publications, 2001.

Davis, Kathleen. *Periodization and Sovereignty: How Ideas of Feudalism and Secularization Govern the Politics of Time*. Philadelphia: University of Pennsylvania Press, 2008.

de Blick, J. "L'œuvre exégétique de Walafrid Strabon et la Glossa ordinaria." *RTAM* 16 (1949): 5–28.

Deetz, James. *In Small Things Forgotten: An Archaeology of Early American Life*, expanded and rev. ed. New York: Anchor Books, 1996.

de Ghellinck, Joseph. "The Sentences of Anselm of Laon and Their Place in the Codification of Theology during the XIIth Century." *Irish Theological Quarterly* 6 (1911): 427–41.

De Hamel, Christopher F. R. *Glossed Books of the Bible and the Origins of the Paris Booktrade*. Woodbridge: Brewer, 1984.

Deleuze, Gilles, and Felix Guattari. *A Thousand Plateaus: Capitalism and Schizophrenia*. Minneapolis: University of Minnesota Press, 1987.

Delisle, Léopold. *Inventaire des Manuscrits Latins de Saint Victor Conservés à la Bibliothèque Impériale sous les Numéros 14232–15175*. Paris, 1869, repr. New York: Johnson Reprint Corporation, 1965.

Derolez, Albert. *The Paleography of Gothic Manuscript Books from the Twelfth to the Early Sixteenth Century*. Cambridge: Cambridge University Press, 2003.

Derrida, Jacques. "Archive Fever: A Freudian Impression." Translated by Eric Prenowitz. *Diacritics* 25, no. 2 (1995): 9–63.

—. *The Postcard: From Socrates to Freud and Beyond*. Translated by Alan Bass. Chicago and London: University of Chicago Press, 1987.

de Vaan, Michiel. *Etymological Dictionary of Latin and the Other Italic Languages*. Leiden: Brill, 2008.

Dinshaw, Carolyn. *How Soon Is Now? Medieval Texts, Amateur Readers and the Queerness of Time*. Durham, NC: Duke University Press, 2012.

—. *Getting Medieval: Sexualities and Communities, Premodern and Postmodern*. Durham, NC: Duke University Press, 1999.

Dixon, R. M. W. *Making New Words: Morphological Derivation in English*. Oxford: Oxford University Press, 2014.

Dockray-Miller, Mary. *Public Medievalists, Racism, and Suffrage in the American Women's College*. New York: Palgrave, 2017.

Dodwell, C. R. *Anglo-Saxon Gestures and the Roman Stage*. Cambridge: Cambridge University Press, 2000.

Doležalova, Lucie. "Latin Mnemonic Verses Combining the Ten Commandments with the Ten Plagues of Egypt Transmitted in Late Medieval Bohemia." In *The Ten Commandments in Medieval and Early Modern Culture*, edited by Youri Desplenter, Jürgen Pieters, and Walter Melion, 152–72. Leiden: Brill, 2017.

Doty, William G. "The Classification of Epistolary Literature." *The Catholic Biblical Quarterly* 31, no. 2 (1969): 183–99.

Doyle, Matthew. *Peter Lombard and His Students*. Toronto: Pontifical Institute of Mediaeval Studies, 2016.

Duarte, Carlos F. *El Arte del Tomar el Chocolate: Historia del Coco Chocolatero en Venezuela*. Caracas: C. F. Duarte, 2005.

Dufour, Philippe Sylvestre. *Traitez nouveaux et curieux du café, du thé et du chocolate*. Lyon: Jean Girin & B. Riviere, 1685.

Duggan, Hoyt. "Some Un-Revolutionary Aspects of Computer Editing." In *The Literary Text in the Digital Age*, edited by Ruth Finneran, 77–98. Ann Arbor, MI: University of Michigan Press, 1996.

Duguid, Paul. "The Ageing of Information: From Particular to Particulate." *Journal of the History of Ideas* 76 (2015): 347–68.

Dyson, George. *Turing's Cathedral: The Origins of the Digital Universe*. New York: Penguin Books, 2012.

Eco, Umberto. "Dreaming the Middle Ages." In Umberto Eco, *Travels in Hyperreality*, 61–72. Translated by William Weaver. New York: Harvest, 1986.

Edgerton, David. *The Shock of the Old: Technology and Global History Since 1900*. Oxford: Oxford University Press, 2007.

Egan, Geoff. "Medieval Vessels of Other Materials—A Non-ceramic View from London." *Medieval Ceramics* 21 (1997): 109–14.

Eisenstein, Elizabeth. *The Printing Press as an Agent of Change*, 2 vols. Cambridge: Cambridge University Press, 1979.

Ellard, Donna Beth. *Anglo-Saxon(ist) Pasts postSaxon Futures*. New York: Punctum Books, 2019.

Elliott, Andrew B. R. *Medievalism, Politics and Mass Media: Appropriating the Middle Ages in the Twenty-First Century*. Oxford: D. S. Brewer, 2017.

Ernst, Wolfgang. *Digital Memory and the Archive*. Minneapolis: University of Minnesota Press, 2013.

Evans, Timothy H. "Folklore as Utopia: English Medievalists and the Ideology of Revivalism." *Western Folklore* 47, no. 4 (1988): 245–68.

Ewalt, David M. *Of Dice and Men: The Story of Dungeons & Dragons and the People Who Play It*. New York: Scribner, 2013.

Fairclough, Norman. *Language and Power*. New York: Longman, 1989.

—. *Media Discourse*. London: Bloomsbury Academic, 2011.

Ferrari, M. C. "Before the *Glossa Ordinaria*. The Ezekiel Fragment in Irish Minuscule Zürich, Staatsarchiv W 3.19.XII, and Other Experiments towards a Bible Commentée in the Early Middle Ages." In *Biblical Studies in the Early Middle Ages: Proceedings of the Conference on Biblical Studies in the*

Early Middle Ages, edited by Claudio Leonardi and Giovanni Orlandi. Florence: SISMEL/Edizioni del Galluzzo, 2005.

Fiesler, Casey, Shannon Morrison, R. Benjamin Shapiro, and Amy S. Bruckman. "Growing Their Own: Legitimate Peripheral Participation for Computational Learning in an Online Fandom Community." *Proceedings of the 20th ACM Conference on Computer Supported Cooperative Work and Social Computing* (2017): 1375–86. doi: 10.1145/2998181.2998210.

Finn, Kavita. *Fan Phenomena: Game of Thrones.* Chicago: Intellect Books, 2017.

Folch, Christine. "Stimulating Consumption: Yerba Mate Myths, Markets, and Meanings from Conquest to Present." *Comparative Studies in Society and History* 52 (2010): 6–36.

Foucault, Michel. *The Order of Things: An Archaeology of the Human Sciences.* London: Routledge, 2002.

Foys, Martin K. "Media." In *A Handbook of Anglo-Saxon Studies*, edited by Jacqueline Stodnick and Renée R. Trilling, 133–48. Malden, MA: Wiley-Blackwell, 2012.

—. "Medieval Manuscripts: Media Archaeology and the Digital Incunable." In *The Medieval Manuscript Book: Cultural Approaches*, edited by Michael Johnston and Michael Van Dussen, 119–39. Cambridge: Cambridge University Press, 2015.

—. "A Sensual Philology for Anglo-Saxon England." *postmedieval* 5 (2014): 456–72.

—. *Virtually Anglo-Saxon: Old Media, New Media, and Early Medieval Studies in the Late Age of Print.* Gainesville, FL: University Press of Florida, 2007.

Fritz, Rolf. *Die Gefäße aus Kokosnuß in Mitteleuropa 1250–1800.* Mainz: Verlag Philipp von Zabern, 1983.

Froehlich, Karlfried. "Walahfrid Strabo and the *Glossa Ordinaria:* The Making of a Myth." In *Studia Patristica 28: Papers Presented at the Eleventh International Conference on Patristic Studies Held in Oxford 1991*, edited by E. A. Livingstone, 192–6. Leuven: Peeters, 1993.

Fuller, Matthew. *Media Ecologies: Materialist Energies in Art and Technoculture.* Cambridge, MA: MIT Press, 2005.

Gabler, H. W. "Theorizing the Digital Scholarly Edition." *Literature Compass* 7 (2010): 43–56.

Galloway, Alexander. *Laruelle: Against the Digital*. Minneapolis: University of Minnesota Press, 2014.

—. "Networks." In *Critical Terms for Media Studies*, edited by W. J. T. Mitchell and Mark B. N. Hansen, 280–96. Chicago: University of Chicago Press, 2010.

—. *Protocol: How Control Exists after Decentralization*. Cambridge, MA: MIT Press, 2004.

Ganim, John. "Medievalism and Architecture." In *The Cambridge Companion to Medievalism*, edited by Louise d'Arcens, 29–44. Cambridge: Cambridge University Press, 2016.

—. *Medievalism and Orientalism*. New York: Palgrave, 2008.

Gartler, Mark. "rhizome," Chicago School of Media Theory, https://lucian.uchicago.edu/blogs/mediatheory/keywords/rhizome/.

Geary, Patrick. *Furta Sacra: Thefts of Relics in the Central Middle Ages*. Princeton: University of Princeton Press, 1978.

Gibson, Margaret. "The Place of the *Glossa ordinaria* in Medieval Exegesis." Reprinted in Gibson, *"Artes" and Bible in the Medieval West*, 5–27. Aldershot, UK: Ashgate Variorum, 1993.

Gillespie, Alexandra. "Unknowe, unkow, Vncovthe, uncouth: From Chaucer and Gower to Spenser and Milton." In *From Medieval into Renaissance: Essays for Helen Cooper*, edited by Andrew King and Matthew Woodcock, 15–34. Woodbridge: D. S. Brewer, 2016.

Giraud, Cédric. *Per verba magistri: Anselme de Laon et son école au XIIe siècle*. Turnhout: Brepols, 2010.

—. "Per verba magistri: la langue des maîtres théologiens au premie XIIe siècle." In *Zwischen Babel und Pfingsten—Entre Babel et Pentecôte*, edited by Peter von Moos, 357–73. Zurich: LIT Verlag, 2008.

Gitelman, Lisa. *Paper Knowledge: Towards a Media History of Documents*. Durham, NC: Duke University Press, 2014.

—. *Always Already New: Media, History, and the Data of Culture*. Cambridge, MA, and London: MIT Press, 2008.

Goddard, Michael. "Media Ecology." In *The Johns Hopkins Guide to Digital Media*, edited by Marie-Laure Ryan, Lori Emerson, and Benjamin J. Robertson, 331–33. Baltimore, MD: Johns Hopkins University Press, 2014.

Godefroy, Frédéric. *Dictionnaire de l'ancienne langue française et de tous ses dialectes du IXe au XVe siècle*, 10 vols. Paris: Vieweg, 1881–1902.

Goffman, Erving. "On Face-Work: An Analysis of Ritual Elements in Social Interaction." In *Interaction Ritual: Essays on Face-to-Face Behavior*, 5–45. New York: Pantheon Books, 1982.

Graham, Margaret A., and Russel K. Skowronek. "Chocolate on the Borderlands of New Spain." *Journal of Historical Archaeology* 20 (2016): 645–65.

Gray, Kishonna L. *Race, Gender, and Deviance in Xbox Live: Theoretical Perspectives from the Virtual Margins*. New York: Routledge, 2014.

Gray, Kishonna L., and David Leonard. "Introduction." In *Woke Gaming: Digital Challenges to Oppression and Social Injustice*, edited by Gray and Leonard, 9–14. Seattle: University of Washington Press, 2018.

Gregory, Rabia. "Black as a Coconut and White as a Tusk: African Materials and European Displays of Christ before Columbus." *Journal of African Religions* 2 (2014): 395–408.

Griffey, Erin. *On Display: Henrietta Maria and the Materials of Magnificence at the Stuart Court*. New Haven: Yale University Press, 2015.

Grivetti, Louis Evan, Patricia Barriga, and Beatriz Cabezon. "Sailors, Soldiers and Padres: California Chocolate, 1542?–1840." In *Chocolate: History, Culture, and Heritage*, edited by Louis Evan Grivetti and Howard-Yana Shapiro, 439–63. Hoboken: Wiley, 2009.

Gross-Diaz, Teresa. *The Psalms Commentary of Gilbert of Poitiers: From Lectio Divina to the Lecture Room*. Leiden: Brill, 1996.

Grusin, Richard. "Radical Mediation." *Critical Inquiry* 42 (2015): 124–48.

Guattari, Félix. *The Three Ecologies*. Translated by Ian Pindar and Paul Sutton. London: Athlone Press, 2000.

—. *Les trois écologies*. Paris: Éditions Galilée, 1989.

Guillory, John. "Genesis of the Media Concept." *Critical Inquiry* 36 (2010): 321–62. https://doi.org/10.1086/648528.

Gumbrecht, Hans Ulrich. *Production of Presence: What Meaning Cannot Convey*. Stanford, CA: Stanford University Press, 2004.

Gunn, B. F., L. Baudouin, and K. M. Olson. "Independent Origins of Cultivated Coconut (*Cocos nucifera* L.) in the Old World Tropics." *PLoS ONE* 6 (2011): e21143. http://dx.doi.org/10.1371/journal.pone.0021143.

Guo, N., Y. Huang, T. Mai, S. Patil, C. Cao, M. Seok, S. Sethumadhavan, and Y. Tsividis. "Energy-Efficient Hybrid Analog/Digital Approximate

Computation in Continuous Time." *IEEE Journal of Solid-State Circuits* 51 (2016): 1514–24.

Hall, Eric. *Internet Core Protocols: The Definitive Guide.* Sebastopol, CA: O'Reilly Media, 2000.

Hardesty, Larry. "Analog Computing Returns." *MIT News.* 20 June 2016. http://news.mit.edu/2016/analog-computing-organs-organisms-0620.

Harriman, Andi, and Marloes Bontje. *Some Wear Leather, Some Wear Lace: The Worldwide Compendium of Postpunk and Goth in the 1980s.* Chicago: Intellect Books, 2014.

Hartmann, Wilfried, and Kenneth Pennington, eds. *The History of Medieval Canon Law in the Classical Period, 1140–1234.* Washington, DC: The Catholic University of America Press, 2008.

Harvey, Colin B. *Fantastic Transmedia: Narrative, Play and Memory across Science Fiction and Fantasy Storyworlds.* New York: Palgrave Macmillan, 2015.

Hawk, Brandon W. *Preaching Apocrypha in Anglo-Saxon England.* Toronto Anglo-Saxon Series 30. Toronto: University of Toronto Press, 2018.

Hayles, N. Kathleen. "How We Read: Close, Hyper, Machine." *ADE Bulletin* 150 (2011): 62–79.

Heng, Geraldine. *The Invention of Race in the European Middle Ages.* Cambridge: Cambridge University Press, 2018.

Hill, Mark O. "Local Frequency As a Key to Interpreting Species Occurrence Data When Recording Effort Is Not Known." *Methods in Ecology and Evolution* 3 (2012): 195–205. doi:10.1111/j.2041–210X.2011.00146.x.

Hockey, Susan. "History of Humanities Computing." In *A Companion to Digital Humanities*, edited by Susan Schreibman, Ray Siemens, and John Unsworth, 3–19. London: Blackwell, 2004.

Hodkinson, Paul. *Goth: Identity, Style and Subculture.* Oxford: Berg Publishers, 2002.

Holden, Richard. "Digital." In *Aspects of English: Word Stories.* Oxford: Oxford University Press, 2014. http://public.oed.com/aspects-of-english/word-stories/digital/.

Hollinger, Veronica. "Cybernetic Deconstructions: Cyberpunk and Postmodernism." *Mosaic* 23, no. 2 (1990): 29–44.

Holsinger, Bruce. "Medieval Studies, Postcolonial Studies, and the Genealogies of Critique." *Speculum* 77 (2002): 1195–1227.

Horobin, Simon. "The Scribe of Bodleian Library MS Bodley 619 and the Circulation of Chaucer's *Treatise on the Astrolabe*." *Studies in the Age of Chaucer* 31 (2009): 109–24.

Hsy, Jonathan, and Julie Orlemanski. "Race and Medieval Studies: A Partial Bibliography." *postmedieval* 8, no. 4 (2017): 500–31.

Hudson, Anne. "'Who Is My Neighbour?' Some Problems of Definition on the Borders of Orthodoxy and Heresy." In *Wycliffite Controversies*, edited by Mishtooni C. A. Bose and J. Patrick Hornbeck, 79–96. Turnhout: Brepols, 2012.

—. *The Premature Reformation: Wycliffite Texts and Lollard History*. Oxford: Oxford University Press, 1988.

Huening, Drew. "Symbol/Index/Icon." *The Chicago School of Media Theory* (blog). Accessed 18 July 2018. https://lucian.uchicago.edu/blogs/ mediatheory/keywords/symbolindexicon/.

Huizinga, Johan. *Homo Ludens: A Study of the Play Element in Culture*. Boston: Beacon, 1955.

—. *The Autumn of the Middle Ages*. Translated by Rodney J. Payton and Ulrich Mammitzsch. Chicago: University of Chicago Press, 1997.

Hutton Sharp, Alice. "Textual Format and the Development of the Early *Glossa* on Genesis." *Mediaeval Studies* 78 (2016): 125–65.

—. "'Gilbertus Universalis' Reevaluated and the Authorship of the *Gloss* on Genesis." *Recherches de Théologie et Philosophie Médiévales* 83, no. 2 (2016): 225–43.

—. "*In Principio*: The Origins of the *Glossa ordinaria* on Genesis 1–3." PhD dissertation, University of Toronto, 2015.

Ingham, Patricia Clare, and Michelle Warren. "Introduction." In *Postcolonial Moves: Medieval through Modern*, edited by Ingham and Warren, 1–15. New York: Palgrave Macmillan, 2003.

Innis, Harold. *Empire and Communications*. Toronto: University of Toronto Press, 2007.

—. *The Bias of Communication*. Toronto: University of Toronto Press, 1951.

—. *Empire and Communications*. Oxford: Clarendon Press, 1950.

Jagoda, Patrick. *Network Aesthetics.* Chicago: University of Chicago Press, 2016.

Jaeger, C. Stephen. *The Envy of Angels: Cathedral Schools and Social Ideals in Medieval Europe, 950–1200.* Philadelphia: University of Pennsylvania Press, 1994.

Jefferson, Judith A., and Ad Putter, eds. *Multilingualism in Medieval Britain (c. 1066–1520): Sources and Analysis.* Turnhout: Brepols, 2012.

Jamieson, Ross W. "The Essence of Commodification: Caffeine Dependencies in the Early Modern World." *Journal of Social History* 35 (2001): 269–94.

Janzen, Daniel H., and Paul S. Martin. "Neotropical Anachronisms: The Fruits the Gomphotheres Ate." *Science* 215 (1982): 19–27.

Jefferson, Lisa, ed. *Wardens' Accounts and Court Minute Books of the Goldsmiths' Mistery of London, 1334–1446.* Woodbridge: Boydell, 2003.

Jenkins, Henry. *Convergence Culture: Where Old and New Media Collide.* New York: New York University Press, 2006.

Jerng, Mark C. *Racial Worldmaking: The Power of Popular Fiction.* New York: Fordham University Press, 2018.

Johns, Adrian. *The Nature of the Book.* Chicago: University of Chicago Press, 2000.

Johnston, Michael, and Michael Van Dussen. "Introduction." In *The Medieval Manuscript Book*, edited by Johnston and Van Dussen, 1–16. Cambridge: Cambridge University Press, 2015.

Jordheim, Helge. "Against Periodization: Koselleck's Theory of Multiple Temporalities." *History and Theory* 51, no. 2 (2012): 151–71.

Kapell, Matthew, and Andrew B. R. Elliott, eds. *Playing with the Past: Digital Games and the Simulation of History.* London: Bloomsbury, 2013.

Kaunisto, Mark. *Variation and Change in the Lexicon: A Corpus-based Analysis of Adjectives in English Ending in -ic and -ical.* Language and Computers: Studies in Practical Linguistics 63. Amsterdam: Rodopi, 2007.

Kendrick, Laura. "Games Medievalists Play: How to Make Earnest of a Game and Still Enjoy It." *New Literary History* 40, no. 1 (2009): 43–61.

Kennedy, Kathleen E. "Gripping It by the Husk: The Medieval English Coconut." *The Medieval Globe* 3 (2017): 1–26.

—. *Medieval Hackers.* Brooklyn: Punctum Books, 2014.

Kerby-Fulton, Kathryn. "Afterword." In *The Medieval Manuscript Book: Cultural Approaches*, edited by Michael Johnston and Michael Van Dussen. Cambridge: Cambridge University Press, 2015.

Kim, Dorothy. "Introduction to the Literature Compass Special Cluster: Critical Race and the Middle Ages." *Literature Compass* 16, nos. 9–10 (2019): e12249.

King, Brad, and John Boreland. *Dungeons and Dreamers: A Story of How Computer Games Created a Global Community*. Pittsburgh: ETC Press, 2014.

Kistler, Logan, Álvaro Montenegro, Bruce D. Smith, John A. Gifford, Richard E. Green, Lee A. Newsom, and Beth Shapiro. "Transoceanic Drift and the Domestication of African Bottle Gourds in the Americas." *Proceedings of the National Academy of Sciences of the United States of America* 111 (2014): 2937–2941. https://www.ncbi.nlm.nih.gov/pmc/articles/PMC3939861/.

Kittler, Friedrich A. *Discourse Networks 1800/1900*. Stanford, CA: Stanford University Press, 2007.

Kline, Daniel T. "Participatory Medievalism, Role-Playing, and Digital Gaming." In *The Cambridge Companion to Medievalism*, edited by Louise D'Arcens, 75–88. Cambridge: Cambridge University Press, 2016.

—. ed. *Digital Gaming Re-imagines the Middle Ages*. New York: Routledge, 2014.

—. "Metamedievalism, Gaming, and Teaching Medieval Literature in the Digital Age." In *Teaching Literature at a Distance: Open, Online and Blended Learning*, edited by Takis Kayalis and Anastasia Natsina, 148–62. London: Bloomsbury, 2010.

—. "Virtually Medieval: The Age of Kings Interprets the Middle Ages." In *Mass Market Medieval: Essays on the Middle Ages in Popular Culture*, edited by David W. Marshall, 154–70. Jefferson, NC: McFarland, 2007.

—. "Introduction: Medieval Children's Literature: Problems, Possibilities, Parameters." In *Medieval Literature for Children*, edited by Kline, 1–11. New York: Psychology, 2003.

Knight, Gillian R. *The Correspondence Between Peter the Venerable and Bernard of Clairvaux: A Semantic and Structural Analysis*. Routledge,

2017. https://nls.ldls.org.uk/welcome.html?ark:/81055/
vdc_100041339211.0X000001.

Koopmans, Rachel. *Wonderful to Relate: Miracle Stories and Miracle Collecting in High Medieval England*. Philadelphia: University of Pennsylvania Press, 2011.

Laird, Edgar. "Chaucer and Friends: The Audience for the Treatise on the Astrolabe." *The Chaucer Review* 41 (2007): 439–44.

Lampert, Lisa. "Race, Periodicity, and the (Neo-) Middle Ages." *Modern Language Quarterly* 65, no. 3 (2004): 391–421.

Latham, R. E., D. R. Howlett, and R. K. Ashdowne, eds. *Dictionary of Medieval Latin from British Sources*. Oxford: Oxford University Press, 1975–2013.

Latour, Bruno. *Reassembling the Social: An Introduction to Actor-Network-Theory*. Clarendon Lectures in Management Studies. Oxford and New York: Oxford University Press, 2007.

—. *We Have Never Been Modern*. Translated by Catherine Porter. Cambridge, MA: Harvard University Press, 1993.

Lauer, Philippe. *Catalogue Général des Manuscrits Latins*, vol. 1. Paris: Bibliothèque Nationale, 1939.

Leclercq, Jean. *The Love of Learning and the Desire for God: A Study of Monastic Culture*. New York: Fordham University Press, 2014.

Leiner, Barry M., Vinton G. Cerf, David D. Clark, Robert E. Kahn, Leonard Kleinrock, Daniel C. Lynch, Jon Postel, Larry G. Roberts, and Stephen Wolff. "Brief History of the Internet." 1997, http://www.internetsociety.org/internet/what-internet/history-internet/brief-history-internet.

Lenco, Peter. "(Re-)Introducing Deleuze: New Readings of Deleuze in International Studies." *Millennium: Journal of International Studies* 43 (2014): 124–44.

Lendinara, Patrizia. "Abbo of Fleury." In *Sources of Anglo-Saxon Literary Culture, Volume One: Abbo of Fleury, Abbo of Saint-German-des-Prés, and Acta Sanctorum*, edited by Frederick M. Biggs, Thomas D. Hill, Paul E. Szarmach, and E. Gordon Whatley, with the assistance of Deborah A. Oosterhouse, 1–15. Kalamazoo, MI: Medieval Institute Publications, 2001.

Levinson, Paul. "McLuhan and Media Ecology." *Proceedings of the Media Ecology Association* 1 (2000): 17–22.

Levy, Ian Christopher. "Texts for a Poor Church: John Wyclif and the Decretals." *Essays in Medieval Studies* 20, no. 1 (2003): 94–107.

Liu, Alan. "Where Is Cultural Criticism in the Digital Humanities?" In *Debates in the Digital Humanities*, edited by Matthew K. Gold. Minneapolis: University of Minnesota Press, 2012.

——. *Transcendental Data: Toward a Cultural History and Aesthetics of the New Encoded Discourse. Local Transcendence: Essays on Postmodern Historicism and the Database.* Chicago: University of Chicago Press, 2008.

Lobrichon, Guy. "Une nouveauté: Les gloses de la Bible." In *Le Moyen Âge et la Bible*, Bible de tous les temps, edited by Pierre Riche and Guy Lobrichon. Paris: Beauchesne, 1984.

Logeion 2, built by Philip Posner, Ethan Della Rocca, and Josh Day, https://logeion.uchicago.edu/.

López, Adalberto. "The Economics of Yerba Mate in Seventeenth-century South America." *Agricultural History* 48 (1974): 493–509.

Lottin, Odon. *Psychologie et morale aux XIIe et XIIIe siècles.* Gembloux, Belgium: J. Duculot, 1959.

Loyn, H. R. *The Governance of Anglo-Saxon England, 500–1087.* Stanford, CA: Stanford University Press, 1984.

Lybbert, Travis J. "The Economic Roots of the American 'Zig-zag': Knives, Forks, and British Merchantilism." *Economic Inquiry* 48 (2010): 810–15.

Machuca, Paulina. "De Porcelanas Chinas y Otros Menesteres: Cultura Material de Origen Asiático en Colima, Siglo XVI–XVII." *Relaciones* 33 (2012): 77–134.

Maddicott, J. R. *Origins of English Parliament.* Oxford: Oxford University Press, 2010.

Mak, Bonnie. *Why the Page Matters.* Toronto: University of Toronto Press, 2011.

Malinowski, Bronisław. "On Phatic Communion." In *The Discourse Reader*, edited by Adam Jaworski and Nikolas Coupland, 296–98. London and New York: Routledge, 2014.

Mall, Andrew. "analog, digital." In *Keywords of Media Theory*, edited by W. J. T. Mitchell, Eduardo de Almeida, and Rebecca Reynolds. Chicago:

University of Chicago Press, 2003. http://csmt.uchicago.edu/glossary2004/analogdigital.htm.

Mallette, Karla. "Beyond Mimesis: Aristotle's Poetics in the Medieval Mediterranean." *PMLA* 124 (2009): 583–91.

Marschoff, María. "La Sociedad Virreinal en Buenos Aires: Un Anàlisis desde la Cultura Material y la Alimentación." *Revista des Indias* 74 (2014): 67–100.

Martin, Cristina Esteras. *La Platería en el Reino de Guatemala Siglos XVI–XIX.* Guatemala City: Fundación Albergue Hermano Pedro, 1994.

Martinez-Lopez, Maria Elena. *Genealogical Fictions: Limpieza de Sangre, Religion, and Gender in Colonial Mexico.* Stanford, CA: Stanford University Press, 2008.

Marx, C. W. "The Middle English Verse 'Lamentation of Mary to Saint Bernard' and the 'Quis Dabit.'" In *Studies in the Vernon Manuscript*, edited by Derek Pearsall, 137–57. Cambridge: Brewer, 1990.

Massanari, Adrienne. "#Gamergate and The Fappening: How Reddit's Algorithm, Governance, and Culture Support Toxic Technoculture." *New Media & Society* 19, no. 3 (2017): 329–46.

Matthews, David. *Medievalism: A Critical History.* Cambridge: Boydell & Brewer, 2015.

Mauchly, John W. "Digital and Analog Computing Machines." In *The Moore School Lectures (1946)*, edited by Martin Campbell-Kelly and Michael R. Williams, 25–42. Cambridge, MA: MIT Press, 1985.

McArthur, J.A. "Digital Subculture: A Geek Meaning of Style," *Journal of Communication Inquiry* 33 (2009): 58–70.

McCarty, Willard. *Humanities Computing.* New York: Palgrave Macmillan, 2005.

McGann, Jerome. *Radiant Textuality: Literature after the World Wide Web.* New York: Palgrave, 2001.

McGlotten, Shaka. "Black Data." In *No Tea, No Shade: New Writings in Black Queer Studies*, edited by E. Patrick Johnson, 262–86. Durham, NC: Duke University Press, 2016.

McIlwain, Charlton. "Racial Formation, Inequality and the Political Economy of Web Traffic." *Information, Communication & Society* 20, no. 7 (2017): 1073–89.

McLuhan, Marshall. *Understanding Media: The Extensions of Man, Critical Edition.* Edited by W. Terrence Gordon. Berkeley: Gingko Press, 2003.

—. *The Gutenberg Galaxy: The Making of Typographic Man.* Toronto: University of Toronto Press, 1962, repr. 2011.

Mead, Jenna. "Geoffrey Chaucer's *Treatise on the Astrolabe.*" *Literature Compass* 3 (2006): 973–91.

Menocal, María Rosa. *The Arabic Role in Medieval Literary History.* Philadelphia: University of Pennsylvania Press, 1987.

Moberly, Kevin, and Brent Moberly. "There Is No Word for Work in the Dragon Tongue." *Year's Work in Medievalism* 28 (2013): 1–9.

Mortensen, Torill Elvira. "Anger, Fear, and Games: The Long Event of #GamerGate." *Games and Culture* 13, no. 8 (2018): 787–806.

Moulthrop, Stuart. "Rhizome and Resistance: Hypertext and the Dreams of a New Culture." In *Hyper/Text/Theory*, edited by George P. Landow, 1–18. Baltimore, MD: Johns Hopkins University Press, 1994.

Murphy, James J. *Rhetoric in the Middle Ages: A History of Rhetorical Theory from Saint Augustine to the Renaissance.* Berkeley: University of California Press, 1974.

Musson, Anthony. *Medieval Law in Context: The Growth of Legal Consciousness from Magna Carta to the Peasants' Revolt.* Manchester: Manchester University Press, 2001.

Nakamura, Lisa. *Digitizing Race: Visual Cultures of the Internet.* Minneapolis: University of Minnesota Press, 2007.

Narducci, Enrico. "Due trattati inediti d'abbaco." *Bullettino di bibliografia e di storia delle scienze matematiche et fisiche* 15 (1882): 135–62.

Nichols, Stephen. "Introduction: Philology in a Manuscript Culture." *Speculum* 65 (1990): 1–10.

Niles, John D. *The Idea of Anglo-Saxon England 1066–1901.* London: Wiley-Blackwell, 2015.

Noble, Safaiya Umoja. *Algorithms of Oppression: How Search Engines Reinforce Racism.* New York: New York University Press, 2018.

Norton, Marcy. "Subaltern Technologies and Early Modernity in the Atlantic World." *Colonial Latin America Review* 26 (2017): 18–38.

—. *Sacred Gifts, Profane Pleasures: A History of Tobacco and Chocolate in the Atlantic World.* Ithaca: Cornell University Press, 2008.

—. "Tasting Empire: Chocolate and the European Internalization of Mesoamerican Aesthetics." *American Historical Review* III (2006): 660–91.

Oliphant, Elayne. "Sign." *The Chicago School of Media Theory* (blog). Accessed 18 July 2018. https://lucian.uchicago.edu/blogs/mediatheory/keywords/sign/.

Ong, Walter. *Orality and Literacy*, 30th Anniversary Edition. London: Routledge, 2002.

—. "The Literate Orality of Popular Culture." In *Rhetoric, Romance, and Technology: Studies in the Interaction of Expression and Culture*, edited by Walter Ong, 284–303. Ithaca, NY: Cornell University Press, 1971.

Oxford English Dictionary Online. Oxford: Oxford University Press. http://www.oed.com.

Pargman, Daniel. "Word and Code, Code as World." *Digital Arts and Culture*, 2003 Online Proceedings. https://www.researchgate.net/publication/228881105_Word_and_code_code_as_world.

Parikka, Jussi. *What Is Media Archaeology*. Boston: MIT Press, 2012.

Pavao-Zuckerman, Barnet, and Diana DiPaolo Lauren, "Presentation is Everything: Foodways, Tablewares, and Colonial Identity at Presidio Los Adaes." *International Journal of Archaeology* 16 (2012): 199–226.

Peacock, Vita. "The Negation of Hierarchy and Its Consequences." *Anthropological Theory* 15 (2015): 3–21.

Pennington, Kenneth, and Charles Donahue. "Bio-Bibliographical Guide to Medieval and Early Modern Jurists." Ames Foundation, http://amesfoundation.law.harvard.edu/BioBibCanonists/HomePage_biobib2.php.

Pérez, Jorge F. Rivas. "Domestic Display in the Spanish Overseas Territories." In *Behind Closed Doors: Art in the Spanish American Home 1492–1898*, edited by Richard Aste, 49–103. Brooklyn: Brooklyn Museum, 2013.

Perry, David. *Sacred Plunder: Venice and the Aftermath of the Fourth Crusade*. University Park: Pennsylvania State University Press, 2015.

Peters, Edward, and Melodie H. Eichbauer. "Canon Law." In *Oxford Bibliographies Online*. doi: 10.1093/OBO/9780195396584-0033.

Peters, John Durham. *The Marvelous Clouds: Toward a Philosophy of Elemental Media*. Chicago: University of Chicago Press, 2016.

—. *Speaking into the Air: A History of the Idea of Communication*. Chicago: University of Chicago, 1999.

Peterson, Jon. *Playing at the World*. San Diego, CA: Unreason Press, 2012.

Petroski, Henry. *The Evolution of Useful Things*. New York: Vintage Books, 1994.

Phillips, Amanda. *Gamer Trouble: Feminist Confrontations in Digital Culture*. New York: New York University Press, 2020.

Phipps, Elena, Johanna Hecht, and Cristina Esteras Martin. *The Colonial Andes: Tapestries and Silverwork*. New York: The Metropolitan Museum of Art, 2004.

Picón, Francisca del Mar Plaza, and José Antonio González Marrero. "*De computo uel loquela digitorum*: Bede y el computo digital." *Faventia* 28 (2006): 115–23.

Postel, Jonathan. "Transmission Control Protocol." RFC 793, September 1981.

—. "Internet Protocol." RFC 791, September 1981.

Postman, Neil. "The Humanism of Media Ecology." *Proceedings of the Media Ecology Association* 1 (2000): 10–16.

Pugh, Tison, and Susan Aronstein, eds. *The Disney Middle Ages: A Fairy-Tale and Fantasy Past*. New York: Palgrave Macmillan, 2012.

Raine, James, ed. *Testamenta Eboracensia or Wills Registered at York Illustrative of the History, Manners, Language, Statistics, Etc., of the Province of York from the Year MCCC Downwards. Part 1*. London: J. B. Nicholas & Son, 1835.

Rasmussen, Ann Marie, and Markus Stock. "Medieval Media." *Seminar* 52, no. 2 (2016): 97–106.

Reber, Vera Blinn. "Commerce and Industry in Nineteenth Century Paraguay: The Example of *Yerba Mate*." *The Americas* 42 (1985): 29–53.

Recanati, François. "Le présent épistolaire: Une perspective cognitive." *L'Information Grammaticale* 66, no. 1 (1995): 38–44. https://doi.org/10.3406/igram.1995.3046.

Reddaway, T. F., and Lorna E. M. Walker. *The Early History of the Goldsmiths' Company 1327–1509 Including the Book of Ordinances 1478–83*. London: Edward Arnold, 1975.

Reynolds, L. D., ed. *Texts and Transmission: A Survey of the Latin Classics*. Oxford: Oxford University Press, 1983.

Rice, Nicole. *Lay Piety and Religious Discipline in Middle English Literature.* Cambridge: Cambridge University Press, 2012.

Rihouet, Pascal. "Veronese's Goblets: Glass Design and the Civilizing Process." *Journal of Design History* 26 (2013): 133–51.

Rivero, Héctor, and Bonnelli Miranda, eds. *The Grandeur of Viceregal Mexico: Treasures from the Museo Franz Mayer.* Houston: University of Texas Press, 2002.

Roach, Levi. *Kingship and Consent in Anglo-Saxon England, 871–978.* Cambridge: Cambridge University Press, 2013.

Robinson, Carol L. "Electronic Tolkien: Characterization in Film and Video Games." In *Medieval Afterlives in Contemporary Culture*, edited by Gail Ashton, 124–33. London: Bloomsbury, 2015.

Robinson, Fred. "*Medieval,* The *Middle Ages.*" In *The Tomb of Beowulf and Other Essays on Old English.* Oxford: Blackwell, 1992.

Robinson, Ian Stuart. *Authority and Resistance in the Investiture Contest: The Polemical Literature of the Late 11th Century.* Manchester: Manchester University Press, 1978.

Rodríguez-Alegría, Enrique. "Eating Like an Indian: Negotiating Social Relations in the Spanish Colonies." *Current Anthropology* 46 (2005): 551–73.

Roylance, Patricia Jane. "Winthrop's Journal in Manuscript and Print: The Temporalities of Early-Nineteenth-Century Transmedial Reproduction." *PMLA* 133, no. 1 (2018): 88–106.

Rust, M. D. *Imaginary Worlds in Medieval Books: Exploring the Manuscript Matrix.* New York: Palgrave Macmillan, 2007.

Saler, Michael T. *As If: Modern Enchantment and the Literary Prehistory of Virtual Reality.* Oxford: Oxford University Press, 2012.

Schreibman, Susan. "Digital Scholarly Editing." In *Literary Studies in the Digital Age: An Evolving Anthology*, edited by Kenneth M. Price and Ray Siemens. MLA, 2013, doi: 10.1632/lsda.2013.4.

Sharpe, Reginald, ed. *Calendar of Wills Proved and Enrolled in the Court of Husting, London, A.D. 1258–A.D. 1688, Preserved among the Archives of the Corporation of the City of London, at the Guildhall,* 2 Pts. London: Corporation of the City of London, 1889.

Shifman, Limor. *Memes in Digital Culture.* Cambridge, MA: MIT Press, 2014.

Shillingsburg, L. *From Gutenberg to Google: Electronic Representations of Literary Texts*. Cambridge: Cambridge University Press, 2006.

Shippey, Thomas. *The Road to Middle Earth: How J. R. R. Tolkien Created a New Mythology*. Boston: Houghton Mifflin, 2003.

Silano, Giulio. "Introduction." In *The Sentences, Book 1: The Mystery of the Trinity*, translated by Giulio Silano, xxiii–xxiv. Toronto: Pontifical Institute of Mediaeval Studies, 2007.

Silvestre, Hubert. "À propos de la lettre d'Anselme de Laon à Héribrand de Saint-Laurent," *RTAM* 28 (1961): 5–25.

Simonite, Tom. "Moore's Law is Dead. Now What?" *MIT Technology Review*. 13 May 2016. https://www.technologyreview.com/s/601441/moores-law-is-dead-now-what/.

Singel, Ryan, and Kevin Poulsen. "Your Own Personal Internet." *Threat Level*. 29 June 2006. *Wired*. https://www.wired.com/2006/06/your-own-person/.

Siskin, Cliff, and William Warner. *This Is Enlightenment*. Chicago: University of Chicago Press, 2010.

Small, James S. *The Analogue Alternative: The Electronic Analogue Computer in Britain and the USA, 1930–1975*. New York: Routledge, 2001; repr. 2013.

Smalley, Beryl. *The Study of the Bible in the Middle Ages*, 3rd ed. Oxford: Blackwells, 1983.

—. "Gilbertus Universalis Bishop of London (1128–1134) and the Problem of the 'Glossa Ordinaria.'" *RTAM* 7 (1935): 235–62 and *RTAM* 8 (1936): 24–64.

—. "Gilbertus Universalis, Bishop of London (1128–34)." *RTAM* 7 (1935): 245.

Smith, Lesley. *The Glossa Ordinaria: The Making of a Medieval Bible Commentary*. Leiden: Brepols, 2009.

Snodin, Michael, and Cynthia Roman. *Horace Walpole's Strawberry Hill*. New Haven, CT: Yale University Press, 2009.

Somerset, Fiona. "Lollards and Religious Writings." In *The Cambridge Companion to Literature and Law*, edited by Candace Barrington and Sebastian Sobecki, 167–77. Cambridge: Cambridge University Press, 2019.

—. "Introduction." In *Truth and Tales: Cultural Mobility and Medieval Media*, edited by Fiona Somerset and Nicholas Watson, 1–16. Columbus: Ohio State University Press, 2015.

—. *Feeling Like Saints: Lollard Writings after Wyclif.* Ithaca, NY: Cornell University Press, 2014.

Steckel, Sita. *Kulturen des Lehrens im Früh- und Hochmittelalter, Autorität, Wissenskonzepte und Netzwerke von Gelehrten.* Wien, Köln, Weimar: Böhlau, 2010. https://doi.org/10.7788/boehlau.9783412213466.

Stein, Peter. *Regulae Iuris: From Juristic Rules to Legal Maxims.* Cambridge: Cambridge University Press, 1966.

Steiner, Emily. *Reading Piers Plowman.* Cambridge: Cambridge University Press, 2013.

Stiegler, Bernard. *Technics and Time 1: The Fault of Epimetheus.* Translated by Richard Beardsworth and George Collins. 21–179. Stanford, CA: Stanford University Press, 1998.

Stirnemann, Patricia. "Où ont été fabriqués les livres de la glose ordinaire dans la première moitié du XIIe siècle." In *Le XIIe siècle: Méditations et renouveau en France dans la première moitié du XIIe siècle,* edited by Françoise Gasparri. Cahiers du léopard d'or 3. 257–301. Paris: Léopard d'or, 1994.

Stock, Markus. "Letter, Word, and Good Messengers: Towards an Archaeology of Remote Communication." *Interdisciplinary Science Reviews* 37, no. 4 (2012): 299–313.

Stock, Markus, and Anne Marie Rasmussen. "Introduction: Medieval Media." *Seminar* 52, no. 2 (2016): 97–106.

St. Petersburg. Hermitage Museum. Antonio Pereda. "Still Life with an Ebony Chest," ГЭ-377.

—. Diego Velázquez, "The Lunch."

Stutzmann, Dominique. "La Bibliothèque de l'abbaye cistercienne de Fontenay (Côte d'Or)." Thesis, École nationale des Chartes, 2002.

Swedin, Eric G., and David L. Ferro. *Computers: The Life Story of a Technology.* Baltimore, MD: Johns Hopkins University Press, 2007.

Taullard, Alfredo. *Platería Sudamericana.* Buenos Aires: Peuser, Ltd., 1941.

Taylor, Andrew. "Getting Technology and Not Getting Theory." *Florilegium* 32 (2015): 131–55.

Taylor, Karla. "Proverbs and the Authentication of Convention in Troilus and Criseyde." In *Chaucer's 'Troilus': Essays in Criticism,* edited by Stephen A. Barney, 277–96. Hamden, CT: Archon, 1980.

Thesaurus Linguae Graecae. Edited by Maria C. Pantelia. University of California Irvine, http://www.tlg.uci.edu.

Thesaurus linguae Latinae. Leipzig: Teubner, 1900–.

Thomas, Ebony Elizabeth. *The Dark Fantastic: Race and the Imagination from Harry Potter to the Hunger Games*. New York: New York University Press, 2019.

Thompson, E. M. *An Introduction to Greek and Latin Paleography*. Cambridge: Cambridge University Press, 1906.

Thomson, Williell R. *The Latin Writings of John Wyclyf: An Annotated Catalog*. Subsidia Mediaevalia 14. Toronto: Pontifical Institute of Mediaeval Studies, 1983.

Toker, Franklin. *Pittsburgh: A New Portrait*. Pittsburgh: University of Pittsburgh Press, 2009.

Trakulhun, Sven and Ralph Weber. "Modernities: Editors' Introduction." In *Delimiting Modernities: Conceptual Challenges and Regional Responses*, edited by Trakulhun and Weber, ix–xxiv. Lanham, MD: Lexington Books, 2015.

Treharne, Elaine. "Fleshing out the Text: The Transcendent Manuscript in the Digital Age." *postmedieval* 4 (2013): 465–78.

—. *Living through Conquest*. Oxford: Oxford University Press, 2012.

—. "The Architextual Editing of Early English." *Poetica* 71 (2008): 1–13.

Tresca, Michael J. *The Evolution of Fantasy Role-Playing Games*. Jefferson, NC: McFarland, 2011.

Truitt, E. R. *Medieval Robots: Mechanism, Magic, Nature and Art*. Philadelphia: University of Pennsylvania Press, 2015.

Tucker, T. G. *A Concise Etymological Dictionary of Latin*. Halle: Max Niemeyer, 1931.

Turing, A. M. "Computing Machinery and Intelligence." *Mind* 59 (1950): 433–60.

Turkle, Sherry. *Second Self: Computers and the Human Spirit*, 1st ed. New York: MIT Press, 1984.

Turner, E. G. *Greek Papyri: An Introduction*. Oxford: Clarendon Press, 1968.

Tyler, Elizabeth M., ed. *Conceptualizing Multilingualism in England, c.800–c.1250*. Turnhout: Brepols, 2011.

Underwood, Ted. *Why Literary Periods Mattered: Historical Contrast and the Prestige of English Studies.* Stanford, CA: Stanford University Press, 2013.

Unsworth, John. "Medievalists as Early Adopters of Information Technology," *Digital Medievalist* 7 (2011), https://journal.digitalmedievalist.org/articles/10.16995/dm.34.

Vail, Leroy, and Landeg White, eds. *Power and the Praise Poem: South African Voices in History.* Charlottesville, VA: University Press of Virginia, 1991.

van der Veen, Marijke. *Consumption, Trade and Innovation: Exploring the Botanical Remains from the Roman and Islamic Ports at Quseir al-Qadim, Egypt.* Frankfut am Main: Africa Magna Verlag, 2011.

—. "Trade and Diet at Roman and Medieval Quseir al-Qadim, Egypt. A Preliminary Report." In *Food, Fuel and Fields: Progress in African Archaeobotany*, edited by Katharina Neumann, Ann Butler, and Stefanie Kahlheber, 207–12. Köln: Brill, 2003.

van Dijk, Teun. *Discourse as Social Interaction.* Los Angeles: SAGE, 2009.

Van Engen, John. "Authorship, Authority, and Authorization: The Cases of Abbot Bernard of Clairvaux and Abbess Hildegard of Bingen." In *Shaping Authority: How Did a Person Become an Authority in Antiquity, the Middle Ages and the Renaissance?*, edited by S. Boodts, J. Leemans, and B. Meijns, 325–62. Lectio 4. Turnhout: Brepols, 2016.

—. "Letters, Schools, and Written Culture in the Eleventh and Twelfth Centuries." In *Dialektik und Rhetorik im früheren und hohen Mittelalter: Rezeption, Überlieferung und gesellschaftliche Wirkung antiker Gelehrsamkeit vornehmlich im 9. und 12. Jahrhundert*, edited by Johannes Fried, 98–132. Schriften des Historischen Kollegs, Kolloquien 27. Munich: R. Oldenbourg, 1997.

—. *Rupert of Deutz.* Berkeley: University of California Press, 1983.

Vernon, Matthew X. *The Black Middle Ages: Race and the Construction of the Middle Ages.* New York: Palgrave Macmillan, 2018.

Vidier, Alexandre, and Léon Mirot, eds. *Obituaires de la Province du Sens*, vol. 3, *Diocèses d'Orléans, d'Auxerre, et de Nevers.* Paris: 1909.

Villanueva, Amaro. *El Arte de Cebar: El Lenguaje Del Mate.* Introduction by Sergio Delgado, Chronology by Guillermo Mondejar. Paraná: Ediciones UNL, 2018.

Villella, Peter. *Indigenous Elites and Creole Identity in Colonial Mexico, 1500–1800*. Cambridge: Cambridge University Press, 2016.

Von Nolcken, Christina. *The Middle English Translation of the* Rosarium Theologie: A Selection. Middle English Texts, 10. Heidelberg: Carl Winter, 1979.

Wallin, Jason J. "Rhizomania: Five Provocations on a Concept." *Complicity: An International Journal of Complexity and Education* 7 (2010): 83–9.

Wellbery, David. "Foreword." In *Discourse Networks 1800/1900*, vii–xxxiii. Stanford, CA: Stanford University Press, 2007.

Wenzel, Horst. "Boten und Briefe: Zum Verhältnis Körperlicher und Nichtkörperlicher Nachrichtenträger." In *Gespräche—Boten—Briefe. Körpegedächtnis und Schrifgedächtnis im Mittelalter*, edited by Horst Wenzel, 86–105. Philologische Studien und Quellen 143. Berlin: Erich Schmidt, 1997.

Wenzel, Horst, Peter Ggöhler, and Tagung "Gespräche—Boten—Briefe," eds. *Gespräche—Boten—Briefe: Körpergedächtnis und Schriftgedächtnis im Mittelalter*. Berlin: E. Schmidt, 1997.

Whitaker, Cord. *Black Metaphors: How Modern Racism Emerged from Medieval Race-Thinking*. Philadelphia: University of Pennsylvania Press, 2019.

—. "Race-ing the Dragon: The Middle Ages, Race and Trippin' into the Future." *postmedieval* 6, no. 3 (2015): 3–11.

Whitaker, Cord, and Matthew Gabriele, eds. "The Ghosts of the Nineteenth Century and the Future of Medieval Studies." Special issue, *postmedieval* 10, no. 2 (2019).

Williams, Raymond. *Keywords: A Vocabulary of Culture and Society*, rev. ed. Oxford: Oxford University Press, 1983.

Winroth, Anders. *The Making of Gratian's Decretum*. Cambridge: Cambridge University Press, 2000.

Witt, Ronald G. *The Two Latin Cultures and the Foundation of Renaissance Humanism in Medieval Italy*. Cambridge: Cambridge University Press, 2012.

Witwer, Michael. *Empire of Imagination: Gary Gygax and the Birth of Dungeons & Dragons*. New York: Bloomsbury, 2015.

Wolf, Mark J. P. *Building Imaginary Worlds: The Theory and History of Subcreation*. New York: Routledge, 2012.

Wormald, Patrick. *The Making of English Law: King Alfred to the Twelfth Century*. London: Blackwell, 2001.

Wynter, Sylvia. "Unsettling the Coloniality of Being/Power/Truth/Freedom: Towards the Human, after Man, Its Overrepresentation—An Argument." *CR: The New Centennial Review* 3, no. 3 (2003): 257–337.

Wood, Robin. "What Did Medieval People Eat From?" *Medieval Ceramics* 29 (2005): 19–20.

Wray, Stefan. "Rhizomes, Nomads, and Resistant Internet Use." http://www.thing.net/~rdom/ecd/rhizomatic.html#THE%20 LITERATURE.

Yeager, Stephen M. "Protocol: The Chivalry of the Object." *Critical Inquiry* 45, no. 3 (2019): 747–61.

—. *From Lawmen to Plowmen: Anglo-Saxon Legal Tradition and the School of Langland*. Toronto: University of Toronto Press, 2014.

Yoshikawa, Naoë Kukita. "The Making of The Book of Margery Kempe: The Issue of Discretio Spirituum Reconsidered." *English Studies* 92, no. 2 (2011): 119–37. doi: 10.1080/0013838X.2011.553919.

Young, Helen. *Race and Popular Fantasy Literature: Habits of Whiteness*. New York: Routledge, 2016.

—. ed. *Fantasy and Science Fiction Medievalisms: From Isaac Asimov to A Game of Thrones*. Amherst, NY: Cambria Press, 2015.

Zielinski, Sigfried. *Deep Time of Media: Towards an Archaeology of Seeing and Hearing by Technical Means*. Translated by Gloria Custance. Boston: MIT Press, 2008.

Zizumbo-Villarreal, Daniel, and Hermilo J. Quero, "Re-evaluation of Early Observations on Coconut in the New World." *Economic Botany* 52 (1998): 68–77.

Parikka, Jussi, xii, 9
Paris, 150
Paris, Bibliothèque nationale de
France, latin 14398, 141, 150
Paris, Bibliothèque nationale de
France, latin 64, 141, 150
periodization, 10–13, 23, 54–55, 59,
60–68, 77. *See also* epochs
Peru, 90, 91, 95
Peter the Venerable, 119–39
Peters, John Durham, 20, 82
Phillips, Amanda, vii, 7
Piers Plowman, 21, 107
Postman, Neil, 80–81
Prague, National Library, XI.E.3, 106
pre-Columbian America, 89–90, 91,
92, 95, 96, 99, 100
presence (bodily or textual), 26, 120,
121, 123–25, 127, 129, 132–39
print culture, 15, 54, 56, 60, 78
print technology. *See* technology
printing press, xiv, 54, 66
programming, 5–6, 26
publics, 6, 56, 69, 71, 72, 77, 85, 121

Ralph of Laon, 144, 145. *See also*
Anselm of Laon
Recanati, François, 136
Regunculae super abacum. See
Thurkill Compotista
remediation, 15, 23, 26, 130, 132
revolution ,15, 54, 59–62, 66, 77
rhizome, 68, 71–73
Robert of Ketton, 43

Roman Empire, 16, 85, 86
Rome, xiv, 14, 15
Roylance, Patricia Jane, 22
Rupert of Deutz, 145

scholasticism, 26, 143, 144, 146
School of Laon, 145–50, 155, 156
scribes, 18, 38, 42, 45, 134, 141, 143,
146, 148–50, 153–54
scriptoria, 10
scriptus, 39
Selden, John, 62, 67, 73, 74
Seneca, 137
sign language (Clunaic), 37, 39, 41
social media, 7, 27, 33, 107
Spelman, Henry, 62, 63, 67
Stiegler, Bernard, 75

tags, 24, 25, 26, 106, 107, 108, 114
TCP/IP (Transmission
Control Protocol/Internet
Protocol), 69–70
technology, xii, xiv, 3, 6, 9, 12, 14, 16,
19, 33, 42, 71, 75, 77, 81, 100, 105,
107, 126, 131
temporality, 22, 120, 121, 125, 132, 133,
136, 137, 138
textuality, 19, 74, 129, 132, 137
Thirty-Seven Conclusions, 113
Thurkill Compotista, 42–43
Tolkien, J. R. R., xii, 6, 7
transparency, 14, 88, 137
Treatise on Laws, 113–14
Turing, Alan, 33

vernacular, 44, 45, 116, 134

verse, 25, 105–15

voice, 13, 68, 107, 123, 131, 132, 134, 138, 139

Walahfrid Strabo, 143

Williams, Raymond, 32

witan (Witengemot), 64, 66

Wyclif, John, 46, 106, 109, 112–15

Wycliffites, 112–16

yerba, 89, 91–95, 96, 97

Zielinski, Sigfried, xii, 9